Europe
at
School

NORMAN NEWCOMBE

A study of primary
Europe
and secondary schools
at
in France, West Germany
School
Italy, Portugal & Spain

METHUEN

First published in 1977 *by Methuen & Co Ltd*
11 *New Fetter Lane, London* EC4P 4EE
© 1977 *Norman Newcombe*
Printed in Great Britain by
Butler & Tanner Ltd, Frome & London

ISBN *hardbound* 0 416 82880 9
ISBN *paperback* 0 416 82890 6

This title is available in both hardbound and paperback editions. The paperback edition is sold subject to the condition that it shall not, by way of trade or otherwise, be lent, resold, hired out or otherwise circulated without the publisher's prior consent in any form of binding or cover other than that in which it is published and without a similar condition including this condition being imposed on the subsequent purchaser.

Distributed in the USA by
HARPER & ROW PUBLISHERS INC
BARNES & NOBLE IMPORT DIVISION

Contents

1 By way of introduction 1

2 Organization 7
*Compulsory school ages – Types of school – Co-education –
Size of classes – Streaming – Boarding places – Terms and holidays
– School hours – The working day – Homework*

3 What they do and how they do it 24
*Attitudes to education – Programmes of the primary and secondary
schools – Standardization of the curriculum – Syllabuses:
the native language, mathematics, history*

4 The teacher and his work: I 40
Some lessons described

Contents

5 The teacher and his work: II 69

Standards – Pupil-teacher relationships – Progress in Spain – Some pupils' views – Conditions of work – The darker side – The teaching profession – Promotion – Retirement – Inspectors – Staff organization – Some teaching techniques – Teaching aids – A rural teacher in Portugal – Teachers' centres – Classroom devices – The teacher's duties – Ancillary workers

6 Testing the work 102

End-of-term assessment – Recuperative work – The Spanish approach to continuous assessment – Fichas – A Portuguese assessment test – Two newspaper reports – A German informal test

7 Buildings and equipment 113

Buildings old and new – School planning – Buildings and their use – Space – Beauty and drabness in the school – Deficiencies – Some attractive new schools – Classroom layout and atmosphere – Laboratories – Sports halls – Other special teaching rooms – Halls, libraries etc. – Miscellaneous rooms – School meals – Grounds and playing areas – Desks – Chalkboards – Teaching aids – Textbooks and stationery

8 Away from the classroom 149

Sport – Clubs and activities – Expeditions and outings – School magazines – Children's writings – Social activities

9 Pastoral care and welfare 160

Role of the form teacher – Relations with parents – The class council – Records and documentation – Marks and assessments – Reports – Recuperation – Educational welfare – Fees and grants – Medical services – Contact with parents

Contents

10 Rules and regulations 185

The approach to discipline in the schools – Some school rulebooks – Sanctions and codes of discipline – Educational democracy in Germany – Problems in Italy – Atmosphere of the schools – Customs and courtesies – Dress – The overall as a working dress – Hair

11 And so . . . ? 214

APPENDICES

I Curriculum in France 221

II Curriculum in Italy 225

III Curriculum in Portugal 227

IV Curriculum in Spain 229

V Curriculum in West Germany 232

VI Numbering of classes 235

VII Working hours 237

VIII Teachers' salaries 239

IX Blueprint for a Spanish school 242

Glossary 244

List of schools 253

Index 257

'Look out, gentlemen, the
schoolmaster is abroad'

LORD BROUGHAM

I
By way of introduction

This study has perhaps been vaguely meditated ever since my first holiday abroad, but only recently did I think seriously of putting it into effect; that I was able to do so was largely thanks to my employers, the Kent Education Committee, who annually allow leave of absence for a term to a few long-serving teachers who wish to carry out some research or project they could not otherwise do. I therefore spent the summer term of 1973 in visiting four European countries whose languages I could make reasonable shift to understand: they were France, Italy, Portugal and Spain, and with the exception of France they form a group of which little seems to be known by English teachers, and about which much of the information is confused or contradictory. Many people suggested that I should find them, educationally, 'pretty backward'... but what *is* 'backward'?

It has been said that you only need to keep your old teaching material long enough and you will find it is once again the very latest thing; and certainly I did not despair of finding in these countries of largely Latin and Roman Catholic culture much that would be useful and interesting. The addition of West Germany, in a separate visit in 1974, was my publishers' idea, and again I am grateful both for the idea and for their encouragement in carrying it out.

My original tour lasted about nine weeks, during which time I visited two different cities in each of my four chosen countries. As I live and work in Maidstone, the county town of Kent, with a population of about 60,000, I felt that I ought to choose places of about the same status and, if possible, size; comparison with familiar standards would thus be made easier. My reasons for choosing the actual towns were varied, and of no particular interest in themselves; eventually the choice fell upon Beauvais and Avignon in France, Cremona and Perugia in Italy, Evora and Braga in Portugal, and Gerona and Jaén in Spain. For the later German trip I had to pick areas where the start of the autumn term was early enough to fall into my own summer holidays; hence Trier, in the Rhineland-Palatinate region, and Emden in Lower Saxony.

I have also been able to incorporate some later material gathered on further visits to Spain, France and Italy, though I must confess one failure in the case of Italy: I had hoped to include a couple of school visits while on holiday in Venice, but repeated letters to the authorities there were stonily unanswered, and a personal call finally produced polite but unyielding refusal on the grounds that authority from the Ministry in Rome would be necessary. I regret this not only for the loss of some further knowledge, but also for the unhappy taste the experience briefly left behind, which I feel sure is not typical in any way of Italian hospitality, though it may exemplify a certain bureaucratic approach!

Deliberately, I confined my visits mainly to schools catering either for primary or for younger secondary children. This was partly because a lot of my own work has been with pupils at the lower end of the secondary range, and therefore also with transfer from primary schools; partly also it was because the upper limit of compulsory education in some European countries is lower than our own, and I naturally wanted to see what the education of the majority was like, rather than that of the smaller proportion who continue past the statutory leaving-age. However, if anything came along which was outside my chosen range I accepted it gratefully, and thus was able to enjoy some memorable visits

By way of introduction

to nursery schools, technical institutes and grammar schools of an academic type.

I have not much use for those visits to schools which involve a conducted tour by the headmaster, who knocks politely on a few classroom doors to allow a brief glimpse of embarrassed pupils being unnaturally virtuous in the presence of their headmaster; therefore I asked to be allowed as often as possible to sit in on lessons and to meet staff and pupils informally. In one case, at the Marist College in Jaén, I got a little more than I had bargained for and found myself left for about half an hour in sole charge of a very agreeable class of boys! My aim was to estimate as far as possible what it would be like to be a teacher or a pupil in the school myself (and in that particular case I certainly found out); to discover how I should have to behave; what would happen if the work done was unsatisfactory; what textbooks I should use; how much homework there would be; whether there would be marks, detentions, weekly tests, uniform, organized games; how much of the work would be practical; what the meals would be like; about school societies, school magazines, parents' associations, desks, satchels, medical inspections, school bells . . .

After making my initial approaches, I asked the authorities of the schools to answer a few preliminary questions; by laborious use of dictionaries and grammar books I tried to make my questionnaire multilingual, but there are many pitfalls for the innocent. Even so simple a word as 'course', for example, does not equate exactly with *cours, curso* or *corso*: or so I discovered when the answers began to arrive! Where I have translated foreign words in this book, as I often have, my aim has been to do so accurately, but I dare not claim positively that no misunderstandings have crept in.

It would be absurd to pretend that a necessarily brief visit tells one everything about a school; if a visitor came to my own school, I know how little I could convey of its real nature, and also how quickly I might try to hurry him past the blemishes. If some of my own kind hosts did likewise I do not blame them. It may be that some readers may accuse me of painting too kind a picture of European schools; but I am unrepentant, for I did indeed admire a great deal of what I saw. I think my information is quite broadly based; in my tours I have visited in all some forty schools, not only in the cities, but also in more rural places, and they ranged from a school with twenty-eight pupils to one of nearly 2,000. Besides schools, I also saw something of the supporting facilities: a splendid Cultural Centre in Gerona, the training facilities and resources centre at Beauvais, and the work of a peripatetic teacher for rural schools in Portugal, to give three examples. I cannot estimate how many individual teachers I met and talked with.

And it was the devotion and sheer decency of the average teacher in every country which impressed me most. Not all of them were brilliant scholars, some were not even specially gifted as pedagogues; but their endeavours were sincere and honest, they loved their pupils, they toiled hard in their interests, they gave them the best they had. I do not think any group of professional people anywhere could surpass them, and if I said less than that for them, I should be betraying them.

I must also pay the warmest possible tribute to the kind and friendly way in which the children themselves received me. I cannot believe that I deserved the obvious delight with which they welcomed an English visitor. May I especially mention Stefano, of the A. Fabretti elementary school in Perugia, who, at the age of ten, interpreted for me one morning (using the English he had learned on visits to his British grandmother) with a cheerful aplomb that few adults would have been able to equal; and that delightful class of girls at the *liceu* in Evora, who at once adopted me and brightened the whole of my stay in their town with their cheerful greetings whenever we met in the streets.

I wish, indeed, that I could name everyone who helped me or showed a kindly interest in my work – innumerable education officers, inspectors, heads and individual teachers, who took great trouble to show me their schools, answer my badly phrased questions and arrange facilities for me. One or two individuals must be mentioned, however: Signorina Rosa-Maria Colombi and Signora Maria-Luisa Casadei, who smoothed my path wonderfully in Cremona; my good friend Carlos de Oliveira of Evora – teacher, artist, fisherman and (with his charming wife) kindest of hosts; another personal friend, Jean Lambert of Beauvais, who gave me much generous help and hospitality; and Señor Jesús Nieto Gil, Inspector of Schools at Seville.

As far as my knowledge and belief can make it so, the information in these pages is correct at the time of writing. But the main body of my visits took place in 1973; the educational and political

By way of introduction

worlds are in a constant state of flux; books take an interminable time to get themselves published; and by the time these words are read, many details will surely have changed. This is especially likely to be true of Portugal, where the events of 1974-5 have brought about a complete change in the country's political leadership and outlook. Much as I should have liked to do so, I have not been able to revisit Portugal to see things for myself, and although a certain amount of information has reached me, some of which I have been able to mention in passing, it has seemed better to let most of what I wrote stand unaltered. Portugal is not a very rich country nowadays, and it seems likely that she will have to manage for a considerable time with the same buildings, equipment and teaching force which she now has, so that the reforms which will surely come must be gradual ones.

Wherever possible, I have used official sources for the factual information, but much of the book is necessarily subjective, and if anyone who reads my comments with personal knowledge feels that he would have reported the matter differently, the discrepancy may be one of viewpoint rather than of fact. As I saw things, so I have honestly tried to report them; if the reader feels I have laid too much or too little stress on a topic, he must blame my sense of what is significant or interesting. There is not much in this book, for example, on public examinations, and nothing at all on education beyond the school level.

I am describing individual schools, but I have inevitably generalized at times from my experiences. I believe it is fairly safe to do so, certainly far safer than it would be in this country, where a tremendous diversity of types of school, and within those types a tremendous diversity of educational philosophies, can co-exist. Under the far more centralized system of, say, France, one secondary school will be much more like another than would, say, a London comprehensive school and one in rural Devon.

Because the individual schools are cut to rather similar patterns, and because the private sector of education on the Continent is either of minor importance or subject to the same regulations as the state sector, there is much less social distinction implied by attending one school rather than another. This is not to say of course that French or German parents do not have anxious worries as to whether little Henri or Heinrich will qualify for admission to the *lycée* or the *Gymnasium*; and, as I shall indicate later, Continental schools are by no means afraid to think in terms of purely vocational education, so that the parents' hopes of a career are closely bound up with the course of study their child follows. But it would take a sociologist rather than a teacher to identify precisely the social stratifications of European schools, and I do not see it as any part of my brief to do so. It would be, anyway, difficult to see this question through English spectacles: German or Spanish snobberies, if they exist, are not the same as English ones! If I had to risk a brief comment, it would be that the situation is vastly different in the Mediterranean–Catholic countries from that found in the more industrialized nations. For, while it may well be that there is a vast gulf between the social expectations and pretensions of (say) the doctor or lawyer on one hand and the unskilled factory-worker or peasant on the other, there is remarkably little reluctance to let their children sit side by side in Spanish or Italian classrooms.

I visited many more schools than are mentioned in the index or the text of this book. Where I felt sure it could hurt nobody's feelings to do so, I have named the schools to which I refer; but where I have felt bound to be critical of a school, I must make it clear that it is not one of those mentioned by name. The occasional unfortunate lesson or unsatisfactory teacher I have left unidentified. I wished to present an honest picture; it would invalidate my book to mention only the good things and none of the bad ones, but I may easily have seen the school concerned, or the teacher, on an untypical off-day. I do not wish to say anything which could detract from the respect which I feel, and which indeed all should feel, for people who labour in so hard a field. Society today pays its teachers a good deal less than it pays to certain other people whose activities largely serve to undo the teacher's work, and I have no desire to lend even my small amount of influence to the destroyers.

For I believe we have not been wrong all these centuries in seeing schools as among the most powerful influences for good which our world has devised. They do not, of course, always succeed; they have their weak links; but until we can think of some more effective way to hand on the knowledge and wisdom of past and present to the generations of the future, we cannot do without schools.

So, to the teachers and pupils of Europe, my sincere affection and admiration.

2
Organization

Se c'incontri per la via,	*If you should meet us in the street,*
Fiocchi rossi sui colletti,	*with red ribbons at our collars,*
Siamo noi, gli scolaretti	*we're the little schoolchildren*
Della scuola elementar'.	*from the primary school.*
Gli scolaretti portano	*The little scholars wear*
Il grado al braccio destro;	*their class-badge on the right arm;*
Davanti al lor maestro	*they trot off to present themselves*
Si vanno a presentar.	*in front of their teacher.*
Con la biro e col pastello	*The schoolboy writes, writes*
Scrive, scrive lo scolaro;	*with pen and crayon; some are*
C'e chi e bravo, chi e somaro,	*good pupils, some stupid, and some,*
E chi, ahime, non vuol studiare!	*alas, don't want to work at all!*
Imparo un po' di storia,	*They learn a bit of history,*
Imparo geografia.	*they learn some geography.*
Cinque anni, e vado via,	*Five years of it, then they're off*
Le Medie ad affrontar!	*to tackle the Middle School.*

I heard this little ditty sung by the children of the A. Fabretti primary school in Perugia; alas, I don't know if it was their own composition, though the somewhat bumpy rhythm and vague rhyme scheme suggest that it may have been. I think I shall always remember it, though, when I see a little Italian boy or girl going off to school in the charming traditional uniform. These are, after all, the things that education is all about; but behind that reality lies a great shapeless mass of administration and organization which, somehow, one has to try to reduce to some kind of order. One feels like a child trying to decide where to start eating a rapidly melting ice-cream which threatens to overflow the edges of the plate before there is time to eat even the first spoonful. But, since one must start somewhere, let us begin with the age at which compulsory education takes place.

Of course, there is education – a lot of it – outside these compulsory years: for example, in our own nursery schools, in the French *maternelles* and in the *educación pre-escolar* of Spain. These schools do a fine job, not only introducing young children to the ideas of reading, writing and counting (and not always, as I saw myself, stopping short of actually teaching them a little of these skills!) but, above all, supplying that food for the young imagination which the concrete deserts of our great housing-estates so signally fail to offer. Whatever preconceived notions I had about the undesirability of taking such young children away from the care of their mothers melted away in front of the reality; on balance, the child gains an enormous amount. And there is also, of course, a vast amount of education continuing beyond the school leaving-age, in the *lycées* and their equivalents, in the technical colleges, in the universities. Only shortage of space prevents me from saying much more of these forms of education; but I must try to confine myself largely to the period of compulsory schooling.

Children usually start school, then, at six on the Continent; at that age the law will in theory intervene if the child is not sent regularly to school. There are remote areas, perhaps, where little Giovanni, Juan or João may be able to avoid the clutches of the school, or where, even, there may be no school for him to go to; but the world is changing fast, and the remotest villages today may find it hard to remain outside the reach of central government. They probably will not wish to do so, indeed, for the peasant often values education more than does the town-dweller; one can see this clearly in that superb little book *Letter to a Teacher*, written by pupils of the remote Tuscan mountain farms;* it is a book one may not always agree with, but some of its comments are among the most penetrating things I have ever read about education.

A curious feature of the Italian system is that a clever six-year-old can start his education in the second form among the seven-year-olds, thus achieving a head start over the average child. Germany proposes to lower the starting age to five by about 1980. With these exceptions, all five countries agree about the start of formal education, but there is much variation at the other end. Italy provides an eight-year period from six to fourteen. So, at present, does Spain, but a plan at present before Parliament would raise the minimum age of employment to sixteen, the effect of which would be to require pupils to do two years of first-grade professional education unless they were already continuing with

Letter to a Teacher by the Pupils of Barbiana, trans. N. Rossi and T. Cole (Penguin, 1970).

a grammar-school course. Even now, Spanish pupils who have not completed the course satisfactorily often stay beyond fourteen to do so. France agrees with Britain in fixing the upper limit at sixteen, though the final year is not necessarily spent in an ordinary school situation; in Germany, pupils must attend school for at least nine years, with the further obligation to attend eight hours weekly of 'vocational education' unless voluntarily continuing in full-time education beyond the leaving-age. As for Portugal, at the time of my visit she was still struggling to raise the leaving-age from twelve to fourteen; her new rulers have much to do.

There is also much diversity in the type of education provided in these six, eight, nine or ten years. The situation is most complex in France and Germany, which justifies my starting with one of the others; I choose Spain because she has recently re-orientated her whole educational programme. One official there admitted frankly that there is still some gap between theory and practice in these reforms; but a good deal of money has certainly been spent. In 1973, 15·4 per cent of government expenditure went on educational and cultural provision. Between the ages of six and fourteen some four million Spanish children receive what is called *Educación General Básica*, usually shortened to EGB. Normally it is provided throughout in the same school, but in two stages, *primera etapa* from six to about eleven, and *segunda etapa* onwards to fourteen. The Ministry booklet states that EGB is not a mere synthesis of the old primary and secondary courses, but is something quite new, based upon six principles: equality of education for all pupils, more individualized teaching, new teaching methods, education by 'areas' rather than by subjects, a new concept of the school as a 'centre', and new leaving qualifications at the end of the course. Many of these points will be dealt with later, but one or two demand explanation here.

By 'equality of education', the Spaniards mean that every pupil shall have an equal opportunity regardless of his family or economic situation. Formerly some children went on to secondary education at about ten or eleven, but a much larger number had only elementary education up to the age of fourteen; now, all will receive an education suited to their aptitudes and capacities, their pace of learning and individual development. Since 1970 basic education has been free, and over the next few years the principle is to be extended to cover free education in the first stage of professional education beyond the statutory leaving age.

EGB centres in the state system are now known as *colegios nacionales de EGB* but it should be remembered that Spain has many non-state (mainly church) schools; these are now integrated into the EGB system but retain their own structures, names and independent identities. I saw something of this system, for example, at the Sagrada Familia school at Ecija, near Seville; this school is connected with the Company of Jesus, and this *patronato* – a word one might translate as 'foundation' or 'sponsorship' – shares the cost of running the school on a 50–50 basis with the state. Independent schools charge fees, but presumably if the Ministry pamphlet means what it says the state will in future meet that part of the fees covering the pupil's actual educational needs: the words are 'whatever may be the educational centre in which the course is taken'.

At the end of the EGB course, pupils who have completed the programme successfully receive the title of *graduado escolar* (literally, 'school graduate') which will be an automatic title to entry, if desired, to the *bachillerato* course, which is more or less the equivalent of the French *baccalauréat*. Those who do not qualify as *graduados* will receive a *certificado de escolaridad*, or school certificate, which is simply proof of having followed the course offered, without comment on the pupil's actual attainment. This certificate entitles the pupil to enter the first grade of professional education. The *bachillerato* course is normally taken in an *instituto de bachillerato* or in the corresponding classes of a private school, and there is now to be only one single, polyvalent course lasting three years, which may then be followed in one further year by the 'COU' – the *curso de orientación universitaria* (university preparation course).

Before the revolution, Portugal had plans to introduce, by about 1979, a system somewhat similar to this Spanish one, with compulsory school for six- to fourteen-year-olds. How far the new political situation will cause this plan to be modified is a matter of conjecture, but the publication in 1975 of new syllabuses suggests that something on those lines is going forward. Primary education is now divided into two 'phases', the first covering the ages from six to eight and roughly corresponding to the first two classes of the old system, and the second running from eight to ten or eleven. Pupils then move into the *ciclo preparatório*, a two-year course which either prepares them for entry into working life at fourteen, or bridges the gap between primary education and that of the *liceu* (grammar school) or *escola técnica* (technical school). I am told that pupils can in fact remain in the second phase of primary school until the age of fourteen if necessary, and that those who even then have not completed the course satisfactorily can continue it in evening classes. Most, however, go into the *ciclo preparatório* at latest by the age of twelve, and some as early as ten. Up to the present, the *liceus* and technical schools have charged fees, though these were quite low, and grants were available to poorer students; whether the new régime plans to make secondary education free to all who follow it, I have not been able to ascertain.

Italy also maintains the division into primary and secondary schools with a break at about eleven; the basic secondary school is called the *scuola media* and provides a three-year course to the age of fourteen; thereafter the pupil either leaves school or proceeds to a higher school such as the *liceo classico*, a more or less traditional grammar school with a five-year course; or a similar five-year course at a *liceo scientifico* or an *instituto tecnico*; or a four-year course in the *liceo artistico*. Any of these may lead on to a university course; but for those not aiming so high there is also the *magistrale*, with a four-year course for those intending to become teachers and leading on to the *magistero* or training college; or there are vocational schools (*tecniche*) with four-year courses also.

Next, let us look at France. Here again the primary/secondary division is observed, with the break at about eleven. The secondary stage begins with four years in a *collège d'enseignement sécondaire* (CES); in the first two years there are at present three parallel courses arranged according to the pupils' ability: the ablest go to Types I or II and are taught by specialist subject-teachers, while the weaker ones go to Type III and continue to be taught more or less on the primary-school method with a single class-teacher responsible for virtually every subject. (This is justified on the grounds that the slower pupils develop better in the more secure atmosphere of the classroom with a single teacher who knows them well and with whom they feel at home; there is something in this argument, though possibly an insufficiency of specialist teachers who can also teach the less gifted pupils may well have something to do with it!)

After the first two years of the CES, more subjects are introduced as options, and instead of Types I, II and III there are now Types I, II and II *aménagée* (not an easy word to translate, but perhaps 'adapted' or 'modified' would do). Type II *aménagée* follows a less exacting curriculum, with extra work in basic subjects, and to it go some pupils from the previous Type II classes together with those from Type III who do not either enter the 'pre-professional class' or remain for a further year in their former class.

This same structure continues for the last year of CES, but some of the less academic pupils will enter courses leading to apprenticeship or professional courses. On paper there is a great deal of flexibility in these various courses, and attempts to reproduce them in diagrammatic form become very complex; in practice, it was my impression that transfer from one course to another was relatively uncommon.

After completing the CES course, pupils either proceed to a *lycée*, a *lycée technique*, a *collège d'enseignement technique*, or one of a variety of specialized colleges; or they continue working for professional or apprenticeship qualifications.

However, it was recently announced that the government has accepted a drastic reform of this system, as well as of the *baccalauréat* examination, and by the time this appears in print change may be under way, though it is said to be running into a good deal of opposition. It is said that the division into three grades has proved to be arbitrary and unjust; children of workers are said to be much more likely than others to find themselves in Type III classes, and very few who get into this stream ever get out of it again.

The new proposal is to have mixed-ability classes, but with subject-grouping for the three major subjects of French, mathematics and the first foreign language, so that pupils can repeat just one of these subjects if necessary, instead of having to repeat the whole year's work should they fail one part of it. Such pupils will be given extra help, and if at the end of the first four-year cycle a pupil is still below the general standard, only then will he be given an extra year to try to fit him for entry to the second cycle. All pupils will be taught by teachers with the same qualifications during the first four-year cycle; these teachers will specialize in two subjects, thus providing the pupil with a transitional stage between the single-teacher primary class and the subject-specialist system of the second cycle secondary school.

Public opinion seems to be rather pessimistic about this proposed system, so it may come to nothing after all; the arguments on both sides resemble those which have raged in this country over comprehensive education, and perhaps the most useful comment one can make is that it might be better, in whatever country, to look more carefully into the reasons why inequality of achievement occurs in the schools, than to devise ever more sophisticated ways of camouflaging it.

Finally Germany. Here the position is complicated by certain differences between one federal state and another, arising partly from political differences: those states governed by the Social Democrats favour a system more akin to the comprehensive than do those governed by the Christian Democrats, which prefer to maintain a tripartite system until more is known about what they consider an unproved system. But pretty well everywhere agreement has been reached on a basic four-year primary school programme, between the ages of six and ten (though in the city states – Berlin, Bremen, Hamburg – this stage normally lasts six years to the age of twelve). Following experiments in Hesse and Lower Saxony, the idea has been developed of following this primary stage (known as the *Grundschule*) with a two-year assessment period, originally called *Forderstüfe*, but now known as *Orientierungstufe*, during which the child's aptitude can be observed with a view to steering him into the most appropriate type of secondary school. Again, party differences lead to different interpretations of this: the Social Democrat areas favour the idea of making it the nucleus of an eventual comprehensive organization, the others see it rather as a refinement of the selection process.

In Emden, I was informed that Lower Saxony proposes that this classification period shall be conducted in classes taught by teachers *from all types of school*, presumably seconded for part-time teaching in this school; the classes will have to take place in some part of the buildings of an existing school, but will not officially form a section of that school. This sounds an admirable idea, enabling a consortium of experienced teachers of all types to observe the pupil for two years and give an unbiased professional judgement on him when the time comes; the organization of the teaching profession in Germany should enable this kind of secondment to work quite well, though I can imagine some problems arising from the differential hours of work and rates of pay enjoyed by teachers in the different types of school. But some of those with whom I have discussed the idea in Germany were rather non-committal as to their hopes of its success.

When the child has passed through this classification stage, in whatever form, he will enter one of three types of school. The *Hauptschule*, attended by anything from 50 to 80 per cent of pupils, provides a course up to the age of fifteen which is really an extension of the basic education provided in the primary school and may, indeed, take place in the same premises, as it does at the school I visited in Zewen, near Trier; such a school closely parallels the Spanish system. Those who do not stay in the *Hauptschule* will move either to a *Realschule*, a kind of intermediate school (it is, indeed, sometimes called a *Mittelschule*, and its leaving certificate is the *Mittlere Reife*); or to a *Gymnasium*, or grammar school. The *Realschule* course lasts to the age of sixteen; the *Gymnasium* course to the age of nineteen, though some have argued for shortening it by one year. Pupils of the *Hauptschule* can, if they wish, stay on to sixteen, take the *Mittlere Reife* as do the *Realschule* pupils, and then go on to a technical college or to the upper forms of a *Gymnasium*. Normally, however, there is no formal examination at the end of the *Hauptschule* course; pupils are merely furnished with a certificate that they have completed the course satisfactorily (if they have!) and this serves as an entitlement to enter upon employment.

Perhaps the gravest objection to our own 11-plus system of school organization, as far as parents were concerned, was that a child who was allocated by the system to a particular type of school appeared to be directed thereby into a channel which would determine his whole future education and his career prospects. It is difficult to assess to what extent this feeling exists among parents in European countries under their different, but by no means entirely comprehensive, school system. I have briefly touched on this matter in my introductory chapter; here I would comment that my visits to schools were deliberately made mainly to those which provided the basic education of the majority of children. There are, however, clearly marked lines leading from the school which provides basic education – the Italian *scuola media*, the Spanish *colegio nacional* or the French CES – to the 'higher' education of the *liceo*, *instituto de bachillerato*, or *lycée*, and from these access to the professions is open. Taking Spain as an example, we have seen how the pupil who has completed the EGB course well enough to be awarded the *graduado* can automatically pass into the *bachillerato* course, and soon this will be free. Only Germany of my chosen countries has something much closer to our old tripartite system, and even there we have seen that the *Mittlere Reife* provides a possible route from *Hauptschule* to *Gymnasium*. If, therefore, the reality matches the promises on the outside of the packet, it would seem that the European pupil receives a reasonably Square Deal; but I do not think one could evaluate the situation justly without living for quite a long time in the country concerned and talking to a great many more people than I had time to meet.

The different countries show differences of practice on the question of co-education. In France almost all schools are now accepting pupils of either sex, even if some of them have not yet been co-educational long enough for numbers to have achieved an equal balance. The same is also true of Germany, though here I did visit one *Gymnasium*, or grammar school, which was virtually a single-sex school, its only girl pupils being a few who had entered as a result of the school's having a co-operative arrangement with the local *lycée française*.

The ultimate in an unbalanced class, however, was probably the one I visited in another German school, which comprised twenty-seven girls ... and one boy – who looked, I thought, tolerably pleased with his lot. Two other establishments which had accepted co-education only in part were the CET at Beauvais, a college specializing in building techniques, where the very small proportion of girls is easily explained by the special character of the school; and the Institution du Saint-Esprit in the same city, which is an independent boarding-school for boys that has begun to admit girls into its top classes.

Spanish schools were formerly almost exclusively single-sex, and probably a majority still are; but newer ones are often co-educational, as I saw at the Colegio Menendez Pidal at Salt and at several schools in Jaén. The situation in Portugal is broadly similar, with integration of the sexes again just beginning to take place; Italian schools, however, are almost always mixed.

A co-educational school, of course, does not necessarily mean mixed classes. One Italian *scuola media*, San Paolo at Perugia, had been forced by timetabling problems to segregate a number of classes (the spanners in the works are often physical education and handicraft, though at the primary stage mixed PE lessons are sometimes found, and a few schools of all types had also found it possible to mix their handicraft classes at least to some extent). Another Italian school, this time a primary school, had all its classes segregated, but was proposing to reorganize on mixed lines in the very near future. One Spanish *instituto* and many of the *colegios nacionales* had one or two mixed classes but the majority segregated (often with male teachers for all-female classes); and the Portuguese *liceu* which I visited had separated classes for younger pupils, but taught the older ones in mixed classes.

The ultimate absurdity, however, was attained by one Portuguese primary school. It was a fairly small school, with only enough pupils in each year-group to make up one single mixed class; but the principle of segregating the sexes was so inflexible that each room contained a group of pupils of the same sex but of two different age-groups. Thus, instead of one properly homogeneous mixed class, every teacher had to struggle with having to direct two distinct activities at the same time. Inevitably the children suffered under this absurd arrangement, the object of which seemed to be to ensure that no little boy ever saw a little girl during school hours except from a safe distance.

It is hard to generalize about the size of classes. One Spanish school, with otherwise impeccable standards, had classes of forty-five to fifty pupils, and classes of about forty are the Spanish norm except where small groups corresponding to an English sixth form are taught. For this reason, valiant efforts are being made to evolve more flexible teaching units, though it is official Spanish policy to reduce all classes to a maximum of thirty pupils as soon as this can be achieved. The problem is not shortage of staff so much as shortage of buildings, and some places are having to resort to two-shift systems even to maintain the present class-sizes. In France I was surprised to see splendidly unflappable women coping with as many as forty-five children in nursery classes, but the general average was much lower – about twenty-five or twenty-six as a rule, though some classes might rise to as many as thirty-five. Portuguese primary classes sometimes reached thirty-seven pupils, but teaching-groups in technical schools and *liceus* rarely exceeded thirty. German primary classes are said to average upwards of thirty, with fewer in the secondary classes; but it was my impression that, if anything, numbers are increasing rather than decreasing, and my German teacher friends often lamented that their classes were larger than they could wish.

The tendency for secondary classes to be smaller than primary ones was, however, reversed in France. Bearing in mind the greater formality of teaching found at the secondary level in France, this is probably the right way round; in any case, it is fairly common for French secondary classes to divide into two halves for some of their lessons to make possible more individualized teaching.

Streaming is not very often found in Continental schools, though the French division of secondary pupils into three 'types' is, of course, one form of streaming. I did see some special remedial classes, again in France; and at one German secondary school I was told that the older pupils were streamed for mathematics and for English. Otherwise, such separation of sheep from goats as there was within the schools related only to the pupils' choice of alternative subjects (which sometimes also amounts to streaming, if the choice is between a more academically demanding subject and an easier option). I say 'within the schools' because it must not be forgotten that none of these five countries has a completely 'comprehensive' educational system.

There is, therefore, often a fairly considerable range of ability within any one class. I recall, for example, one class in an Italian primary school, with a group of highly vocal and quick-thinking pupils at its top end, and one particular boy at the other who seemed quite lost. I wondered about this boy: he did not seem evidently older than the rest of the class, and must presumably have received normal promotions, therefore. Possibly someone had turned a kindly blind eye to the rather rigid Italian procedure of 'no pass, no promotion'.

Staffing ratios roughly corresponded with the figures I have already given for the size of classes; indeed, in primary schools the figures normally must do so, since the primary teacher does not normally receive free periods during his working day, save occasionally in the case of a head teacher. Thus, if the school has ten classes, it has ten teachers: it's as simple as that. Indeed, in Italy, even when a specialist teacher is brought in to teach, say, art or music, the class-teacher must also remain with the class throughout, as he is responsible for all that happens to his pupils: for him, 'there's no discharge in the war'. The one primary school I found where the staffing ratio was better than 'one man to one class' was the unusual little village school at Porcellasco, which will figure rather often in this book; and I sensed some resentment among other teachers about this, for they obviously felt that, given such luxury, they too could have done as well. It is difficult to find precisely comparable statistics, but one set I have discovered may be of some interest: they show that in the primary schools, Spain has one teacher to thirty-five pupils, Portugal one to thirty-four, and Italy one to twenty-one, while in the secondary stage Spain and Portugal have one to seventeen pupils and Italy one to eleven. Figures for England and Wales are one to twenty-eight (primary) and one to nineteen (secondary); but it should be noted that the Continental countries referred to have a large number of part-time teachers in the secondary stage, people who combine a few hours' teaching with some other profession. A set of figures provided by the German authorities shows one teacher to thirty pupils in the elementary schools, one to twenty-three in the *Realschule*, and one to eighteen or nineteen in the *Gymnasium*; these are figures averaged out over the eleven *Länder*, for there are wide variations between the best and the worst figures in each category: plus or minus about five in each case, I suppose. I have no figures for France.

The sizes of individual schools inevitably vary a great deal, but I think it is true to say that in the larger towns very big schools are tending to becoming the rule. Leaving out the occasional very small village school, those primary schools which I visited were not usually very large – only one had over 500 pupils – but among the secondary schools the picture was very different, averaging about 1,000 pupils per school, and in one case rising to almost 2,000. Very few of them were of that intimate size which would allow reasonable hope of any one person having a fair knowledge of every pupil, or even of all that went on in the school. This was certainly one reason why a number of the secondary schools seemed to be rather impersonal places, though I felt that there were other reasons too! (I must, of course, point out that I virtually only saw *town* schools: when the multitudes of small village schools in every country are counted in, it is worth remarking that the average number of pupils in German primary schools comes down to less than 300 per school, in Italian ones to about 130, in Spanish to only just over 100, and in Portuguese schools to fewer than 60; at the secondary level, figures are more equal, with Germany and Spain on about 320–30, Italy about 270, and Portugal about 225.)

Boarding accommodation is found more often abroad than in England, for obvious enough reasons: schools may have to serve large areas with relatively little transport, so that pupils have to stay at the school at any rate during the week. I visited three French and two Spanish schools which had boarding places – indeed, there may possibly have been other schools with boarding accommodation which I did not see. Both the Spanish schools concerned were church schools, run by the teaching order known as the Marist Brothers. Their college at Jaén was a handsome building, not very old, near the city centre. It had about 1,500 pupils and a staff of some forty teachers. 330 of these pupils were boarders, and they enjoyed such amenities as separate small bedrooms for each boy, simply but pleasantly furnished, a play-room with various mechanical and other games available, a play-park in the grounds for the youngest children, a spacious handicraft-room, and even a fully equipped barber's shop. The other Marist College, La Inmaculada at Gerona, was housed when I first saw it in very timeworn buildings, offering much more Spartan accommodation – communal dormitories, a long room full of old desks used for evening preparation, and not a great deal else; I have since revisited this school in its new buildings on the outskirts of Gerona and was much impressed by what they had to offer, even in their partially completed state of Easter 1974.

Of the three French schools with boarders, one was a privately-run school, where I think the boarders considerably outnumbered the day-boys. This school had comfortable accommodation, the pupils sleeping in small dormitories. The other two were both technical schools, which drew their pupils from all over their *département*, and indeed from beyond its limits. Each had some 300 boarders, out of respective totals of 900 and 1,100 pupils. One of them had a particularly notable school hospital, with two wards each holding eight or nine beds, and an additional small isolation ward with room for three patients.

Sometimes, however, the problem of pupils who live in remote areas is better dealt with by providing transport; I was told of one school in the town of Alcalá la Real, in the Province of Jaén, Spain, where no fewer than 1,400 pupils arrive each day in fleets of buses from outlying hamlets and isolated farms. As Alcalá is itself quite a small town, perhaps with 25,000 inhabitants, this vast influx must be quite worth seeing: even allowing for the impressive capacity of the average Spanish bus, it is probably a rather remarkable procession that makes its stately way through the streets of Alcalá. The bicycle, too, plays a big part in school life in Europe; I was considerably impressed by the vast provision made for bicycles in some French and German schools, though I did also come across one in Beauvais which had virtually banned the use of cycles on road safety grounds.

The school term differs somewhat in length and arrangement from English practice. In Germany, the *Länder* stagger their terms in order to even out the loads of traffic on the roads and of holiday-makers in the resorts, and as the schedules of holidays change every so often there is not much point in giving more than a small sample. The exact dates of the holidays can in fact be found, among other places, in the official German railway time-table – a useful provision, in view of the number of trains which are marked 'Schooldays only'. In 1973–4, for example, all schools broke up for Christmas on either 22 or 24 December, but the beginning of the spring term varied from 3 January in Hamburg to 14 January in Baden-Württemberg. The Easter holidays started as early as 11 March in Hamburg, and were over there by 30 March (a fortnight before Easter!) whereas they did not commence until 8 April in Bavaria (where they lasted till 20 April) and in North Rhine-Westphalia (where they went on to 27 April). Children in Saarland and Rhineland-Palatinate began their summer holidays as early as 20 June, and in the latter *Land* they were already back at their books on 1 August, the day when the children of Bavaria *began* their own summer holidays, which lasted until 16 September. It is really quite difficult to find many days in the year when nobody is at school anywhere in Germany! I asked a teacher how he and his colleagues coped with these ebbing and flowing terms – how, for example, they allowed in the planning of syllabuses for the fact that one school year might well be two or three weeks longer than average, and another one, owing to its being the year in which the region moved from one end of the holiday queue to the other, two or three weeks shorter. He shrugged, and said, 'Well, you just get through the work a little faster or a little slower, as the case may be!'

Organization 21

The other four countries normally opt for a long summer holiday and quite short ones at other periods. The intense heat of summer in many regions, and the compensation available in the form of fairly frequent national holidays, saints' days, etc., probably make this arrangement work quite pleasantly. One Spanish school provided me with a detailed calendar for 1972–3: the autumn term began (with programming of courses) on Monday 11 September, actual lessons starting one week later, and continued (with occasional days off) until Thursday 21 December. Resuming on Monday 8 January, term went on to Friday 13 April; and after a brief Easter break, re-commenced on Wednesday 25 April. Actual teaching ended on Wednesday 20 June, but end-of-term tests prolonged the term to the end of the month. In 1974, I saw slight variations on this pattern in some areas, and I would guess that local holidays may need to be compensated for by adding a day or two here and there to the standard term.

French school holidays are fixed on a national basis. Though I understand that some slight changes in the traditional plan have recently been made, the 1972–3 pattern here quoted is reasonably typical: the year ran from 18 September to 30 June, with holiday periods from 29 October to 1 November; 22 December to 2 January; 11, 18 or 25 February to 18 or 25 February or 4 March; and 11 April to 25 April. The main differences from the Spanish system is the later start to the autumn term, balanced by an earlier start in January. However, as the Spanish schoolboy works 5 or $5\frac{1}{2}$ days weekly against the French boy's $4\frac{1}{2}$, he possibly puts in rather more time over the entire year – which does not necessarily mean that he works harder!

The working day can also vary a great deal. An attempt has been made in Appendix VII to provide a comparative table, but it may be remarked here that primary-school pupils work about 27–8 hours a week (less in Italy), but the hours of secondary schools range from a minimum of about 27 in Italy up to (apparently) a possible 40 for some pupils of a Spanish *instituto*. From this time must be deducted the recreational breaks, which are so variable as to defy tabulation. Italian practice seemed to be to call a few minutes' halt when everyone was feeling a little jaded, so that the children might stretch their legs and perhaps eat a bun or sandwich. Spanish schools usually had long breaks of up to half an hour both morning and afternoon, though one school, Martin

Noguera at Jaén, took no breaks at all. Portugal had the pleasant practice of making a 10-minute break at the end of each (notional) hour of work; French practice was much the same as our own, with breaks of about 15–20 minutes midway through a session; and the extremely long German morning was split into three sections by breaks of 15 or 20 minutes. I must add here that to one accustomed to the English system, it is a depressing moment when, at the end of the second lesson of the day in Germany, one's watch records that it is still only 9.30 a.m., with another $3\frac{1}{2}$ hours to go before lunch! But class 12Na at the Emden Treckfahrtstief Gymnasium left me in no doubt that they thought the English custom of making the pupil go to school in the afternoon as well as the morning was little short of barbarous; as they said, if you can't do your homework in the afternoon, you obviously have to do it in the evening, and then what happens to your social life? A tenable point of view, but it is my honest opinion that many pupils in Germany are very tired and lacking in concentration by the time they reach the final stretch of a six-period morning.

Officially, the length of a German lesson is 45 minutes; in practice, there are usually two bells, one a minute or two before the end, the other a few minutes later, to give the teacher time to move from one class to the next. Elsewhere, it is normal for the unit of a single lesson to be one hour, though, as already mentioned, the Portuguese hour is but a notional one. That beastly institution the change-of-class bell is rather less common than in England (though it is general in Germany); one Portuguese school used the old-fashioned hanging bell, tolled by anyone who happened to be handy at the right moment. But the really nasty device was the one used by one French primary school and one Spanish *instituto*: a harsh corncrake blare from a klaxon, used to call the pupils in from play. It frightened me out of my wits every time it went off.

'Homework' is a word which is rather glumly received by pupils everywhere. It seems to be pretty well universal in all European schools, though naturally most evident in the secondary schools and especially their upper reaches. It does not appear to be set to any regular pattern; teachers give pupils tasks to do at home as and when they think fit, and some German pupils told me that it was not uncommon for every one of the morning's six lessons to produce a piece of homework. This may not, however, be a very

Organization

heavy task; for example, one class of beginners in English at this same school were asked to form for homework five questions beginning with the words 'Who ... ?', 'What ... ?', 'Is he ... ?', 'Is she ... ?' and 'Are they ... ?', which would probably not take the average pupil very long to do. Against this, however, I must set the German lady teacher with a class of primary children aged about eight, who told me that she expected them to do on average $1-1\frac{1}{2}$ hours' work each day at home. 'After all', said she, 'they have all the afternoon to do it.' She added that she only sets work that the children have been able to prepare previously in class, and she admitted that personally she thought it would be better if the children returned to do the work under supervision in the afternoon, as it would then be more effectively done. It would also be rather arduous for them after a five-hour morning, I thought!

Two minor and miscellaneous matters to end this chapter. The first is to refer briefly to the long-standing German tradition that every six-year-old starting school for the first time is given a huge paper cornet, almost as big as himself, containing sweets and toys to share with his friends; in one German school I saw photographs of three generations of children from the same families taken probably about 1920, 1940 and 1970; their dress was very different, but the cornets were identical.

Lastly, it may be of interest to mention that a number of days each year are always set aside for the formal enrolling of pupils for the coming year; sometimes this takes place at the end of the summer term – in one French CES at the time of my visit the headmaster was engaged in interviewing every single child who would transfer to his school from the primary school – and sometimes it happens during the few days preceding the start of the autumn term. In chapter 9 I refer briefly to some of the documentation which accompanies this formal registration of pupils.

POSTSCRIPT

In addition to the types of German secondary school mentioned on pp. 13-14, some areas have adopted the *Gesamtschule*, or Comprehensive school, while others use a variant, the *Additivgesamtschule*, or multilateral school. In this last type, regular meetings of staff teaching each year discuss individual pupils and, if necessary, recommend their transfer to a different section of the school.

3
What they do and how they do it

It is traditional to the Englishman that he takes a somewhat sentimental view of the places in which he spends his youth – his school, his college, his sports club or his regiment may all take on a somewhat unreal golden glow in his later memory, whether the reality was enjoyable or not. It was perhaps for this reason that I asked a group of Spanish boys, aged about seventeen or eighteen, if they thought they would remember their schooldays with pleasure and affection. I was unprepared then for their puzzled looks, and for the way in which their natural politeness struggled with an evident feeling that the question was rather an absurd one. They did their best to make clear to me that a school is just a place to which you go to do certain things, just like a shop or a railway-station. The shop offers you boots or bananas, the station sells you tickets and provides trains, and the school . . . well, the school teaches you to read and write, to speak foreign languages, to calculate, to understand something of world history and geography, and all that sort of thing.

An entirely practical and sensible view, of course. These are things which will be of value to your subsequent activities in life, and so a building is provided, and a group of people are assembled there who themselves know how to do these things (up to a point, anyway) and you are allowed to go along there and absorb some of their knowledge and ideas and experience for so many hours a day, so many days a week, so many weeks a year. As far as other time, other activities, are concerned, that is your own affair; the idea that you can feel affectionate towards the place as an institution is difficult to understand, for one does not feel affectionate about the post office or the bank, does one?

Of course, this is too plain a picture to be quite true: it *is* possible for European children to sing in the school choir, write a poem for the school magazine, go with the school on an outing or excursion, or play for the school team in certain games or sports. Children do go to school camps, give parties for their teachers, and borrow books from the school library; they make friends, play informal games, and generally enjoy the society of their fellows; and all these activities make the school far more than just a fact-shop. If the pupil considers the matter in that light, he will feel some affection and warmth towards a place where so many interesting and enjoyable things happen to him. But I think he considers it in that light much less often than does his English counterpart: I read a series of statements in an Italian school magazine, in which children gave their views about their school, and although they mostly appeared to find it a satisfactory place, it seemed to be rather because it was teaching them efficiently than because it was a place of emotional satisfaction. There is, on the whole, no European equivalent of the curious English cult of the 'school story'; a book may to some extent involve school life, as does Alain-Fournier's *Le Grand Meaulnes*, Jules Vallès' *L'Enfant* or Miguel Delibes' *El Camino*, to mention three books at random, but the school is not the central theme, it is neither the hero nor the anti-hero of the story.

Nor is there a place in French or Spanish myth for the utterly Philistine attitude towards education that the otherwise engaging 'school story' engenders: those twin notions that success in sport is far more important than academic achievement, and that the object of every decent schoolboy must be to 'rag' instead of working. Those ideas, themselves the product of the notion that all the best schools are those for 'sons of gentlemen' who can afford to do without book-knowledge, have vitiated the efforts of teachers in this country for far too long; they have no parallel outside Britain – indeed, outside England, for Scotland and Wales see matters quite otherwise. So a book about English school life would probably set the discussion of curriculum and syllabus within an ornamental border of sports, societies, school concerts, farewell presentations to Mr Chips, and appassionato renderings of the School Song; but such of these things as exist in Europe are strictly subordinate to the real job, which is teaching and learning. In my view, after seeing thirty or forty Continental schools, they do this job astonishingly well, and if we are prepared to dismiss from our minds a few deeply embedded prejudices, we can learn much from them.

In the appendices I have tried to summarize the basic curriculum of European schools, and it would be superfluous to set it out here also; in any case, as far as the primary schools are concerned, the programme is rightly kept quite fluid. One of the first schools I saw, the A. Fabretti elementary school in Perugia, may be taken to illustrate this point. It is a mixed school with about 220 boys and girls, and ten teachers. Though situated in an old part of the city, behind a rather dreary wall, it is in fact a fairly recent building. I saw two sessions there, the first with a male teacher, Signor Cicchi, the second with a lady, Signorina Lamoretti.

Signor Cicchi's class were eight-year-olds, and a delightfully alert and lively group; thirteen were boys and nine girls. They were using a method of learning which was quite new to me, based on the composition of short 'dialogues' about topics of interest such as the weather, school life, music, animals, science ... or, indeed, anything else in which an intelligent child may be interested. They make frequent visits to museums and other places of interest, use the cinema a good deal, and have plenty of active pursuits such as music, movement and handicraft. Signor Cicchi told me he used this method simply because he liked it; he was free to use whatever method he pleased. This one certainly called for a lot of energy and resourcefulness on his part, and he showed no shortage of those qualities!

While he talked to me, the class got on busily with its work; I don't say 'quietly', because Italian children are too lively to be quiet for long, but their noise was the right sort of noise, a buzz of positive activity. Some were doing arithmetic, some were drawing and some were in the throes of literary composition, notably one Gianfranco Vergoni, a chubby eight-year-old, who had instantly turned his very fluent pen to a description of myself and my activities. The children were completely involved in their work, and although they moved about the room freely, they were always under control; it needed only a sort of sharp hiss from Signor Cicchi to bring down the level of noise. They had all contributed to a variety of class projects and journals, and their work was of a very high standard, comparable with the very best that an English primary school would produce, and probably superior to it in the matters of handwriting and style of expression, both of which seemed to be very well taught.

Signorina Lamoretti's methods, with her thirty pupils aged about ten or eleven, were somewhat more formal, but for all that, her room had a lively, modern feel about it; it was sunny, the desks were grouped about the room, and the walls were bright with pictures. But in other respects, the atmosphere was more like that of a secondary class; the teacher was dealing with the *risorgimento*, and the pupils were busily taking down notes much as an English grammar-school sixth form might have done. When I arrived, however, Signorina Lamoretti quickly brought the lesson to a neat conclusion, and turned over to learning something about England. The children asked me some very good questions: how was England governed, and what were the Queen's powers? Did we feel happy about being in the EEC? All this was done – for I am not very fluent in Italian – with the help of a boy called Stefano (I never found out his surname) who spoke good English, as he has grandparents living in Reading and often visits them. I very much envied this little boy's skill as an interpreter: how fortunate the child who can grow up genuinely bilingual!

Lessons then resumed, with the class secretary (appointed by the week) completely recapitulating the lesson up to the point at which it had broken off; then a few minutes were spent on grammar, with much enjoyable chanting by rote; this was followed by a little geography, including some reference to current affairs; and the session ended with a performance, *con brio*, of a short drama written by the children, which led to a glorious Mediterranean rumpus with everybody arguing at once about the right way to render the final song.

Such an informal approach might be paralleled in all European countries. Printed timetables exist, but may be viewed sceptically; the good teacher does not pursue a topic when he has obviously lost his class, or abandon one when their interest is still at its height. One school's timetable (Ramon Calatayud, at Jaén) did no more than suggest general headings and the type of teaching-group to be used; both here and at a Portuguese primary school I saw later, there was flexibility in the taking of breaks, so as to permit the teacher as much freedom as possible.

I can, however, quote an actual timetable from the village primary school of Porcellasco, near Cremona. This school (officially the Scuola Pietro Pasquali) has about fifty pupils and five teachers – an unusually lavish staffing-ratio, because it is an experimental 'all-day school' of a type very rare in Italy. The extra afternoon sessions enable the basic curriculum to be extended into a wide range of activities, and one hopes its example is inspiring other Italian schools to follow. Here, then, is the timetable:

	MONDAY	TUESDAY	WEDNESDAY	THURSDAY	FRIDAY
8.30–9.00	Classwork	Classwork	Cinema	Classwork	Classwork
9.00–10.00	Classwork	Classwork	Cinema	Classwork	Classwork
10.00–11.00	English	Classwork	Classwork	English	Classwork
11.00–11.30	Break	Break	Classwork	Break	Break
11.30–12.30	Classwork	Drama	Classwork	Classwork	Drama
14.00–15.00			Work-groups (See below)		
15.00–16.00	Work-groups		Study		Work-groups

On Tuesdays and Thursdays, some children have Choir from 15.00–16.00)

The term 'work-groups' requires a little explanation, for it is a very modest title indeed, seeing that it includes such activities as printing (monotype, woodblock, spray), clay-modelling (under the guidance of a local sculptor), painting, drawing, carpentry, copperwork, needlework, cardboard-modelling, paper-cutting, elementary domestic science, embossed work, collage, linocuts, photography, speech-training, recitation and something called 'techniques of figurative expression', which I take to be some form of instruction in stylish writing. A formidable list for a little rural school of less than fifty boys and girls; but I saw samples of many of these arts and crafts, and was surprised by their very high standard. I saw copies of the little magazine produced by these children: part of it was set up in type by themselves, part was simply cyclostyled; but they have every intention of having the whole thing printed as soon as they can manage it. One sparkling little boy in the fourth class, Vatio by name, wrote with pride of the way he had been detailed to explain the intricacies of coloured woodblock printing to a group of visiting teachers: 'You take a little block of plywood, you make a design on it, and you cut into it with a biro or a cutting-tool; then you take some printing-colours and go over the block with a brush dipped in turpentine. The coloured block, with a white sheet of paper over it, is stamped either by hand or in the printing-press. At the end of my practical demonstration, I could see that the teachers were very interested in this method of printing in colour.'

Moving from Italy to France, I think the summary given in the appendix is more or less self-explanatory; but the English teacher will be interested by the very different weighting given to the different educational disciplines in France: more than a third of the week is given over to study of the native language, and with such an allocation of time, one is a little less surprised that the French do this particular job so well; some may also be surprised to see the generous allocation of time to physical education and games, for (except in rugby football) the French are perhaps not thought of as a major sporting nation. But the standard of physical health of their children is certainly high.

The most interesting feature of the Spanish programme is its division of the work into 'areas', rather than separate subjects: the two areas are 'Expression', which subdivides into language, mathematics, plastic expression (art, craft, etc.) and dynamic expression (physical education and music – an interesting union which also, apparently, exists in Portugal); and 'Experience' (or perhaps 'Experiment' is another equivalent) which divides into the social and natural area and the religious area.

The German school on which the summary in the appendix is based shows a progressive increase in the amount of subject-division: the youngest children have, apart from such activities as physical education and music, only a programme of basic foundation work; those aged from eight to ten begin to study one or two subjects in isolation, while still concentrating largely on the fundamentals of literacy and numeracy; and only in the secondary stage do 'subjects', properly so-called, come into the picture.

Of course, when we move into the secondary school, we find

a more subject-orientated programme. Again, the appendix furnishes the bare details, and I must apologize if they are not presented in a completely uniform way: the problem is that every country has its own individual peculiarities and, furthermore, it has not been possible always to reconcile printed programmes – sometimes showing an actual number of hours worked in each subject, sometimes giving suggested percentages of time to be allocated – with what I personally saw in the schools. However, I believe the figures given are substantially valid.

One point which will immediately strike the English teacher is that the sciences generally receive less time than in our own schools; and where pupils are taught science, it is generally either biology or some form of general science. The specialized study of chemistry and physics (except for a few purely theoretical lessons) tends to be reserved for the upper reaches of education – the top forms of *lycées*, or even the universities. There is also a subject called 'pre-technology' which features in the curriculum of French secondary schools.

Finally, the appendix offers some information about the final stage of secondary education, that leading to whatever may be the university qualification: *baccalauréat, bachillerato, abitur*, and the rest. Here it should be mentioned that the data given for Spain will be obsolete in a few years' time: the former system provided a four-year course called *bachillerato elemental* and two years of *bachillerato superior*, but as two years of the *elemental* are now absorbed in the EGB programme a new scheme has been produced, with the resounding title of *bachillerato unificado y polivalente*.

Discussing the Spanish *bachillerato* programme with some senior pupils, I was left in no doubt that they regard the programme as somewhat heavy, and I am inclined to agree with them. Certainly, our own sixth-form scientists, for example, would feel somewhat irked at having only four hours of actual science in their weekly programme at the age of sixteen or seventeen (or seven hours if we regard mathematics as a science, which only heretics would); for, it will be noted, there is actually *less* science in that year than in the previous one, presumably in order to make room for the philosophy and history of culture courses. Yet, if we accept that education is not just the absorption of a mass of facts, and that an intelligent person's mind may be richly fed by any study that is worthwhile in itself, there may be something to be said for the Spanish programme. For in the last two years of his course, the student will have taken a total of eleven subjects; all of them, including the arts students, will have done *some* science; all of them, including the scientists, will have studied literature and philosophy. Can we say as much for all our own sixth-formers? It is true that the scientist is more hard done by than his arts counterpart, if a narrowly specialist point of view is taken; but in any case, the approach is clearly not the same as ours, for if it were we should be astonished to find the apparent absence of any means to study at this level such subjects as chemistry, geography or economics. Presumably, the acid test would be whether Spain is producing fewer chemists or economists than she needs; but then, are *we* producing too few good lawyers, astronomers or doctors, since we do not offer sixth-form courses in these subjects? The Spaniards appear to feel that an able, hard-working and intelligent pupil will have his or her mind trained just as well by their method as by ours; and much the same kind of approach is taken by the French.

Where the French programme differs both from ours and from the very much simpler Spanish one is in the provision of a very wide range of more or less vocational courses: commercial studies, various kinds of technical course and so on. Perhaps we are too frightened in this country of letting our education have any vocational slant: our ideal seems to be the 'pure' rather than the 'applied' study. The French appear to have no such inhibitions; if they have pupils who fancy the idea of becoming laboratory technicians, they are quite happy to slot them into a course which gives them the chance to practise some of the necessary techniques, such as the making of glass apparatus; at the same time, however, every care is taken to make sure that they also learn plenty of French, mathematics, history, foreign languages and other things that a soundly-educated person should have.

Another feature of the French programme is its 'optional studies'. I do not know how far there is restriction on the number of these which a pupil may take: presumably there should be some limit imposed on a pupil already doing 30 to 32 hours of compulsory studies; but even without these, pupils in most of the course will be studying ten or so different disciplines, which is a commendably broad-based education. However, one must admit that French youngsters complain more about their education, and seem to be under more intense pressure, than most Europeans. This may not only be due to the sheer weight of the programme, but also have some connection with the rather aridly academic style in which some French pupils seem to be taught.

The proposed reforms of the secondary system in France, already referred to, also include some revision of the *baccalauréat* to try to meet some of the most serious criticisms. I have included a brief reference to these proposals in Appendix I.

It will be clear from what I have said that in Europe it is fairly usual for the Ministry of Education to prescribe the curriculum to be followed, at least in broad outline. English teachers often say that such direction would unduly cramp their style, and that such matters are for teachers, not administrators, to decide. No doubt in theory an English school head could decide to devote half the week to the study of cookery and the other half to Finnish grammar, but if he did he would be firmly told by the parents of his pupils, his staff, his governing body and the inspectorate that he had better desist; in fact, therefore, he is by no means a completely free agent.

But if we were to have in this country an agreed curriculum, even an agreed syllabus, the teacher would not necessarily be the helpless victim of the bureaucrats. The teaching profession is well, and vociferously, organized, and educational authorities rightly pay regard to its views. There would, in fact, be real advantages to the pupils: most teachers will have experienced the problem of trying to fit into their school, where French and German are the foreign languages studied, a pupil who has spent the last two years in the study of Spanish; most have had to face an annoyed or disappointed parent whose child has been making good progress in Latin or economics, but must now drop the subject on transfer to a school which cannot provide them. One of the nation's great needs is a more mobile labour force, not least among skilled and specialized people; but many parents must reluctantly decide they must stay where they are because Jeremy's or Jennifer's education must not be disrupted. In most European countries, the transfer of a child from one school to another is easy: if he transfers from the *troisième* of the CES at Crottin-le-Grand to the same class at Limaçon-sur-Mer he will find the class doing more or less the same things there. Hence, no doubt, the origin of the myth that the Minister of Education looks at his watch at 10.30 a.m. and says 'Ah, yes, now they will all be on page 73 of *Histoire de France, Tome IV.*' Of course he does not know anything so boring: schools can choose their own ways of teaching the syllabus, and, with so many imponderables about, the detailed organization of the timetable could not possibly be standardized. Nevertheless, there is undoubtedly much greater control than in England: as an example I may mention that whereas here innumerable primary schools have jumped on the bandwagon of teaching French, the converse has not happened in France, where the Ministry has only approved the carrying out of a limited experiment in certain schools – which may possibly prove to have been a wiser policy.

It is impossible to go into detail here about the content of syllabuses: for Spain alone I have some 500 pages of documentary evidence. (The booklets concerned are full of fascinating material, well-presented and obviously based on deep thought, but they also contain a lot of rather numbing abstractions: the key documents are the two issues of *Vida Escolar* for December 1970 to February 1971 and April to June 1971.) Here I can do no more than illustrate the theme with a few examples.

As a teacher of English myself I was naturally interested to see what the Spanish booklets said about the teaching of their own native language. They emphasize that every teacher, whatever his subject, is to some extent a teacher of the native tongue, and they stress the importance of his own attitude in doing this: 'He must encourage the active participation of his pupils, stimulating them to continual intervention, giving them time for the transmission of their own ideas and thoughts, always respecting them, answering and encouraging their questions.' The teacher specifically concerned with Spanish is then advised on the methods he should use: as soon as the child can form sentences, he must do some written composition each day, and it should include some planning and selection of material. 'Rote' methods such as learning word-lists, or excessive amounts of formal grammar, are discouraged. Literature is studied from the age of thirteen or fourteen, being at first based on texts the pupil already knows through private or group reading, films, dramatization or other means.

The advice concentrates throughout on teaching the pupil to think for himself, to differentiate between essentials and incidentals, facts and opinions. These are admirable principles, and the lessons I saw certainly suggested that pupils do express themselves clearly and even stylishly, with more formal accuracy than their English counterparts; their training has not encouraged them in an impressionistic use of words, but in the formal sobriety which is one aspect of the Spanish character.

The booklet goes on to suggest specific syllabuses. For example, the six- or seven-year-old (first year of EGB) should 'be able to read with understanding simple texts of up to twelve words, divided into two or three phrases, at fifty words to the minute'. At La Inmaculada in Gerona, I was shown a class of six-year-olds, and invited to pick any one at random and ask him to read from whatever page I chose from the textbook in use; I accepted the challenge, and the pupil selected passed with flying colours; later, I heard a little boy of four and a half in the kindergarten of the same school read very nicely, and from these two experiences I am prepared to accept that the syllabus is not merely a pious hope. 'Handwriting', it continues, 'should display clear, uniform shaping of letters, without superfluous strokes, at increasing speed', and pupils should be able to 'compose sentences of four or five words suggested by the presentation of pictures, or as expression of experiences, wishes or feelings'. By the time the Spanish child is ten or eleven, at the age when his English counterpart will normally be moving up to a secondary school, he should know 'the value of variety in vocabulary and the choice of the most expressive words', 'be able to sum up group discussions both during their course and after', 'comment on programmes and announcements broadcast on TV or radio', attempt the 'critical evaluation of the truth and reliability of information received', 'use notes, reference-slips and reference-tables for oral explanation', 'analyse arguments, reinforce or contradict them, and explain consequences' and his reading should have progressed to about 110 words a minute, with 'accuracy and understanding, paying attention to marks of intonation, accent and pause'.

Interesting points from the suggestions for the thirteen- and fourteen-year age group include 'analysis and synthesis of written texts . . . distinguishing the personal and the objective in a report', a certain amount of study of vocabulary and semantics, and of grammar, 'use of simple and compound sentences, juxtaposition and co-ordination, types of subordination, simple transformations of linguistic structures'; and the pupil will also have begun to study literature seriously, with some knowledge of 'principal stylistic devices, and systematic analysis of literary passages'. Some of this may seem to the reader to be rather over-generalized, but there is also a good deal of solid meat in the programme, and there can be no doubt that a pupil who had acquired a good number of these skills would be well-prepared for citizenship. I sadly recall having heard a parent tell me that his son's teacher had airily dismissed the fact that the boy had no idea whatever of the use of punctuation-marks with the words 'Oh, nobody bothers much with that sort of thing nowadays!' Perhaps they should: certainly this view is not shared by Continental teachers. For an example of the standards they try to achieve, I might quote one sentence from a composition written by the little Italian boy Gianfranco Vergoni, whom I have already mentioned: it comes from a charmingly written (and attractively illustrated) dialogue about Spring:

> La stessa cosa è'successa a me: ero vicino al ruscello dove mi aveva dato appuntamento . . . e lei è'arrivata dopo un'ora!
> (The same thing happened to me: I was down by the brook where he had told me to meet him . . . and he arrived an hour late!)

I wish all our bright eight-year-olds were as assured as this little Italian boy in their handling of the colon, the exclamation mark, and the apostrophe, or knew as surely how many c's there are in 'success' and p's in 'appointment'.

Space does not allow me to quote at similar length from the Spanish syllabus in other subjects, but one or two extracts are possible. In mathematics, for example, the work to be covered in the eighth year (thirteen- to fourteen-year-olds) is:

Construction of the set of rational numbers.
Sum of rational numbers. Additive group. Product of rational numbers. The body of rational numbers.
Functions of variable rational. Graphs; equations.
Proportion of segments. Similarity.
Polynomial functions. Polynomials.
The second degree equation. The parabola.
Descriptive study of the hyperbola.

I hope my translations make sense to mathematicians; I am assured, anyway, that the syllabus is good modern maths. I shall refer later to some actual lessons, but I would remark here that – as in this country – not all teachers have taken equally kindly to the recent reforms in mathematical teaching; one elderly gentleman dismissed 'modern maths' out of hand, while another, somewhat more sympathetic, verdict was that 'it teaches them to *think*, but unfortunately not to *calculate*!'

Another subject of which I examined the suggested syllabus rather carefully was the 'social area', covering history, geography and civics. For those who find it easiest to pigeon-hole countries neatly into 'good' and 'bad', and for whom any totalitarian régime is automatically 'bad', it will, I hope, be of interest to learn that one stated objective of the course is 'awakening an attitude of respect for human beings as people, and as members of social and natural groups, and an attitude of tolerance and understanding in appreciating both the resemblances and the differences between peoples'; another is 'the developing of a critical spirit and clear thought about social situations . . . the awakening and development of active participation in the life of the community, with the aim of improving society'.

Even if not every Spanish school succeeds in these admirable aims, it is interesting to know that the Ministry of Education lays them down in black and white as something to be attempted. And judging from the pleasant, intelligent and quite uninhibited way in which pupils questioned me about my own country, and about such portentous topics as the attitudes of young people in Britain towards freedom, I don't think they are doing at all badly.

The general approach of the course is that the child will work outwards from his own immediate environment; at six or seven he thinks of himself, his family, his village, his school; then at ten or eleven he is ready to look further beyond these boundaries, and think about Spain and its people, or of specific topics in the geography and history of the rest of the world. By thirteen or fourteen he is learning quite a lot of modern and contemporary history, not neglecting that of other continents, with at least some study of the culture and politics of China, Russia, the USA and Africa. It may perhaps be an over-ambitious course, and it certainly calls for good teaching; but a pupil who has absorbed even some part of it should be reasonably well-informed about the world and about the issues which will be placed before him as a citizen.

The booklet goes on to offer some advice on method, and one paragraph particularly struck me: it urges the teacher 'to stimulate debate, discussion and study of the government of the school community of which the pupils form a part'. He is also advised to use a system in which each pupil has two notebooks, one for notes, summaries, sketches, photographs, etc, and the other for maps, graphs and the like. Thus he will, in effect, be composing his own textbook and atlas. Teaching should be supplemented with books, slides, films, tapes, magazines, etc. It sounds lively, interesting stuff, a far cry from the rigidly controlled, spoon-fed pupils we perhaps imagined; in it are surely the seeds of a future Spanish democracy?

I have quoted fairly extensively from these documents because they are among the fullest and most up-to-date works of the kind that I have come across. One even more recent is the 1975 syllabus of the Portuguese Ministry of Education. As yet I have only seen the primary school volume, an attractively-produced book of about 150 pages, full of suggestions for useful and interesting activities. Either it was produced with astonishing rapidity after the Revolution, or something of the kind was already in process of gestation; possibly the latter, for what I have already said about Spain should have made it plain that lively and forward-looking ideas in education are not at all incompatible with a political régime well to the right of centre. The booklet does, however, contain many references to the part education can play in the building of a new social order: within the first few pages, we find such statements as 'Education is a road towards the elimination of economic, political and cultural privilege', and 'the proper development of collective work favours a spirit of brotherhood and co-operation indispensable for the building of a democratic society'. The book itself is packed with good ideas, though it may be permissible to wonder whether all of them can be implemented, even by the best teachers in Portugal, until more material resources are made available to the schools, which in 1973 were sadly lacking in them.

With these new programmes may be compared an older document published by the Italian Ministry of Education. This is mainly devoted to statements of principle, and gives relatively little space to actual programmes; most of its advice is on predictable and entirely orthodox lines, with strong emphasis on traditional cultural values. In Italian, some tough literary fare is recommended – Orlando Furioso, Gerusalemme Liberata, even the Divine Comedy, as well as translations from foreign classics like the Song of Roland, the Poem of the Cid, and the Nibelungenlied. I have read some short essays by Italian pupils which certainly suggest that they had gained from reading these difficult works, and perhaps our own school reading programmes err in the opposite direction, of being too unambitious? Another interesting feature is that in the second year of the *scuola media* course some comparative study of Latin is undertaken, using methods not so very dissimilar to our own Cambridge Classics Project.

The Italian mathematical syllabus seemed both lighter and less enterprising than the Spanish one I have just quoted; and that for the history and civics course was stated in the barest possible outline: for example, the twelve-year-olds of Class II are supposed to study 'From the Holy Roman Empire to the end of the Napoleonic Era', which must approach the all-comers record for a quick whisk through world history. Perhaps the sheer confusion of Italian medieval history puts the Italians off any more detailed tackling of the events between about the fifth and nineteenth centuries! Civics are treated fairly lightly in the first and second years, but Class III is offered '... the inspiration and principal features of the Constitution of the Italian Republic. Rights and Duties of the Citizen. Social organizations and their relations with the State. Labour, its organization, defence and security. General ideas of the organization of the state. Principles and organizations of international co-operation.'

One must hope that the actual implementation of all this may be rather less arid than was a civics lesson which I saw one day in a French CES. Here the pupils began by doing a short written test: the questions were 'Is French justice politically independent?' and 'What is the function of the Conseil d'Etat?' The pupils looked as if they did not care very much, and there was some mild protest about the very idea of having a test, but eventually most of them managed to write something. They were then regaled with a dissertation on the functions of the Ministries of Health and Labour, with an inordinate quantity of notes to be copied from the board – and to very little purpose, really, since they all had textbooks containing the very same information. It was a lesson few of them would remember; I fear a subject like civics is perhaps particularly vulnerable to this kind of treatment – yet how interesting it might be made!

A scarcely brighter effort was the lesson I saw at a German primary school with a class aged about nine. This was not a civics lesson as such, but part of the *Sachunterricht* programme, for which I tentatively offer 'general knowledge' as an equivalent. The textbook covered such diverse topics as map scales, elementary science and the subject of this lesson, which was a comparison of the wording of school rules 'then' and 'now', under the heading 'Manipulation: how men are influenced'. I thought it much too subtle for these children, though secondary pupils would probably have found it interesting.

Philosophy is not a subject commonly found on the timetable of English schools, so I was interested to see a philosophy lesson at the Instituto Virgen del Carmen at Jaén. (This is a grammar school for about 1,000 boys, with a staff of fifty, in handsome modern buildings in the newer part of the city.) The course, I was told, included some logic and a little psychology; the pupils were in the final year of the *bachillerato* course. One boy read a paper he had written on political philosophy; it was quite deeply thought, and, I must add, of staggering length, for it took him twenty-five minutes simply to read it out, with one or two very brief pauses when other pupils took him up on a point. An animated discussion followed his paper, with the teacher taking little part, but the other pupils probing the arguments in a most civilized way. This paper was followed by a second one, also quite long, and the speaker's flow of eloquence was not even dammed by the sounding of the bell for lunch at 1.30! As so often with the thoughtful young, it was very solemn, and in need of a little light relief, but the command of language and ideas was most impressive.

In the two following chapters I attempt to give some answer to the question: given that curriculum and syllabus are apparently sound enough, how well are they in fact taught?

POSTSCRIPT

The introduction of Italian pupils to the Study of Latin (p. 38) has now been removed from the curriculum.

4
The teacher and his work:
I

Our glance at a few lessons may as well begin with the foundation of all teaching everywhere, the study of the pupil's own native language. The youngest class I saw doing anything which could be so described was a class at the Ecole Maternelle Jean Moulin in Beauvais. They were nearly six years old, and just about ready to leave the *maternelle* for their first primary school. Strictly speaking, reading and writing are not taught at this age, but the teachers wisely initiate children into the early stages to that they enter primary school with a flying start.

On the board were three sentences: the absence of capital letters is quite deliberate, this being a complication not taught till considerably later:

voici la foire a beauvais

il y a la grande roue

la grande roue tourne

They were in fact topical sentences, as the square at one end of the city did contain a fair with a big wheel, part of the annual carnival. The emphasis in studying these sentences was placed on the *ou* sound occurring in *roue* and *tourne*, and there was much repetition of these sounds to fix in the children's mind the relation between the look of the word and its sound. French cannot be an easy language to learn, with its many diphthongs, its accents, and its innumerable ways of spelling almost identical sounds. The teacher also showed me some albums, *cahiers* of large sheets of paper (probably wallpaper) made up into books. In these were pasted drawings done by the children during the year, concerning the adventures of a little black boy. As the drawings accumulated and more characters were introduced, the children acquired new words in captioning their pictures in big sprawling letters.

German, too, is a language which must present its problems when one is learning to read: those terrifying compound-words are liable to crop up quite soon, and one suspects dismally that the German equivalent of Tank-Engine Thomas may well be ordered by the *Stationsversteher* to withdraw to the *Bahnbetriebswerk* while the *Fahrgäste* are occupied at the *Fahrkartenausgabe*, with discouraging effects on the infant reader. However, there was little sign of this in the lesson I saw at the Grundschule Zewen, near Trier; this is the lower half of an all-age school serving the village of Zewen and a considerable surrounding area, including some outer suburbs of Trier itself. There are 670 pupils, aged from six to fifteen, and it was a cheerful group of thirty six-year-olds under Frau Kremer whom I saw. With gentle patience she led the children through simple sentences like 'Mama ruft Papa', 'Papa kommt'. The class recited some of these in chorus; then Frau Kremer opened the triptych-blackboard to reveal the key words, beautifully written. The pupils had small cards with the same words, and played a variety of games, matching their cards to the words she indicated, using them to fill gaps in sentences as they were directed, or working in pairs to make up question and answer.

I also remember with pleasure two lessons with rather older classes. At the J. H. Fabre school at Avignon (a mixed primary school annexed to the *école normale*, and serving the St-Ruf quarter of the city) a class of seven-year-olds started with a short playlet about some lost keys. Then the teacher opened the board to reveal a story, very clearly written, using many of the same phrases. The children read this aloud in chorus; then the teacher focused their attention on the awkward nasal sound 'oin', in words like 'point'. After recognizing this, they had to look for other examples, and soon spotted 'coin'; finally, they were given some duplicated slips with further exercises on the same material, with one or two little traps to avoid, such as the word 'lion'. Again, I thought, an excellent lesson, with a specific object attained, and plenty of interest and activity for the children.

The same was true of Frau Lörscher's lesson with a class of eight-year-olds at Zewen in Germany. These children could read quite fluently, and had been looking at a passage about plants. Now Frau Lörscher wished them to write something by way of describing the process of transferring a growing plant to a larger pot. A believer in 'learning through doing', she had brought an actual plant along, with all the necessary material for re-potting it, and under her guidance the children, or at any rate some of them, carried out the job very competently. They then worked at a short description of the process on the blackboard, with contributions from a number of the children. The title they had chosen was 'Wir topften um', and the first few lines, composed on the board, ran thus:

> Zuerst suchten wir einen passenden Topf aus. Dann legten wir eine Scherbe über das Bodenloch. Nun füllten wir den Topf halb mit Blumenerde . . .
>
> (First we select a suitable pot. Then we place a piece of broken pot over the hole in the bottom. Next we half-fill the pot with soil . . .)

From here, the children were on their own, and each had to finish off the account by himself; the teacher moved round with help and advice, telling me that there was a wide range of ability in the class and that she knew which children would need a lot of individual help.

I have no doubt whatever that both the Germans and the French are very good indeed at teaching pupils to read and write; perhaps especially the French. They are sticklers for precision; I remember with delight a handicraft lesson at the J. H. Fabre school, during which the kindly lady in charge was meticulously insistent that her seven-year-olds should properly word any question they asked her, and in grammatically correct form; her own instructions to them included, for example, the remark 'Vous allez percer une petite orifice.' Possibly the word 'orifice' is a little commoner in French than it is in English, but that in itself would be proof of how much more the French respect and understand their language than do we our own powerful and expressive tongue.

Also at J. H. Fabre I was impressed by the high standard of the reading-matter offered to quite young children: some ten-year-olds did very well with a passage from André Gide's *Les Nourritures Terrestres*; they clearly understood it, and gave very perceptive answers, though when the young student-teacher in charge tried to take them into a discussion of the style of the passage, they were, not surprisingly, a little out of their depth. But their expressive reading showed beyond doubt how well they understood what they were reading. Later I saw some children aged about nine studying a poem by Jacques Prévert, called 'Pour faire le portrait d'un oiseau' – another example of the good taste and seriousness with which French teachers present their literature.

Later I visited another Avignon primary school, La Barbière-B. Whereas J. H. Fabre was in a rather 'nice' area, this school served a rather intimidating estate of big, featureless blocks of flats. It had a staff of twelve, serving just over 300 pupils. In the lesson under consideration, the teacher was no less insistent on precise expression; she constantly exhorted her seven-year-olds to give 'une petite phrase, s'il vous plaît', if they momentarily looked like giving a single-word answer. Despite this formality, they loved every moment of the lesson, simply jumping with eagerness to give their answers. For such very young children, the standard of their reading was very high, even quite difficult words like 'désagréable' being skilfully negotiated. Indeed, it was interesting that the teacher afterwards discussed with one small pupil (aged seven, remember!) the reason for pronouncing the 's' in 'désagréable' as if it were a 'z'. Without batting an eyelid, the child replied: 'Il se trouve entre deux voyelles, Madame.' Impressive, to find a seven-year-old who knows a vowel when he sees one, and can apply a rule in this way.

Another class in this same school – eight-year-olds this time – also made me blink somewhat by the skill with which they coped with a grammar lesson. First they found subjects, pronouns, and so on; then, believe it or not, they proceeded to a full analysis and parsing of the sentence! I do not necessarily suggest that our children of that age should be doing the same, for English is a far less structured language than French; but I just remind our English teachers of Winston Churchill's remarks on this very subject in *My Early Life*. And how did the class take this rather arid material? Very well, I must report: it was a vigorous and happy lesson.

In contrast to the excellent reading material I have mentioned as being found in French primary schools, the textbook I saw being used to teach Portuguese to a class of nine-year-olds at the Escola São Vitor in Braga was rather pedestrian. (It was a pleasant school, however: a primary and 'complementary' school for 200 boys, serving a residential area near the city centre. A similar girls' school is adjacent, and will eventually be combined with the boys'.) This textbook, the *Livro de Leitura da 3a Classe*, seemed to me rather a priggish production, over-full of earnest passages about saluting the flag and respecting the national anthem. Portuguese textbooks do tend to be rather like that, and classroom walls are often adorned with stirring texts from Camoens – rather as if every English classroom carried bits of Shakespeare's 'This blessed plot' speech! However, today's passage was earnest in a different way, being all about food and nutrition. The usual methods were used at first: teacher reads passage, teacher explains passage, teacher reads it a second time . . . but then came a variant: the boys closed their books, all except one of them, who read the first paragraph while the rest listened; then the next boy took over, and so on until the passage was finished. Everybody had to keep alert, or he would have no idea where to look for the place when his turn came. Then the teacher went through the passage yet again, this time asking the boys questions on the language of the passage: for example, on finding the word 'pão' (a loaf) he would ask 'What's the plural of that word?', and 'What other words do you know with that kind of plural?'. Finally a blond boy called João Paulo was called out to analyse one of the sentences on the blackboard, which he did very competently at the tender age of nine-and-a-bit.

Another class I saw at São Vitor was a fifth form, aged about eleven. They were using Book 5 of a course called *Vamos Ler*, which roughly means *Let's Read!* and I thought this was a considerably better book than the other. It included prose and verse passages and short dramatic excerpts, with grammatical exercises and notes interspersed – just such a book, indeed, as has made many an English teacher's fortune! Of its kind, this was by no means the worst I have seen. The lesson started again with the teacher reading the passage, and after this the boys also read, pretty fluently and with good understanding. Now the procedure varied somewhat: the teacher distributed some test-papers, which had actually been laboriously written out by hand: I can only suppose the school does not run to a duplicator, and if so, it is a revealing fact. There was also a sense of desperate 'making-do' in the materials which the boys used for writing their answers – old diaries, cheap scribbling-blocks and the like. Only a few had actual exercise-books. As the boys worked, the teacher walked round making encouraging noises to his pupils: it was a warm, homely relationship.

When the answers were finished, some of them were read out, with brief comments of approval or criticism, and others were written on the board – very neatly and confidently. Watching the boys at work, I thought that, even if they were what we should consider to be a rather deprived group, they had in fact been very well taught, within the limits of the system, for they were able to answer with speed, confidence and accuracy. Finally, the teacher took one or two boys through some grammatical points; one boy did a full analysis of a quite tricky sentence (nouns and pronouns in different cases, active and passive verbs, and so on), and he did it with great aplomb, as if he were doing a particularly easy conjuring-trick. However, the effect was sadly marred by the embarrassing inability of his lanky successor to put a verb into the future tense – which happens to be one of the very few things I *can* do in Portuguese! But even this lad's work showed correct spelling and well-formed handwriting.

Comprehension lessons, as here, play a big part in the teaching of the native language. In Germany, most of the lessons of this type which I saw seemed to follow an almost identical pattern: a little preparatory discussion of difficult words, a reading (usually very skilful) by the teacher, class discussion of topics arising from the passage, and then a second reading by the pupils themselves. Frau Huck, teaching some eight-year-olds of 3B at the Früchteburg School in Emden, rounded off the lesson by having the children improvise a brief dramatic version of what they had read, prompting them in stage-whispers if they ran out of ideas. The boys, especially, put on a very lively and amusing performance.

Other good lessons of a similar type which I attended in German schools took the form of readings and discussions on current social problems.

The Realschule, Emden, is a co-educational secondary school, intermediate in curriculum between an ordinary secondary school and a *Gymnasium*; there are 940 pupils and a staff of forty-one. There I saw an impressive lesson with some twelve-year-olds on the delicate topic of racial prejudice. Having read a passage about the problems of a coloured boy in the USA, the young pupils asked some very thoughtful questions, the discussion then leading to the preparation of a few key-words and phrases highlighting the attitudes of prejudice; Herr Strybny then read, gently and quite unemotionally, a passage about a rejected Jewish girl, and from this went on to the topic I half-expected and half-dreaded, the treatment of the Jews in Germany itself during the Hitler period. Within the limits imposed by the children's age, the treatment was frank and full. The next day I was at the Gymnasium am Treckfahrtstief, a splendid school of the grammar type just beyond the city centre. Until 1971 this was a girls' school; girls still preponderate among the 1,000 pupils, and there are unusually good domestic science facilities; the school has a staff of about seventy, usually increased by a dozen student-teachers. Here I watched a slight, bespectacled and moustached teacher, with a friendly and informal manner, start his lesson by playing, without comment, a record of a satirical song, 'Deutscher Sonntag' by F. J. Degenhardt. At first the class of fifteen-year-olds did not quite know what to make of it; then, as the humour struck them, they chuckled appreciatively, and when the record ended and Herr Henkelmann started to question them, comments came thick and fast, almost every pupil contributing something, and most of them doing so several times. Their perceptiveness and fluency were alike remarkable; the teacher intervened little, except occasionally to turn the talk into a fresh direction.

Continental schools make a great feature of training their pupils in set compositions, often on fairly well-worn topics – 'Mamma mia' is a great favourite with the Italians! Frequent practice of this kind leads to correct and stylish writing, and even if some freshness is lost, there is always plenty of feeling and warmth. Reading some of these essays, I felt that emotion and personality did come through the rather stereotyped form. After all, one can recognize individuality in Pope or Johnson, even though both use the heroic couplet, or strong personal feeling in Haydn or Mozart despite the strict requirements of the sonata form; it could even be that having the broad outlines of their composition prescribed for them actually gives some children more freedom to develop other sides of their writing.

I saw a slightly similar situation in a French school, but this time at the secondary stage. The school was the CES J. B. Pellerin at Beauvais, a school of about 1,000 pupils with a staff of sixty-one teachers and seven surveillants. It has recently moved from very old buildings into a new school on the edge of the city centre, from which area it draws most of its pupils. Madame Potier began by returning some marked essays, which she gave back in descending order of merit. The three best, with marks of 16 and 15 out of 20, were all the work of girls, the top boy having 14. Marks descended to a melancholy 3 out of 20. The rather unpromising subject was 'A man should not divide his life into two compartments but should instead learn to take pleasure in his work'; but some of the answers I read were thoughtful and well-expressed. The teacher then initiated a discussion on the best way to tackle such a subject, working out a preliminary plan on the board from ideas supplied by the pupils. Her technique was competent, but the very academic choice of subject made the lesson rather boring to me . . . though there was a lovely view of Beauvais Cathedral from the window!

Earlier, at the huge Lycée Frédéric-Mistral at Avignon, with nearly 2,000 pupils and a staff of 120 in its vast buildings, I saw a remarkably good lesson in précis-writing, about my least favourite subject as a general rule. The class had already done some preliminary work by preparing short papers on race relations and allied topics, and now they were studying an article from *Le Monde* on the same theme. For homework, they had written a summary of this article, and two versions were now read out. Discussion followed, some of it very critical of one girl's effort, which was felt not to have liberated itself enough from the original wording. Finally, the teacher offered her own version, which the pupils took down paragraph by paragraph, underlining at each stage the words which carried the transition of thought from one paragraph to the next. An orthodox lesson, but good because it was so well-planned and prepared; the teacher called her class 'rather below average' for their age (about sixteen) but I thought them distinctly good.

A similarly effective teacher was Signor Mainardi of the Scuola Media Virgilio at Cremona. His relations with the class were easy, but he obviously stood for high standards and this integrity had rubbed off on his pupils, whose work was accurate, fluent and stylish. Compared with primary-school work, however, there was that falling-off in presentation one often finds in adolescents, mainly owing to the over-rapid production called for by the pressures of the secondary school.

Literature teaching, or such of it as I saw, was usually less imaginative than the teaching of language. I was, however, delighted to see, during a short visit to the La Salle College in Palma de Mallorca, a class of Spanish boys having great fun with an impromptu drama lesson; they were enacting a murder and the subsequent interrogation of the suspect, and doing it with great energy and fluency.

I felt that the standard of mathematics teaching tended to be more variable than that of the native language; but this may be mainly because I am less knowledgeable about the problems involved. And certainly I saw much to admire in the German lessons, with their insistence on method and precision. Take, for example, a class of about forty twelve-year-old pupils at Zewen. When I joined the lesson, they were observing with, I think, real interest the way in which ideas written in mathematical language can be looked at in two different ways: $(7 \times 12) + (3 \times 12)$ can either be thought of as $84 + 36$ or as 10×12, the answer in either case being 120. A pupil was then called to the blackboard to demonstrate the addition of 18×24 to 2×24; the teacher was insistent on precise layout, setting out the calculation step by step:

$$2.24 + 18.24 = x$$
$$24(2 + 18) = x$$
$$24(20) = 480$$

The actual arithmetic may have been a little elementary, but as a display of method the pupil's performance was admirable. The class then did some examples by themselves; two of them came out to the blackboard and worked on the back of the hinged wings, and as the others finished they came out to compare their work with that of one of the blackboard demonstrators. It was all very quiet and unfussy.

Perhaps a more interesting lesson was that given by Frau Sürm to a class of seven-year-olds at Früchteburg School, Emden. This is a primary school (with kindergarten) and among its 470 pupils are also some fifth- and sixth-year classes overlapping the work of the secondary schools.

It was a skilfully varied lesson, and the children enjoyed it. They began with some additions: in adding, say, 15 to 6, they had to write down three stages: $15 + 6 / \underline{15 + 5} + 1 / 20 + 1 = 21$. This capacity to think in terms of bringing the number up to the next level ten and then adding whatever is left over is the secret of rapid addition, but how seldom one finds children doing it! Next they were shown that there are numbers below 0, a thermometer being used to make this point. Frau Sürm then used a flannel-graph and coloured strips to familiarize the children with the idea of simple fractions, multiplications and divisions; a brown strip occupying eight squares represented a bar of chocolate to be shared fairly by two children, giving the expression $\frac{1}{2} . 8 = 4$ (dots are used as the multiplication sign rather than $\times$). After a little further practice, with the half of 12, 20 and other even numbers, the class was invited to try $\frac{1}{2} . 3$ – which did not appear to cause any alarm to most of the pupils. Finally, judging them to have had enough oral work, the teacher set the class to work out in their exercise-books such tasks as the halving of 10, 2, 8 and 6, and some corresponding multiplication.

The textbook these pupils were using was very colourfully and attractively designed – and quite expensive (12 marks, which at the present exchange rates is about £2). Every child also had his own set of instruments and plastic shapes, and also a set of articles resembling in function the Cuisenaire rods popular in our own schools.

These children, at the beginning of their second year of formal schooling, appeared quite at home with division by 2 and with the related ideas of fractions and multiples. Indeed, they were brilliant mathematicians compared with a class of Portuguese children I had seen the previous summer. This class was within a week or so of the end of its second year of school – some, indeed, were older than that – and, as their school was attached to a teacher training college, they might be thought a cut above the average. In fact, I am afraid I thought their lesson extraordinarily inept.

Not that it was wholly uninteresting, but the interest rather lay for me in irrelevant details, such as the fact that the Portuguese sign for 'divided by' is a simple colon, without the horizontal bar which we use, or that the numeral '1' is written with its top serif extended into a great sweeping upstroke considerably longer than the downstroke.

The entire hour was spent in what appeared to be an activity preparatory to learning to divide by 2. On the blackboard the earnest lady teacher had drawn a stylized representation of the sun, with what turned out to be forty-seven rays around its cheerful face. The pupils were told first to count the rays – more a test of eyesight than anything else, since the rays were drawn very close together and the surface of the board was ancient and pitted. Having agreed on the total of forty-seven, the next move was to count them off in pairs to see if one was left over at the end; I hoped that there might perhaps just be *one* bold child who would cut short the proceedings by saying 'But, miss, forty-seven's an odd number, so there *must* be one left over!' but nothing so enterprising occurred; they just counted away industriously, and the boy who was eventually called on to answer in fact produced the *wrong* total.

Since the Spanish syllabus for this age-group also appears to require 'initiation into division by means of experimental situations familiar to the pupil', I may be overestimating the capacity of the Iberian seven-year-old in thinking that this was rather a poor effort; perhaps the business of counting up rays was just a rather dim example of an 'experimental situation familiar to the pupil'! (The Spanish syllabus does also include 'functional recognition and description of cubes, pyramids and prisms', which I'm sure I never did at that age, so probably it's all relative!)

Later I saw a similar group at this Portuguese school tackling some very elementary mathematics in an end-of-term test; and an older group (pupils aged eight to ten) dealing with areas and perimeters of rectangles. Some of the working-out of these problems produced surprising reactions from the teacher: one pupil gave '140 cm' as the perimeter of a rectangle measuring 18 cm × 42 cm, and she cheerfully accepted this incorrect answer and used it as the yardstick for marking other pupils' work. I was too much of a moral coward to intervene, I'm afraid – either that, or I didn't want the teacher to lose face in front of her pupils.

The teacher and his work: I

I was also surprised to see how laboriously some of the problems were tackled: for example, take this one: I buy a litre of oil for 28 escudos. How much will 2·5 decilitres cost? Everyone solemnly multiplied 28 by 2 and then by 5, and added the results with the appropriate juggling of decimal points; nobody spotted that 2·5 is a quarter of 10 and therefore that a quicker solution is to divide by 4. Perhaps, again, I am making unreasonable demands; but I have in fact noticed that people in countries which have long had the metric system can't do simple arithmetic: I have even seen a post-office clerk in Spain take a scrap of paper to work out the cost of ten $3\frac{1}{2}$ peseta stamps! Our own demented pounds, shillings, pence, rods, poles and perches at least forced us into familiarity with some solid mental arithmetic!

In fact, however, some of our European cousins have their own arithmetical problems, and one of those I had never previously considered cropped up at the J. H. Fabre school in Avignon, where I saw a young teacher helping some youngsters over the problem of the French way of saying numbers like 70, 80 and 90: *soixante-dix*, *quatre-vingts* and *quatre-vingt-dix*. The child meeting these for the first time does not connect them with the numbers they represent, and it becomes especially awkward with the adjacent numbers 79 and 80 (*soixante-dix-neuf*, *quatre-vingts*). The child thinks of the former, perhaps as 6019 (sixty-nineteen), and the latter appears to him as 420 (four-twenty).

The method used involved bundles of sticks. Each contained ten sticks, which were referred to therefore as *une dizaine* ('a ten') and two of these together as *une vingtaine* ('a twenty'). Putting together four twenties they saw for themselves that they had eighty sticks, and after establishing this, the teacher proceeded to show the children that 30 + 50, or 60 + 20, are other ways of making up 80. The children practised these calculations for themselves; then the teacher subtracted one stick from the last *vingtaine*, and showed that she now had sixty (*soixante*) sticks plus nineteen (*dix-neuf*). I am not in the least surprised that children find these things difficult, and I admired the teacher's placid patience in explaining it, with many repetitions of processes until she was satisfied that all understood; but surely the French should do something about this demented piece of semantics? The Belgians have already done so (perhaps that is why the French find it unthinkable, of course!) and it would be a comparatively simple thing to enact, one would suppose. But, of course, human beings are very perverse about things like this; we ourselves had hardly decimalized our coinage before popular usage took a hand and decided that the plural 'pence' should be substituted for the word 'penny', even though the coin itself is clearly marked 'One Penny'. If, however, such a change had been officially decreed, nobody would have taken the slightest notice of it! What the French should do, of course, is to get somebody to write a pop-song with the refrain 'septante, huitante, neuvante, cent!' and have it blaring out of ten million transistor radios.

In the other primary school I saw at Avignon, La Barbière, I watched Madame Pozzéra, a very able teacher indeed, taking her class of nine-year-olds through some quite difficult arithmetical manipulations: using magnetic strips on the blackboard for demonstration purposes, she confronted them with the idea of a person dealing in tables and chairs, eight of the latter at 56 francs each and four of the former at 124 francs. Various pupils came to the blackboard and skilfully manipulated these figures in various ways, such as:

(a) to find the total cost $(124 \times 4) + (56 \times 8) = 944$

(b) to find cost of a table $\dfrac{944 - (56 \times 8)}{4} = 124$

(c) to find cost of a chair $\dfrac{944 - (124 \times 4)}{8} = 56$

(d) to find no. of tables sold $\dfrac{944 - (56 \times 8)}{124} = 4$

and so on. This was an entirely 'traditional' lesson, but firm and efficient none the less; nor is Mme Pozzéra unwilling to use up-to-date techniques even to teach traditional processes, for her room had many good teaching devices around its walls.

Another excellent teacher of the same stamp was the vivacious Signor Bassi, of the Leonida Bissolati school at Cremona. This large mixed primary school has 623 pupils, with five classes in each year, its pupils coming from a mainly residential area of the city. Signor Bassi made much use of simple aids such as wooden squares and triangles, sometimes joined together in pairs by thick rubber bands at the corners so that they could be extended to form various 'solids', twisted to form double pyramids, and so on. I enjoyed his lesson very much, and was almost sorry when he decided the class had had enough, and converted himself instantly into a musician by pulling out a small electronic organ and accompanying some of his pupils who played guitars and recorders. He is a real teacher, and I know exactly why his headmaster remarked in an aside 'he's one in a thousand!' There was a splendid moment when the headmaster had the temerity to argue with him on a point of solid geometry, and the two men went for each other hammer-and-tongs, but with the greatest friendliness and good humour, to the vast delight of the children.

Solid shapes also cropped up in the first Spanish maths lesson which I saw, at the Colegio Nacional Juan Bruguera in Gerona. This school is for boys only, and has 744 pupils aged from six to fourteen, taught by a staff of nineteen teachers plus a headmaster. The building is right in the commercial centre of the city, and a fairly gloomy old building it is, but it is for all that a very sound school. The class was learning how to work out the volume of a cone; the teacher said he was on the whole a supporter of 'modern' mathematics, but preferred to invoke older techniques for certain parts of his syllabus. His class contained forty boys aged about eleven or twelve; the method was quite unspectacular, a pupil working out an example on the blackboard, the class doing a few more in their exercise-books, and the teacher finally running through the work himself amid a chorus of comment and explanation from the boys. They seemed intelligent lads, and worked neatly and effectively by themselves; one boy showed me with great pride a splendid 'rose-window' pattern he had evolved as a geometrical exercise. The textbook in use was bright and attractive. It was an exceptionally quiet lesson, for the teacher had an intimate delivery and that unobtrusive class-control which ensured steady work and a minimum of fuss.

A day or two later I saw another maths lesson in a private school, the Colegio La Inmaculada, which is the Marist Brothers' school in Gerona. At my first visit, this school occupied two or three separate buildings in the old part of the city; its 500 pupils were drawn from all over the city and surrounding areas, and there was a staff of about twenty. The school has now moved to fine new buildings (see chapter 7). The atmosphere of this lesson was rather formal, the boys always addressing their portly and genial teacher as 'Profesor', while he used their surnames. But the style of the lesson was conducive to good work – authoritative without being repressive, and the boys were not afraid to ask questions or argue a point with the teacher. This lesson started with some exposition of geometry (the bisection of angles featured prominently) but when the teacher sensed that the class was growing weary of the subject, he quickly switched to another activity. He divided the class into two teams, and calling out one boy at a time from each team set them to race to answer a problem on the blackboard, working side by side on the two halves of the board. I vividly recall one pair, Soms and Medina. Their problem concerned two vehicles proceeding in opposite directions for fifty-two hours, one at 15 kph and the other at 17 kph. How far apart would they be at the end of their journey? The excellent Soms briskly wrote down as follows:

15 and 17 kph. 52 hours
Distance from city and km difference
$15 \times 52 = 780$ km from city
$17 \times 52 = 884$ km from city
$780 + 884 = 1664$ km difference between them.

It took him about one minute, I suppose, to write this down and trot cheerfully back to his seat; and by that time poor old Medina had just about got the first line down. Game, set and match to Soms. But Medina was not the only boy to have trouble of this kind; I noticed others who seemed quite lively in oral answers but somewhat flustered when required to put their thoughts into writing.

Another interesting arithmetical anecdote comes from this same lesson. A boy was asked to come to the board and divide the number 72765 by 135. All he wrote was:

$$\begin{array}{r} 72765 \\ 0526 \\ 1215 \end{array} \Big/ \begin{array}{r} 135 \\ \hline 539 \end{array}$$

Can you see what he was doing? In case you can't, I give the working below as a footnote,* because I was rather pleased to

---

*The boy first divided 135 into the first three digits, 727, in the usual way; he worked out in his head that it 'goes' 5 times, and that the product of 135×5 is 675. Still working in his head, he says '727 − 675 = 52' and he

find that I could, despite being barely numerate! The method was not peculiar to this school; I saw much the same later at Ecija.

Being now well launched on a description of some of the many lessons I saw, I will risk the generalization that I felt that the majority of schools and the majority of teachers were doing a pretty good job. Lack of adequate facilities, over-large classes, pupils whose environment is inimical to the learning process, can make hay of the best syllabus; indeed, the better the syllabus the more likely it is, perhaps, to break down under such conditions, for a good syllabus must be lively, imaginative, even exciting, and such qualities demand teachers and materials to match them if they are to succeed. So it was that sometimes I saw good teachers struggling against material difficulties that they could hardly be expected to overcome completely. But more often when I had doubts about a lesson, it was because the presentation of the material was too narrowly academic – too much theory, too much rote-learning – and this in itself may often be linked with a shortage of facilities, as when a teacher must try to teach science to his pupils in an ordinary classroom without the facilities for carrying out experimental work of even giving a decent demonstration. It was thus, for example, with one chemistry lesson I saw in Spain, which was a series of listings of formulae on the blackboard – formulae for such substances as platinum bromide or stannous chloride. Incidentally, chemical formulae in Spain appear to be the opposite of ours: sulphuric acid is SO_4H_2; but chemistry teachers will learn with resignation that Spanish boys also confuse manganese and magnesium!

One handsome *scuola media* in Italy could show me no laboratory of any kind, and another, I was told, will have one laboratory in its new building for 600 pupils who, I should guess, will be lucky if they have one lesson a week there. Things were somewhat better elsewhere, but rarely did the provision approach the level of British schools; over the four countries of my first tour, the average was about one laboratory to 500 pupils, and many had no access whatever to special rooms where they could do practical or

---

writes 052 below the 727, bringing down the 6 for the next stage. 135 into 526 'goes' 3 times; 135 × 3 = 405; 526 − 405 = 121; he writes that down and brings down the 5. 135 into 1215 is exactly 9. The divisor and the quotient are both written down at the right. How odd to do all the really difficult bits in one's head!

experimental science. Even Germany, with her splendid scientific traditions, does not reach the level of laboratory provision which we have come to expect: the *Realschule* at Emden, for example, has four laboratories for its 940 pupils; and even the lavishly equipped Treckfahrtstief Gymnasium, with over 1,000 pupils, had less scope for practical work than we should expect, though its science block was in other respects superb. Each of the three separate sciences had, as it were, a suite of rooms, comprising lecture theatre with terraced seats and a demonstration bench for the teacher; preparation and store rooms; an office for the teacher; and a single practical laboratory, beautifully designed and generously equipped.

At the *Realschule* I saw a very effective biology lesson; the class, aged eleven or twelve, had been asked to mount and label the flower of a pea in their exercise-books as homework, and now Frau Ringewaldt, using a large plastic model which could be taken to pieces, got one of the pupils to check over the parts of the flower for the benefit of the others. From this they proceeded to discuss the functions of the various parts, and then the way in which the plant grows, which led naturally to consider climbing-plants in general. The children were intelligent and found the topic interesting, and it was significant that whereas at the start of the lesson the teacher's voice was almost lost against the hideous squeaking of some very ramshackle rotating stools, before long the children had forgotten to fidget and were fully absorbed.

Another biology lesson in a German school had little interest for me because it was much less well planned and the pupils contributed very little; but I thoroughly enjoyed a physics class at the Wallschule, Emden; this is a secondary school (*Hauptschule*) with some 550 pupils in nineteen classes, with a staff of twenty-seven. Pupils stay here to the age of fifteen, and the buildings are rather antiquated, though well-equipped; it is, indeed, just the kind of school which might be very bad, but is in fact pretty good. Herr Böhme, in charge of this class of eleven- and twelve-year-olds, was young, casual in manner, dressed in jeans; but one instantly sensed technical and professional competence. Using an overhead projector in preference to the blackboard, he wrote up the headline 'Wir bauen einen Tauchsieder' ('We make an immersion-heater'). Skilfully extracting the suggestions entirely from the children, he compiled a list of requirements – wire, a thermometer, a beaker, some water, a couple of crocodile-clips, two lengths of cable and a source of current; rapidly he sketched the required arrangement of these items, and without any fuss the class divided into six groups to construct their apparatus. There was considerable excitement as first one group, then another, reported that their water was heating satisfactorily; the lesson ended with a few quiet minutes in which they made written notes of the work done, with a diagram. The lesson had nothing unusual in its form and content; its attraction lay in the skill with which it was presented and executed.

Laboratories of themselves will not ensure good teaching, and the well-equipped biology laboratory of one French secondary school gave me the most disastrous lesson of my whole tour. From its initial conception to the last detail of its execution, it was an Awful Warning. The syllabus apparently decreed that the class, about sixteen boys and girls who were anyway in rather a surly mood, must learn all about smallpox. Don't ask me why: I should suppose that any person needing to know about the subject could read up all he required in about ten minutes from an encyclopedia. It was a hot day in late May; it was a Friday; and the lesson was the last one, beginning at four o'clock and continuing until five – a time when most English pupils are already home. So everything was against the unhappy teacher, who had indeed warned me that her class was liable to prove rather difficult.

But, this was not the only lesson this teacher had with those pupils, and much of her work with them was surely bound to be more interesting; why not, then, postpone smallpox to a more propitious time, when she and her class would be fresher – or, if smallpox it had to be, give them a token ten minutes of it and then let them do something exciting with all that splendid apparatus? Best of all, why not just forget the whole thing and take smallpox as read? We went, however, remorselessly through the whole sorry hour, with a full exposition of the symptoms, their incubation period, the progress of the disease, its prevention, its cure, its statistics. There was one moment of hope, when a projector was switched on, but this was only to show the class a single horrific slide of a baby suffering from the disease, a picture of such repellent nastiness that some of the pupils giggled hysterically. Wearily, they made notes of all this boring stuff – and some of the technical terms were at least impressive, such as 'scarification', which sounds as if it would add insult to injury. My sympathies went mostly to the pupils who had to endure such a lesson, but I spared a little too for the teacher who felt obliged to deliver it, for the real villain of the story is the person who devised the syllabus.

The moral may be that anyone laying down a scheme which someone else has to teach should be required to imagine himself giving lessons on it to a difficult form of adolescents on a very hot Friday afternoon from four to five o'clock. If he plays this game of make-believe honestly, he may learn to avoid including such unappetizing morsels in his syllabus. As a matter of interest, I checked through the Spanish and Italian syllabuses to see if their authorities also inflicted smallpox on the young, and I am happy to report that both countries seem able to do without it, though I admit that I did sit in on a Spanish class which was having both poliomyelitis and cancer, which sounds an even more lethal combination. But there the teacher had had the good sense simply to tell the pupils to read it up in their books, so they got it all over quite quickly, even though I noticed that he gave them a short test on it afterwards.

I saw a far, far better biology lesson, however, at the Instituto J. V. Vives in Gerona, Spain. This is a school of the grammar type, catering for boys and girls from the age of about fourteen upwards; there are some 1,600 pupils, with a staff of about eighty, and the buildings form a fine modern complex on a hillside overlooking the newer part of the city. The biology class I saw was one of the most memorable experiences of my tour; it was a mixed group of hefty adolescents aged about seventeen, and most unexpectedly the teacher was a lady with that aristocratic demeanour one might associate with pouring out China tea from a silver pot on the terrace; but it was immensely cheering to see the brisk and almost elegant way in which she coped with her forty teenagers. She had them just where she wanted them – beautifully under control; her manner was warm and friendly, with touches of amusement here and there. While the class got on with some of its own work, she told me a little of her system; she generally alternates practical with theoretical lessons, whereas some of her colleagues prefer to split their classes, twenty of them doing practical work while the other twenty do revision studies. Her laboratory was excellently equipped, with an abundance of microscopes, dissecting instruments and so on; next door, there was a well-stocked biological library and a small museum, whose interesting collection of specimens included a live uromastix, a most baleful-looking lizard emanating from Africa, for which the Señora appeared to have rather an affectionate regard. This creature had been presented by a former pupil, and someone had taken some magnificent photographs of it which were also on display in case the beast itself was not sufficient. There was also an aquarium, a set of incubators and much more. The archives of the laboratory included the test work of every single pupil in the school for the whole year, arranged in files with coloured identification tags, and these were available for inspection at any time in case of query. It would be hard to imagine a more complete laboratory-complex in a school.

In the laboratory itself, the work-benches were topped with a hard, shiny black plastic material which looked as if it would be an excellent working surface; though no expert, I should say that its fittings were complete, and what I certainly did feel sure of was that the room had much more elegance than one usually finds in laboratories.

The class were studying heredity, and had been carrying out some experiments with drosophila, a fruit-fly with interesting reproductive habits. The teacher called out a tough-looking lad with a pleasant face behind his incipient beard, and got him to demonstrate his findings on the blackboard. He did so quite confidently, drawing good, clear diagrams, but at one point his explanation came unstuck, and the teacher briskly demonstrated to him why: I think his dominants and recessives had somehow got themselves transposed. Next a neat little girl was called out to try her luck, but she quickly became confused, and it was delightful to see how naturally and amiably this excellent teacher put both her students right, her manner adapting itself exactly to the requirements of a cheerful, resilient lad and a rather shy girl, and sorting them both out without offence or passion. I was sorry when this lesson ended, for it had been a first-rate demonstration of both teaching technique and human understanding.

Another quite good biology lesson was in the *scuola media* at Soresina, a small town near Cremona. This school has about 600 boys and girls, some of whom are in two smaller branch-establishments. The buildings were old and cramped, and there was no laboratory provision; but a new building was well under way, and in this there will be laboratories. This class, a second form, was fortunate in its teacher; he had a clear, quiet and relaxed manner, and obviously got on well with his pupils. He was also their mathematics teacher, for the *scuola media* normally expects its mathematicians to be able to teach the science course. A rather attractive textbook was in use, with very clear pictures and diagrams; its approach was rather formal, with Latin names used for all the species mentioned, but in contrast to this the teacher's own approach was at a 'story-book' level. I heard some of the children recapitulating their past work, which they did very confidently and in well-rounded sentences; and some searching questions by the teacher made clear that these answers were not just 'parroted'. A rather similar type of lesson in a Spanish school was much less successful, I thought, mainly because the teacher failed to present the topic – the workings of the human heart – in a way that aroused more than a tepid interest.

But the most astonishing science lesson I saw anywhere must be the one conducted in the Portuguese primary school of São Vitor, at Braga; indeed, I would call this a quite touching experience. It began straightforwardly enough, with some revision of past work, followed by a little purely theoretical physics, concerning levers and balances, done with the aid of blackboard sketches. But then came the great moment: the teacher took some primitive apparatus from a cupboard, and actually prepared to perform a couple of simple chemical experiments.

If you have read H. G. Wells's great comic novel, *Kipps*, you will find something in the early chapters very like what I am about to describe, the only difference being that in my case nothing went wrong to cause the uttering of any improper expressions by the teacher. All the rest was there, though: the excitement of the pupils when they realized what was about to happen, the primitive arrangements, the thrilling smell and the awed sense that something very modern and significant was taking place. But Wells was writing of his own boyhood in about 1880, and I saw this happening in 1973: it does make a difference.

By looking at the children's textbook, I eventually worked out what the purpose of these experiments was (of course, the teacher did explain it to the children, but I find spoken Portuguese hard to follow at the best of times): it seems that they were connected with the human digestive system and with the salivary glands. In the first experiment some oil was floated on water in a jar; in another, a simple filtration was performed; in the third, some mysterious substance was heated in a test-tube and the results displayed to the class. The apparatus was as simple as could be: a test-tube, a jar, some filter-paper, a length of tubing, a spirit-lamp, and a pair of wooden tongs with which to hold the hot glass tube. There were frequent delays for fetching water from a distant tap; once the spirit-lamp went out and nobody at first could find any more spirit to refill it. One felt the utter impossibility of doing a job for which none of the needful materials were supplied. And how much better, of course, if the boys had been doing the experiment: the teacher let them help as much as possible, but it was a poor substitute for actually doing the thing. I know Portugal is not a rich country, but can she be so poor that her children cannot be served better than this? A friend to whom I described this scene shortly afterwards said 'Oh, well, Salazar was all against educating the masses: it is all going to be quite different now we have Caetano, you'll see!' We shall never know, I suppose, whether this optimism was justified, for Caetano was followed by Spinola, and Spinola by Costa Gomes, and . . . I should not care to prophesy beyond that. I had, I think, already detected some signs that there were stirrings down in the forest, with promises of reforms on the way, and if (it is, unfortunately, a very big 'if') Portugal is granted political stability, under whatever leader, I think she may follow the example of her larger neighbour Spain in moving into a brighter educational dawn. Portuguese teachers, if perhaps limited, are sound enough in technique, and could not be more dedicated in their outlook; what they need is a decent amount of money spent on their schools. Those secondary schools which actually exist at present seemed to me to be excellent in their thoroughly traditional way; the trouble is that most Portuguese get only an elementary education, and the major effort must surely be put to remedying that state of affairs.

Strangely enough, the poverty of the material provision for that science lesson was only emphasized by the surprisingly high quality of the textbook in use: it had good photographs, clear and attractive diagrams, and, sadly, plenty of experiments for the children to do themselves . . . if only they could!

English must be just about the most popular subject with

European pupils, and in one Italian *scuola media* the headmaster was eloquent on the difficulty of diverting some pupils from English, which they wanted to study, to French, which they didn't; his problem was that he had too many French teachers and too few who could teach English. Certainly, the first English lesson I saw there did not suggest a very high degree of pedagogical skill; I had been asked to help give the pupils some conversational practice to prepare them for a forthcoming examination, but the lady in charge of the class well-meaningly sabotaged all my efforts to get a fluent dialogue going by her anxiety to correct every little mistake as it was made. I despair of trying to convey the comic exasperation we all felt; no pupil could utter two consecutive words without an intervention, and all idea of communication was totally lost, as was any sense of the intonations and rhythms of actual speech. Her right course, surely, would have been to let them talk, mistakes and all, making notes as they did so of any really serious fault which must afterwards be corrected. Her own accent, too, was somewhat suspect, and she spent far too much time on one or two star pupils while the rest became bored and fidgety. Later, however, a group of very determined boys proved tough enough to hold their own even against her volubility, and we did manage some kind of useful dialogue in the final ten minutes. Teachers of language must ask themselves what they are really trying to do!

I was rather disappointed in general by the standard of the English teaching I saw, and I began to wonder whether the old idea of ourselves as the world's worst linguists is not rather exaggerated. There are noble exceptions: I have recently seen some most competent pupils at Frankfurt, for example, some of whom were discussing problems of style and interpretation as freely as any native English speakers. The great problem – especially for the French – seems to be intonation, our verbal melodies being perhaps more varied than most; I did, however, meet one French teacher who had studied in the north of England and had splendidly caught the accent of Yorkshire.

Though pupils often write very accurate English, a correct pronunciation seems much rarer: I recall a German fourteen-year-old declaring that 'Jayp'n is a cowntry in Arzhia; so is Cheena', and, while he was perhaps exceptionally far adrift, there were many others whose spoken English was fairly unintelligible

– quite as many, I would think, as there are English pupils whose French would make no sense to a Frenchman.

Obviously, it is much easier for Latins to catch the feel of each other's language, and one of the most brilliant lessons I saw was given by a young Spanish teacher, Señor Miguel, at the Institution du Saint-Esprit in Beauvais. This is a Catholic boarding-school, with about 500 pupils in a modern block on the outskirts of the city, and about 350 juniors in an older building in the city centre. I was accompanied to this lesson by a friend who teaches English in the same school, and we agreed that in one year Señor Miguel's class had progressed to a point that we should have been more than pleased to achieve ourselves. His method was to show colour-slides of everyday life in Spanish-speaking countries, and to base on them some simple question-and-answer drills, using formulae like 'Pienso que . . . me parece que . . . me pregunto si . . .' ('I think . . . it looks to me as if . . . I wonder whether . . .') to introduce their answers. Inside this framework, vocabulary was acquired by constant use and repetition, and the boys' confidence in the material thus acquired was remarkable. I think 'twinned' towns could undertake a useful project for each other in producing sets of slides for such lessons.

Textbooks were generally attractive and well-arranged, but I felt that their content sometimes gave a strange impression of English life. A visit to England will be more concerned with double-decker buses, Marks and Spencer's or fish-and-chip shops than with the Boat Race, Beefeaters, or top-hatted Etonians, but it was these latter institutions that appeared most often, as well as historical material about the Norman Conquest which would interest an Italian child about as much as the struggles of Guelf and Ghibellin would appeal to his English counterpart. Likewise, some of the audio-visual courses I met in France seemed to miss the boat by relying so heavily on a certain type of voice which is not so much standard (less still average!) English as, shall we say, standard North Oxford Prep School; these children are not even Janet and John, but rather Joanna and Jeremy. There were also too many examples of those curious exercises which suggest that their inventor was not really quite sure what he wanted to test: I saw one class hopelessly bogged down by an exercise which made great play with the difference between 'Dick is reading a book' (subject–verb–object) and 'Dick is reading in his bedroom' (subject–verb–adverb phrase). Fine, if one really wants to emphasize grammatical analysis, but useless for any other purpose, particularly in learning a virtually uninflected language; it merely meant that children were rebuked for giving answers which were perfectly good, natural English, but didn't fit the required grammatical pattern.

The approach to the teaching of English in French primary schools has been far more cautious than the converse process here, and I am told that the experiment has in fact been virtually dropped, having failed to produce the expected results. Certainly, I was not very impressed by what I saw; it is true that the children seemed to be enjoying their lessons, and could repeat what they heard on the tapes with fair accuracy, but I do not think they really understood what they were doing. A voice on the tape might say 'What a pretty dress!' as the screen showed a bride in her weddinggown and another lady looking entranced; but 'What a pretty dress!' is only one of many possible reactions to such a picture, and I could see that some pupils were missing the point quite widely. Intonation again was a problem, and one made worse by the fact that not all the teachers themselves had good intonations, so that many pupils were picking up inaccurate sounds. These courses, too, seem to forget that circumstances may alter intonations: if I say 'He's not very clever, is he?' my intonation will vary according to whether I am feeling sorry for him, being scornful of him, contrasting him with another person, or considering another speaker's judgement of him.

I did, however, see a good audio-visual lesson at the CES J. B. Pellerin in Beauvais; this first-year class of pupils aged eleven and twelve were obviously learning thoroughly as well as enjoying the process. I also saw some good lessons at the *liceu*, or grammar school, in Evora, Portugal. This is a mixed school of about 1,200 pupils with a staff of about sixty; the school works in the handsome buildings of the Old University, operating a two-shift system. In two days I saw seven English lessons. One was a very boring affair based wholly on grammatical routines, with the questions laboriously written out on the blackboard and copied into the pupils' notebooks, but the others were good. For example, one class which had done two or three years of English were discussing fluently that entertaining passage in *My Family and Other Animals* where Gerry Durrell has an unfortunate contretemps with some scorpions, and their laughter and eager comment made it plain that they understood thoroughly what they had read. In another class, a comprehension method was used, rather than translation, to deal with a story; this class later used me to practise their spoken English, and began rather startlingly by asking me what I thought of their teacher! This was in fact only an innocent attempt to get me to do a bit of their homework for them, for the young Senhor Rosa had told them that in the next lesson he would be asking for their frank criticism, in English, of his teaching methods (yes, in pre-revolutionary Portugal!) and they were simply hoping my answers would provide them with some useful vocabulary.

In all the Portuguese English lessons not a word of Portuguese was used, except in absolutely unavoidable situations. This is official policy, I was told, and as long as it is not carried to excess, it seems a pretty sound one. Certainly, from my own point of view it was a godsend, for Portuguese is not an easy language, owing to the quite remarkable lack of resemblance there sometimes is between the sound of a word and its appearance.

The same emphasis on 'direct method' teaching is to be found in Germany, where one rarely hears a word of German uttered during an English or French lesson. The standard of English teaching was high, with intonation again something of a problem (the common sound of 'a' as in 'cat' is one that the Germans appear to find especially elusive). Some ingenious and amusing methods were in use: a class numbered as two football teams and provided with a ball to throw from one to another, as a means of drilling the English numerals as a game; some entertaining little rhymes which the children obviously enjoyed; a jolly cartoon of a sheriff and a gangster (both these words, having been adopted into the German language, were already familiar to the pupils, as were also 'boss', 'whisky', 'revolver' and 'teenager', which at least made a change from the pen of the gardener's aunt!) There was also a very busy lesson at the Emden *Realschule* in which the room was turned into a market-place and pupils dashed hither and thither buying goods, chatting to shopkeepers, and so on. But, fun as all this was (and competent as the children were, too) one or two touches were curiously dated, such as the 'newsboy' crying out 'Morning Post! Horrible murder in Leeds!' – I wonder when the author of that one last heard such a thing actually being done!

Still, these were good, lively, imaginative lessons, and teachers like Herr Zimmer at the Zewen school, or Frau Strybny at the *Realschule*, are obviously delivering the goods most effectively. I cannot say the same, I fear, for one German teacher I saw, whose lesson with a class of thirteen-year-olds was a failure from start to finish; he began by allowing the pupils to get well out of hand by spending a considerable time going round and checking each pupil's homework – a fairly perfunctory check it was, too, little more than the scribbling of the teacher's initials at the foot of the page, with no real attempt to point out errors. It was a lively and energetic class, which needed plenty to occupy it, and of course, it had nothing while this went on, which it did for some twenty minutes. Having thus lost his grip on the class, the teacher never regained it, and the boys took their revenge on him by working a number of childish improprieties and cheeky references to the teacher himself into the sentences they were asked to invent to illustrate the uses of the relative pronoun. An embarrassing exhibition altogether.

Equally unsatisfactory, and for similar reasons, was a German lesson I saw in a French school – the same which had shown me the smallpox lesson, indeed. Again, the first fifteen minutes went in returning corrected work to pupils; admittedly, it had been carefully marked this time, but the same problem arose of the pupils who had nothing to do while waiting their turn. It would anyway have been hard to bring them back to work after this; but I don't think this teacher was trying very hard in any case, because the rest of the lesson was a confused revision of unrelated grammatical points, all treated entirely in a vacuum without the least implication that the words or phrases might actually convey any meaning. It was the kind of lesson I thought had disappeared decades ago, given in apparent ignorance of tape-recorders, records, projectors, dramatic or conversational methods, or anything else that a good language teacher today takes for granted. The pupils were bored, inattentive and probably learned nothing.

But a formal lesson need not be unsuccessful: at the *scuola media* at Soresina, Italy, I found a third-year French class which had made excellent progress in two or three hours weekly over a period of less than three years; they were fortunate in their teacher, who had an excellent French accent and a sound technique. The lesson began with a dictation; then the class moved on to making notes – in French – from an exposition, also in French, given by the teacher on the subject of the dictation. That the class, in so short a time, had progressed to the point of being able to make notes in French, and, as I saw for myself, clear, accurate French too, spoke well for the way they had been taught. If this lesson would seem to some English teachers over-academic in its content, due allowance must be made for the limited allocation of time, which does not allow for anything more imaginative.

Other good lessons, with somewhat older pupils, were those I saw in the two Spanish *institutos de bachillerato*. At J. V. Vives in Gerona, a class of fifteen-year-old girls had a very well-varied hour of activities: first a 'missing-word' test; then some lively oral question-and-answer, with really quick-fire exchanges; and lastly a corporate working-out of a French crossword puzzle on the blackboard. Except that the girls incessantly chewed gum, which I can't regard as an enjoyable sight, I thought them a delightful class, and very bright, though the teacher assured me seriously that she had had to work very hard with them as they had not been well-taught previously, a complaint I seem to have heard rather often from teachers! At Virgen del Carmen in Jaén, the teacher was the director of the school himself, and the class a group of over thirty eighteen-year-old boys. This was again a quite orthodox lesson, but very competent indeed; the passage was read, quickly translated by one of the pupils, with occasional suggestions or emendations by some of the others, and then a very fluent discussion took place. The students seemed very eager to learn, and to seek information when it was not specifically being thrust at them, and this in itself mitigated the one fault I felt in the lesson, that some of the pupils on the wings of the class were in danger of being overlooked. The director skilfully manipulated the topic so as to bring me into it and thus stimulate a discussion of English educational ideas. We continued to use French as the language of our discussion, of course, and the change of subject showed how thorough had been the students' mastery of vocabulary, for I do not recall their ever being at a loss for the word to express their meaning. Obviously, their teaching had been most effective (even allowing for the family resemblance of French to Spanish) and their teachers might well be proud of what they had achieved.

As well as these lessons in modern languages, I also saw a few

Latin lessons. The Spanish one was largely based on the affinities of Latin with Spanish and, like our own Cambridge Classics Project, the emphasis was on translation from, and comprehension of, Latin, rather than on plaguing the pupil with the doubtfully valuable task of translating from his own language into a dead one. In the CES J. B. Pellerin, at Beauvais in France, I saw a class of beginners – eight boys and thirteen girls – using a most attractive-looking textbook. But its charms were, alas, somewhat illusory, for the colourful modern layout thinly disguised a very traditional approach, full of grammatical niceties about parisyllabic and imparisyllabic declensions and so on. The lesson began with the return of test-papers, in the traditional 'descending order of marks' method which must cause many a sinking feeling in the stomach; it then continued with a missing-word exercise, some of which I thought decidedly difficult. The compiler had, perhaps, been over-ingenious in devising this exercise, and its aim was not always clear to me. The lesson ended with some grammatical points, not closely related to what had gone before. The German class was the one I have briefly mentioned already as containing one lone boy among twenty-seven girls. The book, called *Ianua Nova*, slightly resembled the French one in appearance; it was very well-illustrated, but quite orthodox in its text, and the plan of each chapter was more or less identical – an introduction, a text to practise the new construction, exercises on grammar and syntax, a German–Latin translation exercise, a fairly long text for comprehension work, and a shorter one for further practice. Much of the lesson comprised oral translation, and I noted a great emphasis on producing stylish as well as merely correct translation. The constructions under review were participial phrases and ablative absolutes, and each time one occurred in the passage the pupil translating was expected to isolate it and identify it. It was a good, thorough, scholarly sort of lesson, but it did not fire the imagination; however, the pupils were the same ones whose English lesson (the one based on the satirical song) also impressed me, and so stimulating and articulate a group could not be boring, or bored, however academic the material.

5
The teacher and his work: II

It is difficult to sum up so many different lessons, and perhaps one should not even attempt to do so. But this I will venture to say: when it comes to teaching the fundamental things of the curriculum, most European teachers do it very well indeed. Their lessons are carefully prepared, they have mastery of such techniques as setting out notes and sketches on the blackboard, they expect, and they get, high standards of co-operation and performance from their pupils. They do, in other words, a thoroughly *professional* job; I do not doubt that a visitor to Europe would see poor lessons, as I sometimes did myself, but I feel sure that the good ones greatly outnumber them. I am not (I hope) 'the idiot who praises with enthusiastic tone All centuries but this and every country but his own', and I do acknowledge that our own contributions to education have been immense: but perhaps more in the field of developing the whole personality than in the methodical cultivation of basic skills? And these, surely, should be achieved *before* the rest, for it is little use having original, fresh, personal ideas if we cannot express them intelligibly. When we do decide to tackle the problem of the large numbers of near-illiterates in our midst, I am convinced we must look to Europe for some lessons in how to do so.

Perhaps we might widen the basis of teacher-exchange, indeed, so that not only those who teach languages, but also those in other disciplines, could have more opportunity to compare notes with teachers in other lands. It would be a two-way traffic: France could do with seeing some of our best Nuffield Science teaching, for example, while we might do well to make the acquaintance of such people as the fierce but kindly lady in a French classroom whom I heard chiding a small boy who (having been asked what substances might be measured in cubic centimetres) had said 'des poisons, peut-être, Madame?' and had been firmly corrected with 'plutôt, des produits pharmacéutiques!' One must yield more than a grudging admiration to the tenacity with which French teachers preserve the purity of their native tongue. Nor are there any concessions in the wording of some of the material the children use; take the following sentence from a work studied by some eight-year-olds at Avignon:

> Les troupeaux de bergerie constituent la très grande majorité du cheptel ovin des campagnes françaises; leurs déplacements sont rélativement minimes.

None of this prevents the teachers from having, for the most part, very pleasant and easy relations with their pupils. The atmosphere during actual teaching sessions never struck me as in any way authoritarian; it is true that some of the customs, such as the Italian one of standing to answer a question, may superficially seem so, but in practice there is much fun and friendliness in the classroom. Many illustrations come to mind: the pupils of the *liceu* and the technical school, both at Evora, chatted informally with their teachers and crowded round me to practise their English; discussion ebbed and flowed vigorously in the seminar-type lessons I attended in the *institutos de bachillerato* at Gerona and Jaén; most Italian primary classes were splendidly happy places; and the enthusiasm of the children at La Barbière, Avignon, or the *école normale* annexe at Beauvais could only come from a relaxed and pleasant atmosphere. The primary children at the Zewen and Früchteburg schools in Germany were bouncing with life and energy; a question from the teacher, and up went a dozen or more hands, each child eagerly clicking his or her fingers in the hope of being noticed the sooner, and sometimes emitting little moans and squeaks of eagerness to emphasize the fact of knowing the answer.

I should not, of course, in any way imply that bad relations between teacher and pupil never exist; I have already referred to one or two lessons where pupils showed some degree of contempt for their teacher, and sometimes one saw thoughtless or brusque behaviour by teachers also; it would be remarkable if one did not. Now and then, especially perhaps in Germany, I saw pupils behaving rather oafishly to one another, and sometimes even a visitor under the escort of a teacher was elbowed out of the way by a rush of pupils. But the predominant impression remains one of happiness, natural good manners and orderly freedom, and I cannot help it if this disappoints those hoping for further evidence of the Awfulness of the Young.

I felt very much at home in foreign classrooms. There, as in England, the primary school has the edge over the secondary in such matters as the variety, liveliness and colour of its atmosphere. There, as in England, one can see project work, class discussions, visual aids, oral and written comprehension exercises, special provision for backward pupils and all the other educational commonplaces. But I also had some surprises, the greatest perhaps being the exciting ferment which pervades present-day education in Spain. There, more than anywhere, I found such things as open-plan schools, team-teaching techniques, individual work assignments and flexible work-groups. The average age of Spanish teachers seems to be quite young; at the Sagrada Familia school in Ecija, for example, I was told it was twenty-six or twenty-seven. One teacher said she felt her country was trying to do too much too quickly; she may have had a point, but then, if one waits cautiously for every possible contingency to be covered, does one ever start at all? The middle-aged headmaster at the Colegio Nacional Menendez Pidal at Salt, virtually a suburb of Gerona, admitted to feeling real trepidation at the thought of quitting his old (and squalid) building to move into a purpose-built open-plan school nearby, but he said that his colleagues were as keen as mustard, and he was sure they would see him through triumphantly. When I went back nine months later there certainly seemed to be an atmosphere of purpose and contentment among the 600 pupils and sixteen teachers.

The Spanish Ministry of Education's periodical *Vida Escolar* is a most attractive and informative production, containing some detailed schemes for the better utilization of the limited teaching-force, for the improving of curriculum and for its presentation in more compelling ways, for the more accurate evaluation of children's work and progress, and – most important – for the creation of techniques to bring the weaker pupil up to the required standard without his being forced, as in the past, to repeat part of the course. The magazine also contains reports of actual classroom experiences; surveys of particular aspects of education (one is 'Children and the Cinema', for example); studies of interesting experiments, such as a couple of projects on Education for Peace; reports of conferences, book reviews, and much discussion – now and then rather heavy-going – on educational philosophy. The more practical and factual articles are often excellent; as a sample, I mention just two.

The first (issue of Sept/Oct 1972) is 'Techniques in teaching-communication' by Alberto Mediavilla. This sets out clearly the different arrangements of seating required for ordinary lessons, for conferences, for a symposium, a seminar, a small group-discussion, and so on. It is a valuable reminder that flexibility is vital to good teaching, and that a school needs space, and easily-movable furniture, if it is to do its job properly. Merely to replace the traditional rows-and-columns by a new arrangement is not enough; one must be able to create fresh arrangements for fresh needs. For example, I noticed in one school that pupils were encouraged to work together on a job, each helping the other; schoolmasters used to shudder with horror at this, but it seems to me good sense, and much more Christian than a dog-eat-dog approach. Obviously, for this one needs to be able to move single desks together easily. The school concerned, incidentally, was the Martin Noguera, at Jaén, a *colegio nacional* for about 640 boys and girls, housed in a new open-plan building with magnificent mountain views.

The second article discusses ways of making the study of a foreign language more interesting and effective, and to provide the pupils with constant reminders of vocabulary. The author, Ricardo Jordana, discusses in an entirely practical way such matters as the use of the contents of the room and things seen from the window, the best type of blackboard to have (magnetic, revolving, glass, triptych, etc.) and ways of using it, files of pictures, wall-charts, flannelgraphs, cut-outs of the human face to demonstrate the right position of the tongue, 'kangaroo-pouch' charts, flash-cards, matching-cards, notices and labels, calendars and clocks, weather-boards, helpers' charts, birthdays charts, a model stage, toy telephones, games such as snakes-and-ladders, crosswords, wall-newspapers, picture-dictionaries, exchanges of letters and tapes, collections of objects like bus tickets or stamps, use of maps and railway timetables, gramophone records, tapes, slide-projectors, overhead-projectors, films, the language laboratory, radio, television, electronic teaching-aids and heaven knows what else: I have rarely seen quite so many ideas crammed into eleven pages! Señor Jordana gives a bibliography of nine items, seven of them published in Britain and the other two in the USA – one up to us, in fact! But all credit, too, to Señor Jordana for having studied all this material and condensed it so brilliantly into one utterly practical article. Any teacher who read it would surely find one or two ideas new to him, and I have referred to the article at such length to indicate the determined efforts Spain is now making to catch up.

As will be gathered from all this, I am hopeful about Spain, though of course there is still much to be done there. If she can manage to keep political stability, the keenness of the teachers and administrators would go far to overcome the inheritance of past poverty and political strife, especially as she continues to climb up the industrial league-table. The pupils themselves, when I talked to them, seemed to be conscious of the ways in which their schools are still lacking, and could be improved. Another group of pupils with something to say on this subject are those writing in *Il Formicaio* of 26 May 1973. This is the occasional magazine of the Scuola Media Virgilio, at Cremona in Italy. This is a school of 900 boys and girls, with a staff of seventy-eight, in handsome modern buildings serving a residential district near the River Po; there are also two small detached sections in other premises. One boy regrets the lack of 'educational visits' and draws an unfavourable comparison with what he calls the 'more positive' English school. Another asks why his education is in effect only 'part-time', and demands more out-of-school activities. One or two demand the total abolition of the *voto*, or mark-system, but another sturdily defends it as the best way to ensure that pupils really work. The most radical boy, one Maurizio Mazzolari, calls for the abolition of homework and its replacement by a longer school day, the improvement of foreign-language teaching and the introduction of exchange-visits to other countries and for the teaching of 'the working of modern mechanical devices like cars, nuclear reactors or electronic calculators'. Another boy adds his voice to those asking for longer school-hours, saying that 'it is almost impossible to learn a foreign language well on three lessons a week, to cover the immense Italian syllabus on five, or learn much history and geography with only four hours between the two'. He adds the thoughtful comment that 'history and Italian aren't really just theoretical subjects, but they will soon become so if more time is not found for them'. This boy is expressing what I have myself said, that the combination of a short working day and a very wide syllabus leads to too much being attempted in too little time, so that lessons, especially in the secondary school, become too aridly academic.

But the overall effect of these boys' comments is undeniably encouraging; they *want* education, and value it, and they appreciate good teaching, which they feel must be firmly grounded in the real life of today.

Anyone who reads these pages carefully will quickly deduce that some teachers are very much better than others – as if he didn't know that already! In this country, we often hear it said that some schools only allow the brightest pupils to be taught by the 'best' teachers, while the less able ones make do with the rest; after over a quarter of a century in the profession, I should say that this does indeed sometimes happen, but perhaps less often than some people suppose. And anyway, what is a 'good' teacher? Not necessarily one who possesses all the proper qualifications; the holder of an impressive doctorate can be an unmitigated disaster in the classroom, and a so-called 'unqualified' teacher absolutely superb. If, then, one French CES informed me that its Type I and Type II classes were taught by *professeurs*, while the Type III pupils sat at the feet of *instituteurs* (the term normally applied to primary school teachers) it need not be inferred that Type III were necessarily getting a raw deal; an *instituteur*, as I hope I have shown, may be very good indeed. But it must be admitted that he is paid less than a *professeur*, which perhaps reflects on the esteem in which somebody or other holds him.

It should also be acknowledged that many European teachers are working on a temporary or part-time basis; sometimes they are professional people supplementing their salaries by teaching for a few hours a week in their special subject – foreign languages, for example. Again, they may be excellent teachers; but of course they are not likely to have the same pedagogical expertise, or the same pastoral interest in their pupils, as the full-time professional has. Spain, for example, in 1972 had a total teaching-force of about 178,000 people; of these, some 10,000 were in the part-time, or temporary, category; 7,000 were listed as 'special statute', a category which includes, among others, teachers of religion, physical education teachers, and those teaching 'political education'. Over 50,000 more are listed as 'contracted teachers', which presumably includes the very large number of men and women in religious orders who teach in the private church schools.

I can do no more than report what I saw myself, and that was that the general standard of teaching was of very high professional competence, and that it seemed to be very fairly distributed among classes of all types. With the general tendency of classes to be unstreamed, this is in any case to be expected. Since so many European teachers were very kind to me, I can perhaps try to repay part of my debt by trying to convey something of the general flavour of the profession, and I begin with an extract from *Il Formicaio* for April 1970, in which a second-year pupil, Massimo Lattanzi, writes a 'Memory of My Teacher':

> A character who will always be dear to me is my teacher, a man who gave me much, and to me was more than just an instructor; he was a friend. Of medium height, his face already bearing some signs of age, and his moustaches always in disarray, he was ever there, seated behind the wooden desk pitted with worm-holes, waiting each day to teach us delightful and fresh ideas. Thanks to him, I went willingly to school; he made even difficult things fun to learn.
>
> I remember, and always shall, his affection for us all, even those who drove him to despair; he once gave a large and very handsome fretwork box to a boy who would not work,

as an inducement to greater effort, and then, seeing that the boy continued to be much as before, did all he could to help him learn a manual craft.

Sometimes he rebuked us, but never unpleasantly; even when a morose look came into his eye, his expression showed his underlying kindness. We had this same teacher for four years (having had a lady teacher in our first year, of whom I only have a vague memory because I was so young when I knew her).

My best and most vivid memory of him is of our final day in the elementary school, when we gave him a tangible proof of our gratitude. We were all around his desk; he sat with his head bowed as if he did not know how to thank us; then he gave us some final advice.

The bell sounded, putting an end to five long years of school. Now I am in the middle school, and I meet him sometimes in the street. The last time I did so he left me with a thought that pleased me very much: 'I'd love to be back with you lads of 5A because – I don't know why – you were my favourite pupils.'

I believe that passage to be entirely sincere; the Italians are an affectionate people, given to displays of emotion, but you do not need to be in a place long to sense its atmosphere, and in classrooms such as those of Signor Bassi at Leonida Bissolati, Signor Fracassi at Porcellasco, and Signor Cicchi at A. Fabretti I felt that real affection was present between teacher and pupils. I do not deny that there may be classrooms where the atmosphere is very different – like the one reported in *Oggi* of 26 February 1975, whose teacher required the class to hiss any pupil whose work was inadequate; or those of some of the people Aldo Bernardini came up against in his work at Pietralata; or again, those against which the Barbiana pupils sometimes cry out. But let us not forget also that the Barbiana children had Father Milani, who inspired them to write their marvellous little book. On the whole, Massimo's essay rings true to my ears.

If Italian teachers *were* bad, I do not know that I could wholly blame them, for they labour under many very disadvantageous conditions. Their pay is poor; the schools in which they teach are often dismally inadequate places. Many of them have to take on other work such as private coaching* to enable them to live decently, while many others are married women who are working as teachers to supplement their husbands' income, and thereby pay for the rather higher standard of living to which they aspire. Their security of tenure is by no means impregnable: until a teacher has attained a certain seniority, he is liable to be directed from one school to another, even to a lower-paid post. An Italian friend wrote to me one summer holiday mentioning that she had just received a letter from the authorities (in August!) to say that she would be teaching in the autumn term at a *scuola media* instead of her present *liceo*. Italy is just about the most bureaucrat-ridden country in Western Europe (I should not care to speak for points further East) so that the Ministry, it is said, can sometimes take so long to fix the dates of the holidays that the term is almost over before the schools hear of the decision; and a school in need of a teacher in a certain subject, and already possessing someone with adequate qualifications and a willingness to turn his hand to it, may yet not employ him to do so until permission has slowly ground its way out of the Ministry in Rome. As for applying for a new post, it seems to be a process roughly comparable to requesting permission to help oneself to a few bars of gold from Fort Knox.† All in all, Italy may well have better teachers than she deserves.

The primary school teacher in Italy rarely has any free time during his working hours, as he must remain in charge of his pupils throughout the day. I was told that a teacher conscientiously opposed to taking his class for religious knowledge might exchange with another teacher willing to do so, and I presume that this would be an exception to the general rule. One's sympathy with the teacher who never has a free period is, however, somewhat tempered by the fact that the working day is so short:

---

*This situation also exists in Portugal and probably elsewhere. I do not know whether other countries find it necessary as West Germany does to include in the regulations a ban on teachers giving private coaching to any pupil whom they actually teach at school.

†I should have liked to support this statement by quoting a few extracts from a curious periodical called *Ultimissime della Scuola e dei Concorsi*, which carries detailed 'models' for applying for new posts, transfers, changes of subject, etc.; but they are so tediously boring and verbosely bureaucratic that it would be sheer cruelty to the reader to do so. As they have to be seen to be believed, maybe you will not believe me.

indeed, the Barbiana pupils report – with scathing comments on the fellow's insensitivity! – the case of one teacher who was asked by an audience of parents why he had not established a *doposcuola* (the extra afternoon classes for helping backward pupils to catch up with their work); he burst out indignantly 'You don't seem to realize that I teach a good eighteen hours a week!' This, as the boys acidly point out, to an audience of workers who rose each morning at four o'clock to catch early trains, and farmers who frequently worked for eighteen hours a day ...

The discrepancy is not hard to reconcile, of course: in our own country I know any number of splendid teachers, people who will cheerfully spend hours of their own time on school duties, or in helping some pupil who is in trouble, but who are good Union (or Association) men and will cry out passionately against any attempt to put an extra five minutes on to the school day or an extra duty into the year. We are all frail human beings. Indeed, while agreeing most vehemently with most of what the Barbiana book says, I think perhaps its young authors are a little hard on teachers as a whole: they are not the mean-souled and unfeeling people they sometimes depict, but just rather puzzled people, well-meaning but not always effectual, confronted with forces they sometimes fail to understand or cope with.

I feel this the more strongly, perhaps, after reading part of an article in *Corriere della Sera*, the Italian daily newspaper: only part, alas, because this section appeared in the issue of 8 May, and that was the day on which I left Italy, so I never saw what followed. It was a long, thoughtful, article, occupying almost a whole news page, another evidence of the seriousness with which many European newspapers treat matters our own press gives little attention to. The article called the situation in many Italian schools 'chaotic', and there were statements like 'I was terrified on my first day as a teacher. Control of the class was impossible, the uproar hellish. You could hardly ever find a point of contact, or arouse interest in a pupil. The sound of the end-of-lesson bell comes as a breath of freedom.' Much is made of the problem of the inadequacy of teachers: they are shockingly ill-paid – the teacher described in the article lives in a two-roomed flat in a slummy quarter of Rome, and travels in on an old motor-cycle which he parks well away from his school so as not to be jeered at by his pupils, almost all of whom have far better machines, or even cars. It is hard, therefore, to get decent teachers; those who do exist are often older men bewildered by a world which seems to be crumbling before their eyes; understandably, they opt out of any attempt to understand it. Or they may be younger men with no real wish to teach who simply cannot find the better-paid research posts to which they really aspire. Absenteeism is rife; one post may have as many as three holders, the actual one being on paid leave while his replacement is on sick leave and the substitute-substitute, there for a brief period to earn a little money, has not the least interest in the job. Small wonder, says the writer, that the pupils, the real victims of the system, have become disillusioned and therefore rebellious. The article indicts the entire Italian educational administration as sluggish and cumbrous – and certainly, my own small contact with it does not lead me to dissent from that at least!

The article in *Oggi* of 12 June 1974 is equally worrying. In it, the head of a *scuola media*, himself a teacher's leader, says 'It is useless to conceal that teachers are suffering a deep frustration, placed as they are between hammer and anvil, between pupils in revolt and a total lack of direction from the State, which has for many years left the schools to look after themselves. One proof of this state of mind is found in the fact that absenteeism among teachers is greater than that found in any other category of state employees.'

These pictures are, indeed, very different from what I saw myself. Allowing for the tendency of all newspapers to heighten the colours a little, it is clear that I only saw part of the picture in Italy: the schools I visited catered almost entirely for juniors and the younger adolescents, and it is everywhere the mid-teenager who is 'difficult' and rebellious; I saw only schools selected for me by the Italian authorities; and I visited only schools in moderate-sized cities of fairly middle-class status (though Perugia does have a Communist administration, which may perhaps argue a more proletarian populace!).

For another picture of the darker side, I turn to a very remarkable little book, published in Lisbon: it is a small collection of children's writing, much of it of intense poignancy, called *A Criança e a Vida* (The Child and Life), edited by Maria Rosa Colaço. In her introduction, Senhora Colaço tells how she came to the big city, 'holding in one hand my teacher's diploma, and in the other, my terror'. The school to which she was sent was:

> an old first-floor building in a street dirty with salt, old bills and dampness. The children had absolutely nothing in common with those little dears in white pinafores whom their mothers entrust to the schools as if they were delicate porcelain. I recall our first meeting with such emotion that I doubt if I can find words to express it: I opened the door, and in they came, forty-five of them, and there weren't enough desks, nothing like enough, even when I sat them down three to a desk and put five of them at what was supposed to be my own table. The headmaster came in and said 'Well, there's your kingdom, and here are your little people; if you have trouble, and I shouldn't wonder if you did, the police-station is at the end of the road. And I'm at your disposal. As for immediate needs, well, it's like this: you must decide from the start whether it's to be you or them. No illusions, if you want to survive. I'm sorry to give you the dregs; but make the best of it.' Then he went out; and there I was, face to face with the unknown. The silence which enfolded me was heavy, expectant; in the midst of it, *they* were; and it was early morning. Carved by wind and sea, they came from the boats moored beside the dock, from the shanty-town, from God knows where. In their hands, instead of books and satchels, they brought – I don't know why – leaves of the plane-tree, and branches of flowering almond; and the Autumn gilded their hair. They were living seeds of the purest liberty, and they had no preconceived ideas, of words, or of anything else. I looked at them in silence, one by one, for a long time. Then I picked up the ruler which the headmaster had given me as a protection, and I said to the one who looked as if he was the oldest 'Right, we'll start with you!' Then I couldn't think what else to say to them. But the hunger for affection was in them, just as were the sun, the rain, and the hardships of their life. And, since we were primary school children, poor and all alone, we established there and then a clear and reasonable understanding. That is how we became firm friends; friends for always.

Out of this apparently unpromising start, Senhora Colaço and her pupils achieved a splendid little book of beautiful and moving poetry. I wish I could quote extensively from it, for it is evidence both of the problems facing some European teachers, and of the devotion and love with which those problems are often overcome.

Full discussion of such matters as teachers' salaries and professional qualifications must be beyond the scope of such a work as this, but I have quoted a few figures in an Appendix which may perhaps at least give a rough idea of the situation. Exactly comparable figures are not easy to obtain, and in any case, mere figures mean little unless one knows what standard of living the salary will buy in each country, and how it compares with what may be earned in other professions. But certainly some European teachers are only moderately paid.

They do, however, often do rather well in the amenities provided for their use. I saw, for example, some very comfortable staff rooms, the palm probably going to a Spanish one, that of the Instituto Virgen del Carmen at Jaén, which had both a comfortably furnished lounge with attractive pictures, a tank of fancy fish, and other delights, and a stately room for formal staff-meetings, equipped with three big tables in U formation, leather ceremonial chairs, and a positively ducal throne for the director! The new Colegio La Inmaculada at Gerona has small staff-rooms on every floor, and each class-teacher has his own office adjacent to his classroom, for quiet work and for interviewing parents or pupils. Staff libraries, for study and reference, are commonly found; and in France another pleasant amenity is the separate dining-room for those few of the staff who choose to take their midday meal at the school. One less attractive feature, however, was the occasional inadequacy of the German staff-rooms (one big school had space for only half its large staff); and I found the formality of the German staff-room at break somewhat strange: chairs are ranged along a big table as if a committee-meeting is about to take place, and each person sits down at his own place, unable to talk except to his immediate neighbours: occasionally somebody organizes the brewing of a pot of tea or the preparation of instant coffee, and in one school there was even a small room especially for this purpose – but, alas, I was told that nobody ever troubled to use it! This is a little less surprising, perhaps, when one realizes that German teachers are only required to attend when they have an actual class to give, so that relatively few of them ever have any spare time which they spend on the premises.

The traditional English teacher's gown seems to be growing rather rare in this country, and there is no European equivalent at all. Most Italian teachers dressed rather formally; those of Spain were often more casually dressed, with even the priest-teachers of some church schools wearing pullover and slacks in the classroom; and Germany had the most casually dressed teachers of all – I recall jeans, miniskirts, vividly coloured flared trousers, and even a caftan and beads! France and Portugal shared the feature that many teachers wore a *blouse* – a plain coloured or white smock or overall – as their working-dress, an adult version, in fact, of what their own pupils wore. I am told that this is sometimes done in Germany too, though I never saw it myself.

Admission to the profession is a fairly straightforward matter. In Spain, under the new Act, an applicant to teach in a *colegio nacional* must hold the *bachillerato superior* (after a seven-year high school course) and have done three years in the training college, which now has university status. Alternatively, students who have done a full university course may also teach if they hold the Certificate of Teaching Proficiency, obtained by taking a short course (often less than a year) which may run concurrently with other courses. To teach at higher levels demands a similar procedure, unless the student aspires to teach in a university, when he will require a doctorate. The French requirements are similar: *baccalauréat* plus training course for primary work, and degree plus training for those aiming to teach in CES or *lycée*. In every country, I think, new entrants must serve a probationary period: in Germany this appears to be two years.

Once established in his profession, the teacher can move up the educational ladder just as he can in this country, though there is nothing quite like the weekly scanning of the advertisement columns of the educational papers. In Germany, vacancies are advertised in official publications. Normally, the route towards professional advancement is fairly precisely mapped-out. In France, a teacher's name may be placed on the *Liste d'Aptitude* (a name which explains itself) and thereafter he moves up by way of *professeur certifié* to the rank of vice-principal (called *sous-directeur* in CES, *censeur* in a *lycée*) on his way to the final goal of a headship. In Spain, there is a system of *oposiciones*, or public examinations for promotion, and I have more than once seen newspaper advertisements of coaching for these examinations, or of the sale of model test-papers for the candidate to practise his skills. The new Act, however, has provided an alternative route by which a proportion of posts will be filled by teachers who have the appropriate qualifications and favourable reports from the Inspectorate.

When the post of director, or headmaster, of a Spanish school falls vacant, the staff of the school submits to the authorities a list, in alphabetical order, of three candidates for the vacant post, and from this list the Inspectorate selects one, who is then offered the nomination to the vacancy. There does not appear to be the same inhibition against promoting one of the existing staff of the school as one finds in Britain.

A Spanish teacher may retire at sixty-five if he wishes, and must do so at seventy. If retirement is brought about by ill-health or handicap, he retires on full pay; otherwise, if he has served twenty years he receives a state pension which is 65 per cent of his pay at the age of sixty-five or 80 per cent at the age of seventy. There are additional payments from the teachers' pension fund, to which all state school teachers must, and many private-school teachers also do, belong. It may even happen that the total retirement pay of a teacher is higher than that which he received while working. In France there appear to be different retirement ages for different types of teacher: between fifty-five and sixty for those in primary schools, sixty for the CES teacher, and sixty-five for his colleague in a *lycée*; in each case the retirement pay is 75 per cent of the final active salary. Portuguese teachers do not normally retire before seventy; their pension has been officially described to me as calculated on the formula 'salary minus 6 per cent multiplied by the number of years and divided by four', which is even more baffling than such things commonly are. I have no information for Italy.

The little that I have learned about the work of the inspectorate in Europe has been incidental to my main purpose. I did form the impression that it was rather more divorced from the work of the practising teacher than in Britain; indeed, it seems that in some countries one can become an inspector with very little, if any, actual classroom experience, the role being seen as a purely administrative one. I should not wish to imply that any great number of inspectors are seriously out of touch with what goes on in the classroom, though doubtless some are. In Spain, at any rate, their work is increasingly seen as the promotion of fresh thought about the technical aspects of teaching and school organization; they visit schools fairly frequently, run seminars and courses, and generally try to act as counsellors to the teachers with the object of pointing the way to better-quality teaching. It used to be their duty to see the work of every individual teacher about once a year; nowadays, however, this aspect of their work takes second place to the concept of working with groups of teachers engaged in new projects or special problems. However, they still have influence over the individual teacher in the allocation of the special merit awards which may help him in his quest for promotion to a higher or better-paid post and, as we have already seen, in the selection of candidates to fill vacant headships. Whatever the powers of the inspectorate may be, however, one thing I did notice: in Spain the local inspector wanders in and out of schools, making himself thoroughly at home, with very little diffidence about the possible reactions from the headmaster or staff.

It may be partly a result of the more formalized professional structure that there seemed to be few of those charming and slightly eccentric 'characters' who form a large part of every Englishman's memories of school. I saw one or two, but my notes contain over and over again phrases like 'quietly competent', 'a good classroom manner', 'absolutely on top of his job', 'cheerful and relaxed', 'lively, confident and humorous'. That is to say, most of the teachers I saw were simply excellent professional men and women.

Relations between heads and assistant teachers varied slightly from country to country. Portuguese heads seemed to do quite a lot of class teaching; they mingled informally with their colleagues at break, and were very accessible to pupils. In Spain, too, I met many heads who took a share, even if sometimes a reduced one, of the class teaching; and at the Frücht eburg School in Emden, Germany, Frau Thiemann, the headmistress, had about eight teaching periods a week with her own class and several with another. French heads, even at the primary level, seem to do rather less teaching, though Mme Figuière of La Barbière at Avignon obviously enjoyed doing a good deal of classroom work. The Italian system of grouping several schools into a *circolo didattico* under one head must make him a more remote figure, though there is possibly the compensation that teachers in the other schools of his group have rather more freedom of action.

In fact, Italian heads can do little more than advise their colleagues; they have no power to give them orders. Likewise, in Germany, the head has little real authority over his staff; he cannot enter a classroom without the teacher's permission, or direct his activities in any but the most general way. Nevertheless, in the German schools I visited, relations between heads and other teachers seemed very healthy; one assistant warmly praised her headmaster as the best she had ever worked with; and one head described his staff as 'exceptionally young – only two are older than I am – but they are very good indeed, especially in the way they adapt to new situations'.

Serious shortages of staff do exist in some areas; the head of the Treckfahrtstief Gymnasium at Emden told me that there was an overall staff shortage of about 28 per cent; of his own staff of seventy-two teachers, only about half were full-time qualified staff, the numbers being made up with unqualified people, half-timers, or people past the retirement age who had returned to help out. Another school in the same town was working, a fortnight after the start of the school year, on temporary timetables worked out from day to day, because staffing problems had not been resolved in time for a permanent arrangement to be made.

Save for the occasional teacher of art or music, it is rare to find specialization at the primary level, the usual practice being what the Spanish grandly call *la monodocencia*, which one can only translate as 'having the same teacher for everything'. The Früchteburg school in Germany varies this pattern, the teachers working with their own class for anything from twenty-two down to six hours weekly, according to age and to the demand for the teachers' specialist skills elsewhere in the school. *La monodocencia* has clear advantages with younger pupils, especially if the teacher can stay with the class for several years as quite often happens (see Massimo Lattanzi's description for an Italian case; I refer to it also in commenting on a Portuguese school; and it is common for German teachers to keep their classes for two years). It was, however, surprising to see the principle taken to the lengths of requiring an elderly and somewhat rheumatic teacher to do his gallant best with physical education, or an obviously non-artistic lady trying to instil colour-sense into her pupils, or even a cheerful male teacher trying his hand at elementary dressmaking with his girl pupils. This kind of thing is surely not in the best interests of the pupils. In Italy, incidentally, it appears that the class-teacher at the primary stage is always responsible for his children, and must therefore stay with them even when the specialist art or music teacher is actually giving the lesson; and since, presumably, nobody is very enthusiastic about paying two people to take the same class at the same time, this must help to encourage the doctrine that the class-teacher must turn his or her hand to anything, however unsuitable.

La polidocencia – the use of the specialist teacher – begins to appear at the secondary stage (or stage 2 of the Spanish EGB) where education is usually very much on subject lines. Spain, however, is eagerly embracing the idea of the teaching-team. In the Sept/Oct 1972 issue of *Vida Escolar*, Señor Juan Navarro Higuera proposes a plan for using a group of six teachers as a team, one each for Spanish and the modern language; mathematics and science; social studies; aesthetic and technical education; religious instruction; physical education. For a small school which could only run to one class in each year-group, this would be an impossible idea, for there would only be three teachers in all for stage 2.

In the following issue, Señor José Costa Ribas produces a scheme covering the whole eight-year EGB course with a staff of nine teachers, one of whom is the director and does only eight hours' teaching weekly. The teacher of the first class spends the whole of his time with his pupils; those of classes 2–5 each have one speciality which they teach for about five hours to other classes; those of classes 6–8 have a single specialized 'area' which they teach to all three classes in this top area of the school. Rather conveniently for Señor Costa's purposes, the director takes all the upper classes for their weekly art lessons.

Individual allocations of subjects and classes can obviously vary according to circumstances, but the basic idea is that the babes of the first class should have their own class-teacher all the time; the children aged seven to eleven (second to fifth forms) have their class-teacher for about three-quarters of the time, but have the advantage of specialist teachers for the more specialized subjects; and those in the secondary section, aged eleven upwards, have specialist teaching throughout. Judging from the extensive treatment given to the principle in the literature, it seems to be a fairly new idea on the Spanish educational scene, but it is obviously a practical and sensible one. The article goes on to explain how timetables may be constructed on this basis, and how in fact every teacher does twenty-nine hours a week, the difference between this figure and the totals shown in the table being the teacher's allowance of time for 'organizing and guiding' activities. Even the first-year class teacher has four hours for this; and who shall say that he does not need it? Indeed, it may be appropriate to mention at this point that one of the strongest impressions I brought away from the French *maternelle* schools I visited – and these, of course, deal with even younger children – was the immense amount of time the teachers must need to prepare all the material which their children use.

The article also suggests grouping the eight years of the EGB course into 'cycles'; this can be done, it is suggested, in one of three ways:

(a) four cycles each of two years;
(b) first class separately; then three two-year cycles; then the top class separately – thus giving five cycles in all;
(c) three cycles, respectively containing three, two, three years.

Within these cycles teaching-teams can operate, and the pupils can be divided into groups of various sizes for their activities: large groups, with the whole cycle under one, or perhaps two, teachers; discussion groups, where all members of the teaching-team are required; and individual or small groups, working by themselves, but with one or two teachers available all the time to help them. Thus, with careful organization, four classes will be controlled by four teachers for a certain period of actual teaching-time, but the average time spent by each individual teacher on direct teaching duties will not be more than about 80 per cent of the time. The rest will be available for preparation of material, marking, pastoral care or whatever else is necessary.

Modern methods of organization such as these also seemed to be going on in one of the Italian schools I saw; but in general the organization of teaching-time, except in Spain, seemed distinctly traditional. So did the actual teaching-methods used, though of course they were not necessarily the less competent for that. But sometimes one found the individual teacher using less formal methods, and even though perhaps few of them will be wholly new to readers, they may form an interesting part of the general picture.

One of the more unusual methods was the 'dialogue' approach which I saw in use at one Italian primary school. I am not sure whether this method would be used on all occasions by the teachers concerned, or whether it applies in all classes, but it was certainly not confined to just one teacher. The principle seemed to be that pupils wrote 'dialogues' on whatever subject was being studied, and that these were then acted out by groups of pupils, used as a basis for further class discussion and exploration, and so on.

This same school also used quite a lot of 'free activity' methods, as did one or two schools in other countries. One of the less happy examples of this (to my eyes, anyway) was in a Portuguese primary school. The teacher, young, enthusiastic and intelligent, had invited me especially to come and see this lesson, and when I entered I saw he had written on the board something to this effect:

Today . . . shall we read a book from the class library?
          do some problems?
          draw a picture?
          write a composition?
          learn some spelling?

Proudly he told me that the children would choose the activity in which they knew themselves to need most practice. I must be a cynic, however, for I interpreted quite differently the sight of about forty children almost all of whom were looking through picture-books; to me, it seemed that they had just chosen a pleasant and undemanding activity, and that was all. Two or three only were doing something active – drawing or writing. Free it certainly was, but of activity there was precious little.

More interesting to me were some of the lessons I saw in Germany, where ingenious little games and really positive activities were often used to sweeten the pill of learning; against a number of such lessons, however, I must set an equal number where the teaching seemed to me unnecessarily stereotyped – slavishly following the course-book, or planned to a pattern which repeated itself over and over again in different schools. I lost count of the number of times I sat through the programme 'teacher reads passage; class discusses some difficult words; teacher asks a few questions; class reads passage a second and a third time; bell goes for end of lesson'. It is, of course, a good and useful plan in itself; I merely felt that I had had it rather too often.

But project-work, in one form or another, was generally of a very high standard. Much Italian teaching is done in this way, and often leads to the production of very attractive little magazines containing the best of the children's efforts; in France and Spain also a number of schools have enthusiastically adopted the methods developed at Bar-sur-Loup in the 1920s by Célestin Freinet, who placed the school magazine at the very centre of the teaching programme. I brought back two very pleasant examples from the Pestalozzi primary school at Perugia, a school of about 300 pupils and twelve teachers, serving a modern quarter of the city not far from the main station. One, of some fifty duplicated pages, was on *The Discovery of History*, while the second concerned *Carnivals and Masks* and included some very entertaining research into old customs and traditions, some of them gathered from interviews with older people. Twelve boys and twelve girls had signed their names to this effort, and the text was most mature for children of primary school age; I should not hesitate to say that the general standard of literacy was much above that of the average English class of the same age. Yet my impression of these same children during oral work had not led me to expect such fine written work, for there had been the most terrific uproar, with everybody contributing at once, often at the top of the voice, except for a few who had seemed totally uninvolved and who offered nothing whatever.

They certainly knew how to argue: one tall youngster, perhaps showing-off a little for my benefit, was particularly vocal, and at times was obviously getting much the better of his argument with the teacher, herself a delightful ebullient personality. I had seen a similar virtuoso display of oratory from a class a year younger in this same school; to say 'I was lost in admiration' is the precise truth, for I have to take my Italian a great deal more slowly than these lively, fluent youngsters would permit. But even I could recognize the range of vocabulary and expressive gesture they were displaying.

If these Italian schools were sometimes almost *too* lively, it is perhaps a fault on the right side. In a more restrained way, too,

German children were remarkably effective in the cut and thrust of classroom discussion.

In general, as I had expected, I found the primary schools to be colourful and interesting places, but there was perhaps less movement in them than in their English counterparts, save in Italy and in those Spanish schools where the new methods are already well-established. Elsewhere, on the whole, the children tended to stay firmly anchored in their desks unless called out specifically by the teacher for some reason. This reason would most often be to make use of the blackboard, and I am sure that European children have more experience in writing on the blackboard than do English pupils. For example, a teacher will set the children to work some examples on paper, and finally call one or more of them to the board to demonstrate what they have done. The demonstration is usually given with considerable confidence and a good sense of how the board should be used for exposition. Sometimes there will be two children at the board together, competing to produce the better or quicker answer to a problem, as in the Soms–Medina contest already described.

The usual system in German schools is just a little different; when the class is given its exercises, one pupil will be detailed to do his work, not on paper, but on one wing of the triptych-blackboard, using the side which the class cannot see. At the end of the allocated time, his effort is exposed to view, and the rest of the class compare his work with their own. I formed the impression that it is usually a pretty reliable performer who is called out to demonstrate in this way, rather than one liable to make mistakes. However that may be, and whatever the method used, I think it is good teaching technique to use the blackboard in this way: children will find it more interesting to watch one of their own number than the teacher, and will be more closely involved in the various stages of the demonstration; if he inadvertently makes an error, everybody gleefully points it out, and it is thus quite properly associated with error, whereas a teacher's 'deliberate mistake' runs the risk of imprinting a wrong answer on the pupil's mind simply because the teacher is normally supposed to be the one who gets the answers right. This is one respect, at any rate, in which the traditional blackboard has advantages over more modern apparatus such as the overhead projector.

The walls as well as the blackboard can be most valuable

teaching-aids, as primary school teachers everywhere seem to know. The secondary schools seem much less ready to use wall-space effectively, however. Almost anything may be used to awaken interest: pupils' own work, newspaper or magazine cuttings, reproductions of good pictures, photographs, posters, diagrams, charts, enlarged replicas of stamps or coins, all these and many more were in use, making most primary classrooms a joy to enter. Portugal was the sad exception to this (could it again be a lack of the funds to obtain suitable materials?) but even there one quite common decoration did appear – notices bearing sententious maxims from Camoens, or good advice from the teacher, such as 'PORTA-TE BEM NA AULA!' (Behave yourself well in the classroom!) Of rather more universal application was the large notice I saw in one German classroom: 'Die Erde hat KEINE Notausgang!' (The Earth has NO emergency exit!)

One simple and obvious use of the wall which I do not recall having seen before, was to be seen at the J. V. Vives school in Gerona. Here some of the rooms had a large white rectangle painted on one wall to enable it to be used for projecting film-strips, etc., without the provision of a screen. The quality of projection may not be quite as high as with the screen, but the gain in time and money is obvious.

Projection of all kinds – films, film-strips, colour-slides, overhead projectors and so on – was very widely practised in all the countries I visited. Again, Portugal had the least to show; I was told that there is a central collection of material in Lisbon, but teachers in such places as Braga or Evora need something much closer to hand. However, an attempt is being made to bring visual aids to the remoter schools of Portugal by means of special peripatetic teachers, and I was fortunate to be able to accompany one of these, Senhor Carlos Oliveira, a kind personal friend, on one of his expeditions from his base at Evora.

We left about noon, and drove some twenty miles to the isolated village of São Gregorio, whose village school is just about the simplest and most basic structure imaginable. It is a standard building of the type called 'Centenary Plan School', comprising one big classroom, a small cloakroom where the twenty-eight boys and girls left their big straw hats at the start of the day, and their neat white pinafores at the end of it, and a row of four toilets. There was no running water, just a well close at hand; but there was electric light and power. Theoretically the school had the four classes of the normal primary school with pupils aged between six and ten, but with so few children and only one classroom, the children were in practice required to work together for most of the time in a single group. The teacher's life must be rather a lonely one, with no other adult at hand with whom she can compare notes or to whom she can turn for help.

To this little school we had taken two educational films: the first was about the territory of Angola and its oil production, and the second one on the islands of San Tomé e Principe. The children obviously found it all very exciting – even the preliminaries of setting up the apparatus and improvising (with their help) a suitable blackout – and I was told that later the teacher would use the content of these two films as the basis of future geography lessons.

After showing the films, Senhor Oliveira played the children some recordings which he had made on his portable tape-recorder of children singing local songs; with this introduction, he was eventually able to break down their shyness enough for some of them to sing one or two of their own songs into the microphone. I gathered that his duties include the preservation of as much material of this type as he can pick up on his rounds.

When the children had gone home, after this – to them – exciting afternoon, we had a picnic meal, a sort of belated lunch or early high-tea, in the school, and then transferred our equipment and ourselves to the village hall, where we were to give a repeat performance of the films, together with others, for the adults of the village later that evening. It was of no use to stage this before about 9.30 p.m., for the men would not have returned from the fields and had their own meals earlier than that; and in any case, we had to organize a house-to-house search for a spare bed-sheet to use as a screen for our film-show! By the time we returned to Evora it was past midnight: Senhor Oliveira works these extremely long hours on five, and often six, days every week, but he is obviously a happy man, doing a worthwhile job.

I suppose a basic literacy is about all children will get from a school of this kind – and certainly their work, or such of it as I saw, suggests that they had achieved a good measure of this – but there can hardly be scope for more. They were not unintelligent children: the lively interest on their faces showed that; but I doubt if any of them will ever proceed to any kind of higher education. Yet what is the alternative? The stock answer, I suppose, would be to load them into a bus and educate them together with hundreds of similarly-situated children, in a big new school at Arraiolos, the nearest town. But is it always right to uproot children in this way? The way of life at São Gregorio may not be easy, but it is healthy and sane; if these children miss some good things of life by their isolation, they miss not a few bad things; and probably they know much of which the town child is totally ignorant.

But we are digressing somewhat from our visual aids. Some particularly good facilities for these exist in France and Spain, and I should like to mention briefly two fairly typical examples which impressed me very favourably. At Gerona, in northern Spain, there is a magnificent *Centro Cultural* in an ancient building which has been tactfully modernized for the purpose. It contains a fine concert-hall; various rooms for meetings; a film-projection room; recording-studios; facilities for making filmstrips, tapes, transparencies and similar aids; an extensive library of records and audio-visual aids, all available for loan to schools (both state and private) throughout the province. Numerous courses and cultural activities are held in the evenings, and the building swarms with youngsters every night. There are numerous full-time and part-time helpers to run the Centre, and I thought it a wholly admirable enterprise for a medium-sized provincial city of no great wealth to have set up.

The other similar centre was at Beauvais, in France, where in the Centre Départemental de Documentation Pédagogique I found a very comprehensive library of pedagogical works, with an elaborate index of relevant magazine articles and pamphlets; a gramophone-record library, with facilities for copying records for educational purposes; a library of slides; a television studio under construction, to be used for teacher-training – enabling, for instance, a lesson to be videotaped so that the student teacher may watch himself in action and diagnose his own mistakes, or the lesson to be relayed to a class of other students watching in a separate room; a language laboratory for teachers taking refresher courses; a small printing department producing educational and other material by offset-lithography; and, of course, the usual rooms for meetings, film-shows, etc. We could use more establishments of this kind in our own country, where teachers' centres seem to be only half-heartedly accepted, and are often expected to operate on a shoestring budget instead of being recognized as a key area of the educational service.

I have already referred briefly to the use of audio-visual material for teaching languages; I had plenty of evidence also of its use in other ways, and also of the occasional preparation of audio-visual material by the pupils themselves. One such example was at the Colegio Nacional Santo Tomás at Jaén in Spain, a quite small school with about 280 boys and girls and a staff of seven teachers and the headmaster; it occupies an attractive modern building on an ancient site. The pupils there were making a film about school life; and I was also shown a series of slides on biological subjects, for which they were making a tape-recorded commentary themselves. In a rather different category, but also interesting, was the French primary school which was having one of its lessons filmed to be used as teaching material for the local teacher training college: I believe I inadvertently made a brief appearance in this film myself!

Also perhaps classifiable as visual aids were the delightful glove-puppets in use at the École Primaire La Barbière, in Avignon. The plays they performed had been largely written by the children themselves, and the standard of presentation achieved was almost professional, the diction especially being very clear and lively.

Turning to other teaching techniques, I was pleased to see some laudable attempts to break down the hard and fast barriers between subjects. This is, of course, almost a commonplace of good primary education, though it is worth sparing a word for the French primary school which was basing a lot of its work for the term on the imaginary adventures of a coloured boy in Africa, through which delightful agency the small children were learning to read and write, picking up quite a lot of simple geography and science and even a little arithmetic, and being stimulated to produce some splendidly colourful paintings. An interesting example of the same approach adapted to secondary use was at the Scuola Media Virgilio in Cremona, whose handicraft teacher showed me how his pupils were required to take any practical job through all its stages: to describe the idea (involving thereby their Italian work), to produce a plan of it (drawing), to cost all the materials

The teacher and his work: II

required (arithmetic), actually to carry out the job (handicraft), and finally to produce a detailed report on their methods, the problems they had encountered, etc. (Italian again). The examples I saw were excellently done, and I cannot imagine any better way of relating what is done at school to the practical life of the world the pupil will be entering.

But most often, the methods in use were entirely traditional, though thoroughly sound and undoubtedly successful. Some aspects of this traditionalism, however, were less admirable: especially the immense amount of note-taking which goes on everywhere, and not only in the secondary school, either! I am not criticizing the use of notes to help the pupil arrange and clarify his ideas; this is a good use. But I see little virtue in scribbling down lists of facts which are more conveniently available in the pupils' textbooks; notes should supplement, not repeat, what is available elsewhere.

Very interesting to me were the small details of classroom practice, possibly traditional in one country and quite unknown in another. For example, there is the useful Italian system of appointing one pupil as class secretary for a week at a time; it is his or her job to keep a note of work done and give a brief oral summary of the previous lesson at the start of each period. This is good training for the pupil and a useful reminder for the rest of the class; I do not say 'for the teacher', for he has his log-book. Class monitors of other kinds are quite common; in Germany I saw them cleaning the blackboard and tending the classroom flowers, while a class of eight-year-olds at Miguel de Cervantes, Ecija, had nine monitors, two each for tidiness, tables and blackboard, one for the door and two as general class leaders.

There is little that corresponds to the English system of school prefects, however, though in France *les grands élèves* do play some part in running out-of-school activities. Pupil representation on various committees is, however, quite usual in France and Germany; at the Emden Wallschule, for example, I saw the agenda of a forthcoming committee meeting to which were invited the teaching staff, plus three parents and three senior pupils. The meeting was timed for 4 p.m. on a Monday, and the agenda scarcely looked such as would bring the pupil-representatives back very willingly to do their overtime: discussion of some points in the new school laws of Lower Saxony, details of elections, reports on a working-party which had been discussing 'school development planning', and so on. It seemed rather forbiddingly abstract, and I was not really surprised to learn that the contributions made by the pupil-representatives are rarely very significant. Indeed, I can imagine nothing more likely to still the agitation for pupil representation on governing bodies than a few such meetings!

Just as many English schools have adopted forms of 'School Council' to give pupils a forum for expressing their ideas, so have those of Germany, but in a much more highly formalized and structured way. The regulations for the *Gymnasien* (grammar schools) of Rhineland-Palatinate devote several pages to a detailed exposition of this type of organization, from the election of the *Klassensprecher* (spokesman) for each form, through the *Klassensprecherversammlung* or assembly of class representatives, whose chairman is ex-officio the *Schülersprecher* and so on. To an English teacher it seems a little heavy-handed, and I have heard disquieting tales about the actual operation of these committees, a matter which is briefly discussed in chapter 10.

At the Evora *liceu*, in Portugal, I noticed that each class had its class delegate (one of whose jobs, for example, was to compile each day a list of absentees, referred to by their class numbers and not by name); the *délégué de classe* is also a regular feature of French schools. He is expected to assume command of the class at times when no teacher is present, and to do all kinds of general dogsbodying for the teacher, much as our own monitors or class prefects do. One CES, for example, allows its *délégués de classe* (after notifying the *Surveillant-Général*, needless to say!) to hold class meetings and conduct approved educational activities in their classrooms without the presence of a teacher.

Now for a few quite different types of classroom practice. I saw, and approved, a useful little dodge employed in many French schools for doing quick practice tests. Each pupil keeps beside him a small slate or something similar (an old book-cover served quite well) and a piece of chalk. When the teacher put his question to the class, each pupil wrote his answer on the slate and held it aloft for the teacher to check. This was a useful compromise between the oral test where only one pupil at a time is involved and the rest slumber peacefully, and the written test involving the teacher in detailed marking.

Not that some teachers haven't learned ways of avoiding that wearisome task: one day, when observing a lesson in a Spanish school, I heard the teacher call out about half a dozen numbers, apparently at random. The pupils thus indicated handed in their test-papers with resigned expressions on their faces, while the rest, perhaps thankfully, tore up theirs. Thus the teacher was able to cut his marking by, say, 80 per cent, while the pupils' studies were enlivened by the mild excitement of a kind of lottery!

A teacher's duties are often very carefully defined, either legally by the state or by the individual school. I possess a 16-page booklet from the Colegio La Salle in Gerona which makes interesting, and rather thought-provoking, reading. The school concerned is one of the many schools run by the Christian Brothers; it occupies well-equipped but rather ponderous buildings in the centre of Gerona, and has a staff of forty-eight teachers ministering to nearly 1,200 boys aged from six upwards. It is, of course, a private, fee-paying, school.

The booklet begins by defining the purpose of the school and the responsibilities of the teaching body: '. . . society will save itself only if it respects dignity, freedom, and human rights . . . and if it does not give in to the lures of selfish and nihilistic philosophies, but affirms its faith in life and in what gives meaning to life, the certain knowledge that there exists a just and good God'. And, later, 'Teaching is a profession and at the same time a wonderful vocation, requiring special gifts of heart and soul, very thorough preparation, and continual readiness to adapt to new ideas.'

Almost a page is devoted to the concept of Freedom:

> . . . the development of liberty in the educational context requires the first principle of authority: this authority is exercised by having a reason for decisions, and by expressing that reason wherever possible, so that decisions are not seen as arbitrary. The active participation of pupils in school life involves every level and every activity; it can best be encouraged by bringing up to date tried and tested methods, within the range of both active and group pedagogy: the teacher explains and examines, while teaching his pupils to investigate individually or as a team. A limitation in the use of coercive methods, either in examinations, in marks or in

punishments, is implicit in this plan; what is most necessary is to get pupils used to weighing-up situations, events and their own conduct, so that they can defend themselves against the external pressures that limit their freedom in a consumer society. Similarly, they should learn not to set themselves up capriciously as unthinking judges of everything.

That is a message every teacher, surely, can respond to: that we must urgently do all we can to arm our pupils against a very sick world, and equip them to play their part in finding, as we must, a cure for its sickness. The booklet then goes on to cover various practical points, and finally launches into the following broadside:

> Once the teacher is in the presence of his pupils, he must give himself up joyfully to his noble mission. Therefore, he will:
> - use the most appropriate method for each age and subject;
> - try to awaken the pupils' initiative, encourage teamwork and insist on receiving work correctly done;
> - devote class time to explaining the topic, stimulating personal study or checking work submitted;
> - make fair and permanent assessments of work, which he will require his pupils to do regularly and often;
> - return work to them marked on a system previously made known to and understood by the pupils;
> - attend punctually to any task assigned to him, and not absent himself save for grave cause and with prior notification to the person in charge of his department;
> - inform the Moderator if he should know that he will be unable to be present at any class;
> - refrain from smoking in class;*
> - appear before his pupils with an external appearance appropriate to his position as a teacher;
> - avoid any excessive familiarity in word or attitude which might compromise the prestige of his position;
> - be punctual in ending lessons, to facilitate the recreation of his pupils, and their ease of movement;
> - not leave the room until all his pupils have done so;

*Not all Spanish schools make this demand of their teachers; I was a little surprised to find that many teachers smoked during lessons at the two schools I visited in Ecija in 1975.

– ensure that in the classrooms there is work, good relations, and tidiness, as a precondition of happy coexistence and the fruit of a progressive educational development.

If a headmaster posted that on an English common-room noticeboard, he might surprise his colleagues; but seriously, is there anything in it which an honest and scrupulous teacher would not accept as part of his duty? Even the sentence that at first may seem most prim, that prohibiting 'excessive familiarity', is in fact a very wise one: it does not say that a teacher shall not be friendly, kind, helpful, understanding, or even affectionate; it simply advises him to be mindful of his position towards them. If a teacher treats a pupil with undue familiarity, he must either allow the pupil to return the compliment, which creates obvious difficulties, or he must let it be thought that he values the pupil's dignity less than his own, which would be a base attitude. To be respected, one must respect others.

We then read of various duties of the pupils themselves which the teacher must oversee; and then the booklet turns to that curse of the teaching profession, the staff meeting, stressing its importance as a contribution to the making of school policy. I confess that I have not had the experience of attending a staff meeting in a European school, but this booklet makes them sound not much different from our own; as will be seen later (chapters 9 and 10) in many European countries there are also staff meetings of a different kind, for the assessment of pupils in individual forms, or for consideration of pupils charged with the graver kinds of disciplinary offences. Contact with parents is also stressed:

> the meeting-place for appointments is the college reception room. Teachers should be careful in all their relations with parents; in the content, form and presentation of correspondence; in the issue of invitations to interviews; and in reply-int to parents' requests. As parental participation in the educational work of the school becomes greater, so will the degree of care needed.

Perhaps it is rarely that the teacher's obligations and duties are formally set out in print in this way, but no doubt most schools have less formal ways of doing the job, and whether or not the little handbook had anything to do with it, the La Salle College struck me as a very well-run school. Similarly, the Früchteburg School in Emden kindly sent me a copy of its standing rules for teachers; these were of a strictly practical nature, covering such matters as supervision duties, punctuality, the clearing of classrooms at break, tidiness of the premises, etc. One characteristically European feature was the insistence that pupils should be accompanied to the exits, and that the teacher must regard his supervisory functions as beginning about a quarter of an hour before, and ending about a quarter of an hour after, the actual period of the day's lessons.

I should add a word about the various ancillary helpers who help with the running of the schools. Some, of course, have much the same functions as in England – secretarial, catering and cleaning staff – and, just as here, the smooth and happy running of any school owes much to them. I several times found male staff performing duties which here would normally be done by women: very capable male cooks in charge of the kitchens in several French schools, and a brisk young male secretary in one Italian school. Am I being a male chauvinist if I see in this a sign of the great respect for gastronomy in the one country and for bureaucracy *per se* in the other?

But one or two ancillary positions not found in English schools certainly merit mention. First, I was very impressed to find that secondary schools in several of the countries I visited had the full-time services of a librarian. While I accept that it is very much the responsibility of a subject-teacher to advise a pupil about his reading, it does not seem to me to follow from this that he is also the best person to do the administrative work of the library. If he is to have an adequate teaching programme, he cannot possibly have time to do all the routine tasks of librarianship – ordering books, cataloguing and indexing, checking the stock and so on. Except in a few enlightened areas, we stingily refuse to admit in this country that school librarianship is an occupation distinct both from teaching and from ordinary librarianship, and we try to get two men for the price of one by combining them. In one sense the French do this also, since their librarian often acts also as an archivist maintaining the school's records; but this is a duty more nearly allied to librarianship than teaching is, and consequently may be a justifiable addition to the librarian's duties, which otherwise will at certain times of day be fairly light.

France can also offer us another interesting ancillary worker: the *surveillant*, who, I think, is only found at the secondary level. This is generally a young man or woman, often an intending teacher, who assists the actual teaching staff in precisely the way the name suggests: by surveillance of the pupils outside the classroom. The teacher is regarded as a professional man, and in theory at any rate as a scholar; it is thus seen as a waste of his valuable time and skill to employ him in parading corridors and playgrounds to keep order. Quite a reasonable attitude, one may think: it makes good economic sense to employ as profitably as possible the time of those you are paying to use special skills. For the same reason, one sometimes finds that a school has a technician available to do work like duplicating test-papers or preparing teaching material; one feels that our own teachers might well press for the wider introduction of such help, for improvement of working conditions can be a great incentive to better standards of work.

Finally, there are all the *concierges*, *bidelli* and their kind; whatever their titles, they are almost universally found, sitting at counters inside the entrance-hall, or inside little glass cupboards, for the purpose of asking your business, locking and unlocking doors, carrying messages about the building, or just standing around with indulgent or menacing looks, according to temperament, as the children come in or go home. They can be dragons, or they can be perfectly charming; and they work very hard, often, I suspect, for a fairly low wage. One cautionary word: do not be, as I was, misled if you see on the door of a room in a German school the word *Hausmeister*: he is not a part of some vertical system of pastoral care. He is in fact the caretaker, and perhaps the word is not inappropriate.

6

Testing the work

I have said just a little in passing about the examinations – *baccalauréat, bachillerato* and so on – which might loosely be termed the 'grammar-school-leaving' or the 'university-qualification' type, and now I must add a few pages on those other little-loved institutions the internal school examinations, for these at any rate aim, even if they do not always achieve their aim, to provide their own answer to the question of how well the school is doing its job.

The traditional practice in many countries has been for the tests or examinations to be set in June before the pupils leave for the long summer holiday; those who reach a satisfactory standard are then promoted to the next class, or to the next stage of their education, while those failing to attain that standard are set extra work to be done during the holidays, followed by a further test on their return in the autumn. If this is still not productive of a good enough mark, it has been the custom to keep the pupil down for another year to repeat the whole course. The Barbiana book, *Letter to a Teacher*, has some rather horrifying things to say about

Testing the work

this system: it presents a very interesting series of tables, one of which (Table E) shows that in 1963 there were 454,094 Italian school children who were thirteen years of age. Of these, 23,835 (5 per cent) had already got into a *scuola superiore*; 153,945 (33·9 per cent) were in the third year of the *scuola media*, 130,350 (28·7 per cent) in the second year *media*, and 82,715 (18·2 per cent) in the first year *media*. That still left 63,249 thirteen-year-old pupils still in the elementary school (13·9 per cent) of whom 525 – admittedly, not a vast number over the whole country, but still 525 unhappy lost souls – had not progressed beyond the first year of elementary school. About a third of the 63,249 thirteen-year-olds still enduring this primary school education were in classes below the top one, so that they would, if they held out long enough and did not just give up – have at least one more year to do. But, of course, in fact a great many of them *do* just give up, unable to endure putting on primary-school uniform day after day, facing elementary text-books which they have ploughed miserably through time and time again, watching little boys and girls four or five years younger outstripping them. The Barbiana pupils make a number of trenchant comments on this system of repetition which, even if one did not agree with them, would surely be worth pondering. For example, they ask angrily:

> What do you gain by making the school hateful and by throwing (these children) out into the street? Are you afraid of . . . your colleagues in the upper schools? Or the education officer? If you are so worried about your career, there is a solution: cheat a little bit on your pupils' tests by correcting a few mistakes while you are walking up and down between the desks . . . Perhaps you fear your own conscience instead? Then your conscience is built wrong. 'I would consider the promotion of this child injurious to the good name of the school', wrote a principal in his report. But who *is* the school? We are the school; to serve it, is to serve *us*. 'To pass a bad student is unfair to the good ones', said a sweet little teaching soul. Why not call Pierino aside to say to him, as Our Lord said in the parable about the vine-trimmers, 'I am passing you because you have learned. You are twice blessed: you pass, and also you have learned. I am going to pass Gianni to encourage him; but he has the misfortune not to have learned.'

One sees the immediate objection: human nature is not so spotless that there would not be some diminution of standards if the lazy pupil were always allowed precisely the same pass as the industrious one; consequently, I doubt if one could do quite as the Barbiana pupils suggest; and possibly they wouldn't either. But in some situations, I am all for their approach: we must be sensitive to the slow pupil, the earnest plodder who takes a long time to get there but may in the end be all the better for having done so the hard way; to the pupil who is reasonably able in some directions but has blind spots in others; to the pupil whose home circumstances, emotional problems, psychological development, or physical health are retarding his progress. This is especially true in the primary school, where after all the content of the work is not so vast that, if the child is helped, it could not be recovered fairly quickly. In one French primary school (École Raoul-Aubaud, at Beauvais) I saw a young teacher doing some admirable remedial work in mathematics with a dozen or so boys and girls: it was a pleasure to see how confidently these children were tackling the work with his patient and understanding help, and his sound technique, to guide them. A class of this kind, limited by regulation to a maximum of fifteen pupils, seems to be a standard feature of the French primary school system.

The class with the large age-range does still exist, though modern thought is against it and it must surely disappear soon: in one Spanish school, I saw a class where most of the pupils were aged between ten and twelve, but there were a few as young as nine, and one or two as old as fourteen; and in Portugal I saw one strange situation, where a first and second class were combined in one room with one teacher, the former having pupils aged six, seven and eight, while the latter had pupils up to almost twelve years of age. I particularly tried to observe the work of the twelve-year-old, and (while I admit one short visit is not really adequate evidence) I would have thought him entirely educable and certainly not in any way mentally subnormal: I wonder what his story was?

The German approach to this matter seems still to be fairly conservative. Discussing the topic at the Emden *Realschule*, I was given to understand that pupils are continuously assessed on a six-point scale. If a pupil has, say, two very bad grades (presumably a 6) and is also less than satisfactory in his other subjects, his teachers discuss his situation, and by majority vote they decide whether or not he must repeat the year's course. A 6 in German makes it virtually certain that he will repeat. A pupil may be required to repeat twice, but not in consecutive years. The regulations for *Gymnasien* in Rhineland-Palatinate provide that if a pupil's persistent refusal to perform his work adequately makes it impossible to give him an assessment, his report will be in the form *nicht feststellbar*, which means 'cannot be assessed' and that this is regarded as equivalent to a grade 6. The German system at least avoids the worst features of the Italian procedure, but many teachers still find it unsatisfactory, though I saw little evidence of any serious attempt to re-think the problem.

France may have moved a little further in the way of reform: in one French school I saw a notice giving the decisions of the *Conseil d'Études* on the examination results: 410 pupils had been concerned, and of these some 250 (61 per cent) had won promotion without any reservations; another group, though not having reached the required standards, were nevertheless to be promoted in their own interests; another sizeable group had been granted conditional promotion provided that they satisfied a further test in September; three would have to leave the school altogether; and this only left a few who would return in September to the same forms they had left in July.

Spain, however, is grappling much more drastically with the problem. In future, a Spanish pupil not reaching the required level *will* be promoted, but will be compelled to do additional remedial work in weak subjects as well as following the new course. Some of this work is done in extra periods at the end of the day, but most is now covered by the use of individual work-assignments, or *fichas*.

I saw this system operating effectively in several Spanish schools. At the La Salle College in Gerona, a class of juniors aged about eleven were working from duplicated task-sheets, issued fortnightly. They tackled them in their own way and at their own pace, but each task had to be shown to the teacher as it was completed. He sat at his desk, quietly receiving a steady procession of small boys bearing their *fichas*: in marking them he used a colour code and a series of three grades, which might be rendered 'Outstanding', 'Very Good' and 'Satisfactory'. If the work was not at least up to the lowest of these levels, it was marked in the appropriate colour to show that it must be done again. Thus each pupil received his share of personal attention; each one progressed at his own speed; and the teacher knew that they were all working, and how they were working. In principle, of course, it is a simple system, based on such models as the Montessori and Dalton plans. It needs a good understanding of the pupils' needs, and much preliminary preparation, to ensure that it works well. The pupils, for their part, have some measure of freedom to plan their work, can see exactly where they go wrong, and how to put matters right, and can see themselves making positive progress.

The *fichas* here were home-made, duplicated sheets; but, predictably enough, educational publishers have not been slow to see the possibilities of the method, and at the Menendez Pidal College in Salt (Gerona) I saw a great deal of work being done from rather expensive loose-leaf printed sheets. The format of these seemed to me to be too large for convenience, and the books quickly became floppy and dog-eared as a result; they cost from 100 to 190 pesetas per book (say 75p to £1·35) and, of course, could only be used once. The newly built La Inmaculada College in Gerona was using small duplicated sheets which seemed a much more sensible proposition. One of these which I brought away as a sample will serve as an illustration of the method; it was being used by a sixth class, of boys aged from eleven to twelve years, and it was headed 'Week 23', which presumably implied a weekly issue of the assignments. It covered the whole week's work, in every area of study, and the general layout of each area was similar, starting with a brief statement of the objectives and content of the week's work, then referring the pupil to the textbook or work-sheets he would need for his studies, and finally setting out three levels of work to be covered. For example, in history the objective was stated as a study of the role played by the Church and the monastic orders in the middle ages; the detailed content was listed as 'First appearance of the Monastic Orders – Saint Benedict and his rule – The monks in Europe – Cluny – the Cistercians – the Mendicant Orders'. All this was to be found described on pages 165 to 171 of the textbook, and after studying these, there were eight pages of *fichas* with specific questions and tasks to be done. To achieve the minimum level, boys had to complete pages 189, 190 and 195; for a medium level, pages 191, 194 and 196 were to be added; and the star pupils who aspired to

Testing the work

a maximum level would also cover pages 192 and 193. Provided that the work is carefully graded – and I have no reason to imagine that it was not – this seems a very sensible way of dealing with a class of pupils of widely varying ability, and making sure that even the weakest cover the essential work, while the ablest are stretched to the full.

Very interesting was the assignment of work in the social studies section, which comprised a practical exercise in leadership as part of the study of the theme of government: the boys were required to draw up a programme of physical education for their class designed to include certain specific exercises or techniques, and to be prepared to carry them out or direct others of the group in doing so; here the *ficha* was even sufficiently practical to include a footnote reminding the boys to bring their PE kit on Friday afternoon!

Also attached to the collection of *fichas* given to me were some *fichas de control* containing some short test-questions which the pupils could use for self-assessment. I thought these were, by our standards, rather vague and very academically worded questions ('What is an electric current?' or 'Name and give an example of each one of the subdivisions of the numeral pronouns') but I am bound to say that the pupils seemed quite at home with the system. English teachers may ask sceptically whether the pupils were really being effectively taught by this system: I think they *were*, and it was most impressive to see the purposeful and busy way they were all working at their assignments. It is obvious, however, that not all teachers have adapted completely to methods so different from those traditional to them; for example, in one school I saw the lesson end in a general class discussion and correction of work *en bloc*, which seemed to me to lose much of the point of a system which permits pupils to work at different rates.

The Ministry booklet which sets out the principles of the method mentions five kinds of *ficha*, some of which I have already referred to in passing. First is the *ficha directiva* which is the sheet of instructions telling the pupil what to do and how to set about it; then the *ficha de información* which may contain passages for study, explanatory notes, documents, lists of data, and so on; next, the *ficha de recuperación*, or remedial work sheet; then the very useful *ficha de desarrollo* (or extension-sheet) given to the more able pupil to help him explore the work to a deeper level, or discover some aspect of it which it is not necessary or desirable for the whole class to study; and finally, the *ficha de control*, or self-testing sheet.

The system of continuous assessment is carried on also through the *bachillerato* course, right up to the level of the university entrance course (COU); the teachers collect their data throughout the year, and meet at least five times in every school year to discuss and standardize their assessments. At the end of the year, the pupil with more than two unsatisfactory assessments on his final report is liable to have to repeat the year; with only one or two, however, he will be promoted, though he may have to do extra 'recuperative' work. In the COU course, the university authorities work together with the teachers of the school to moderate the teachers' own assessments, and a 'partially negative' assessment will involve summer holiday work to recover, while a 'completely negative' one will involve repetition of the year.

However familiar such ideas may seem to many readers, they are probably quite strange and new to the older and more conservative teacher in Spain, especially perhaps if he works in a village or small town remote from refresher courses and contact with other teachers. The younger men and women, however, see in these new approaches some very worthwhile opportunities; it was heartening to see the keenness and vigour with which they were starting their careers in a profession which can hardly be a goldmine to them (though the teacher has always been held in some honour in Spain, I think).

Perhaps 'continuous assessment' will eventually render superfluous the traditional type of formal examination; at present, however, the European pupil has as much reason as his English counterpart to view the end of the summer term with gloom. In one Spanish education office, I saw great piles of papers waiting to be sent out to the schools, while in a primary school at Braga I watched a pleasantly primitive example of the more informal type of examination – the end-of-term test or *prova*.

The actual conduct of this examination, to one brought up in the English tradition, was rather strange, with the teacher constantly walking up and down the rows of desks, pleasantly encouraging the children's efforts, and even now and then giving a little fatherly advice. It appeared, nevertheless, that the actual layout of these end-of-the-year promotion tests was something of a hallowed ritual. Each child was given a large sheet of paper, about the size of a double sheet of foolscap. About a third of the first side was left blank, to be used later in the drawing test. A line was then drawn, and below it the words *Prova de Passagem da 3a a 4a Classe* (Promotion Test, 3rd and 4th Class) were written. The first actual test was the *Copia*, or *Caligrafia*, which simply meant the copying out of a passage in the pupil's neatest handwriting. The children were apparently invited to decide for themselves which passage would be used, though they all had to do the same one; the shortage of textbooks meant that there was a good deal of sharing. The handwriting test was then ruled off, and the place and date of doing it were written at the foot of the page, together with the pupil's full name, which was often surprisingly long and florid. This done, the pupils then went back and filled the space that had been left blank with a drawing on a set theme, using whatever medium they had available: the actual standard of art was fairly primitive, I must say!

On this particular occasion, the teacher then took in the test-papers, but inquiry showed that on a subsequent day he would be returning them to the children for further tests to be done on the pages so far not used. These would basically be tests of Portuguese and of mathematics, with perhaps a little elementary history, geography or science according to the age of the pupils. In another Portuguese school I happened to arrive on the day of the arithmetic test; again the level was very elementary, with such questions as 'multiply 4 by 9'; 'add 14, 17 and 15'; 'divide 30 by 5'; and 'take away 23 from 41'. There were only a few problems, and of about this standard of difficulty throughout; nevertheless, the children – aged about eight, I think – seemed to make fairly heavy weather of them.

It was also in Braga that I saw in the local newspaper two rather entertaining items concerning school examinations. The shorter of the two concerned a Deplorable Situation at one of the local primary schools, and I translate it as it was given in the newspaper:

Problems of a Teacher

The teacher of the primary school of the Alegria district, São Vitor, Senhora Rosa Cortez Gomes Amorim, having a pupil of nine years of age called Fernando Maria Mesquita Gouveia da Silva, in the first class, who was not attending school or making any progress, and since she wished that he should take his promotion-test, saw the child's mother; but the boy did not appear. She then decided to call in the police; and Constable 219, getting hold of the child's mother, made her see her responsibility in the matter and acted in such a way that the child did come back to school, and took the test.

That is the complete report, unfortunately; I do not know therefore how the admirable Constable 219 brought home to the erring lady the fact that little Fernando Maria Mesquita Gouveia da Silva, no less, had better get back to school and do his stuff. Nor does one know whether he had any useful contribution to make when he got there; one fears that his paper may have been more or less a beautiful blank after all. But then, seeing that little Fernando etc. was a nine-year-old working with the six-year-olds, it was presumably by no means the first time he had taken this same test; one can see the poor child as just that kind of miserable failure the Barbiana pupils wrote about. It may not, of course, be as simple as that: more likely, perhaps, poor Senhora Rosa Cortez Gomes Amorim had reached the end of her patience with an idle babe who supposed that by playing truant he would escape what was coming to him. Constable 219, however, comes out of it rather well.

The second newspaper cutting was headed, in the sort of type that might announce an earthquake or the arrest of a pop star for bigamy:

IN THE SEVENTH YEAR:
THE WRITTEN EXAMS HAVE BEGUN.
ORGANIZATION:
AN EASY START FOR EVERYBODY.
THE 'CICLO PREPARATORIO' ALSO CHECKS
UP ON WHAT THE PUPILS KNOW.

There follows an article, occupying half a page of the paper (not tabloid size, either), plus a couple of photographs, to tell the expectant nation that the official exams are on, and interviewing some of the pupils about their first day's ordeal. The first paper, apparently, had been on the 'Political and Administrative Organization of the Nation', hence the otherwise rather cryptic second headline. The article reveals that among the questions were ones on the method of electing the head of state, the unity of the republic, the stages in the enactment of a law, the concept of nationality, the powers of district councils and similar exciting topics. One pupil is quoted as telling a reporter 'I don't know how they could set such an easy paper: I could do it all, and I only swotted three hours!' He probably failed, if experience of my own pupils is anything to go by!

There were further interviews with candidates after the other papers of the day (one wonders if the reporter had camped out all day on the steps of the examination-room to catch the little victims at every stage); but even then the newspaper was only halfway through its task; there were also the exams of the *Ciclo Preparatorio* to report on (Portuguese language at 3 p.m., history and geography of Portugal at 5 p.m. – on a blazing June afternoon . . .) as well as some sage observations by the headmaster of the school concerned. (How had his pupils fared? He could not say until their papers had been marked . . .)

Rather comic, perhaps? Yes, but it is a sobering thought that in Portugal half a page of a newspaper can be devoted to an educational topic; Italy can do equally well in this, the Bari paper running a regular column, 'In The Schools', with news of the activities and problems of many individual schools.

Apart from the Portuguese examination described earlier I also saw one other school examination in progress: this was at the Colegio Nacional Ramon Calatayud in Jaén, Spain, where I was vouchsafed a brief glimpse of a big room (two classrooms whose dividing partition had been drawn back for the purpose) in which about a hundred boys and girls, supervised by two young teachers, were writing an essay on one of three subjects in elegant copperplate handwriting on a blackboard in front of them. Apart from the desks being somewhat closer together, the conduct of this examination was exactly in accordance with our own practice, and so, I think, was the exuberant relief with which the pupils emerged at the end of their ordeal!

Informal tests, of course, are of everyday occurrence in most schools, but to round off this chapter I quote with awed respect and just a little amusement a specimen kindly given to me by a very good teacher in one German *Hauptschule*. It was a test of elementary English grammatical constructions – verb-forms and such like – and as a test it was admirable. What awed me was the attendant ceremonial; a page of type-written instructions for the administration of the test; then the test itself; then a marking-sheet with spaces for entering individually the marks for each question, totalling them, and converting the score to one of the six grades which are used in German schools for assessment (this conversion being on different scales for each of the three classes taking the test); then a detailed marking-key; and finally a whole foolscap sheet of analysis and evaluation of the test for the benefit of the teachers marking it, showing them precisely how to convert the raw mark to a percentage, with the aid of Gaude-Teschner's Percentage Conversion Tables, and offering them precisely-formulated explanations of the special merits of the process. What gave the whole document its particularly joyous flavour (to me, if not to the pupils) was the heading of the first of the nine pages: Informal Test. I hope my good friends in that school will not mind my saying that I should find one of their Formal Tests more than I could take.

POSTSCRIPT

My comments on the Italian system of 'repetition' (pp. 102–3) need to be modified in the light of new regulations now coming into force. In the primary school, there will be no examinations for transfer from the second class to the third; there will be no 'repeat' examinations in any year; and the repetition of a whole year's course can only be required of a child once in his primary school career.

7
Buildings and equipment

The word 'school' may mean either the building or the life that goes on inside it; but these two senses are anything but separate, for the physical environment of the school matters enormously. Pupils and teachers have the right to expect certain standards: a building agreeable to live and work in; adequate space for, and provision of, essential equipment and materials; reasonable quiet for their work; comfortable and convenient movement; a safe and healthy structure; flexibility and adaptability for the needs of the future.

In the course of my tours, I saw buildings which ranged from the sublime to the unspeakable – once or twice, indeed, I saw a 'before and after' situation, with the same teachers and pupils in old and new buildings. Age is not necessarily bad in itself; Spain and Portugal particularly can show handsome ducal palaces, convents and the like now adapted to educational uses. At Evora in Portugal, the *liceu nacional* occupies the buildings of the Old University, with spacious marble corridors, two elegant Renaissance courtyards, precious azulejo tiles and stately wooden pulpits from which university lecturers once held forth. Tortosa, in Spain, has a beautiful convent, built in the sixteenth century to house converted Moorish maidens, where now smocked schoolboys play boisterous games of football in the patio. Children who spend their school lives in such places surely gain emotionally from the experience of being surrounded by beauty, even if the buildings are seldom quite ideal for present-day purposes; either their architectural integrity is respected and the school goes without its gymnasium or laboratories; or the balance of the ensemble is spoiled by additions and annexes.

Then, of course, there are the more recent 'old' buildings: the less wealthy countries have all too many of these still inflicting their dark staircases, cramped classrooms and gloomy basements on the children of today. Not that all the older schools are bad, by any means: at Emden in West Germany two of the schools I visited, the *Wallschule* and the *Realschule*, occupied buildings of an earlier generation and, even if they did not perhaps compare with the many fine modern schools elsewhere in the town, they offered quite respectable facilities. Since over 90 per cent of Emden's buildings suffered in the second world war it is an almost completely new town, with only a few isolated survivals of its pre-war appearance, so it is perhaps rather ironic that these two massive and rather unbeautiful blocks remain; but they do, and usefully. The *Wallschule* dates from about 1906, and in earlier days was an academic high school; then during the war it served as a hospital; now its third incarnation has taken the form of an ordinary secondary school. There are several storeys in a plain style or architecture, and, despite its age, it offers quite lofty and spacious rooms which are as comfortable as many more recent buildings can provide. Skilful adaptation has provided such amenities as science and language laboratories; there is even an assembly hall – rather unpredictably located on the top floor – though it is rarely used as such. Somewhat newer, but still far from modern, is the *Realschule*, a colossal block mainly of four, partly of five, storeys, in a style one might call Moorish-geometrical; it looks as if an architect of the 'thirties, briefly wearying of constructing barracks for Goering's Luftwaffe, had taken a holiday in Granada with eccentric consequences to his style. Yet even this monstrosity is quite pleasant internally; it is not large enough to accommodate all the present pupils, unfortunately, but

Buildings and equipment

for all that there is little sense of congestion, for the teaching-spaces which do exist are monumentally large, the corridors and staircases amply wide.

But most schools occupy more modern buildings, and in my travels I naturally saw a large number of these. Perhaps one type of the more modern school may be represented by the São Vitor Primary School at Braga in Portugal. Though fairly recent in date, this building is wholly of the past in its architectural thinking; basically, it is just a two-storey building, half of which is at present devoted to boys, half to girls (though the 'iron curtain' is due to come down shortly). The sharply rising terrain allows the provision of two playgrounds, one at the level of each storey of the building. When you enter you see simply a series of near-identical classrooms, opening off quite wide corridors, on one side only. Nothing else is provided (except, of course, necessary toilet facilities) for nothing else was felt to be required: the school is seen as a series of classes, each with one teacher, who in fact moves up through the school with his class. So, when little Jose-Pedro or his sister Ana-Maria enters the school and occupies a desk in, say, Room 2, there he or she will stay for the next five years or so, assuming that normal progress is made. It is a comfortable and homely arrangement, of course, and excellent for the child's sense of security; but it is not really adapted to the educational needs of today, for which a gymnasium, a library, a laboratory, a visual-aids room, and rooms for the teachers to carry out interviews and pastoral work are all desirable – to say nothing of the possibility that the whole concept of teaching children in groups of thirty throughout the day may be totally wrong!

But when this school was built, the idea of the *aula* – a Latin word which Spain, Portugal and Italy all use for 'classroom' – was paramount. Your school has eight classes? Very well, then you will need eight classrooms, and the only problem is how we arrange them for you: is it a cramped site where we must put four rooms on one floor and the other four above, or is it possible for us to spread ourselves all along one level? Then you build on a small entrance-hall, add a few sanitary amenities, and there's your school. All over Europe there are schools basically like this, sometimes ugly and primitive, sometimes airy, handsome and delightful. As we saw at São Gregorio in Portugal, a small village school may need even less; but a large town school of, say, 400 or more pupils, with more than one class in each year, will need something larger, enabling you to spread yourself to the extent of providing one or two luxuries. If it is a secondary school that you have in mind, you will probably make provision for science work, for handicrafts, and for physical education; but even there your general rule will be that x classes require x classrooms.

The actual building which emerges from this specification may be almost anything from a great barracks of five or six institutional-looking floors, to a cluster of linked chalets. Individual needs, and the peculiarities of sites must be the controlling factors, though some general principles may be laid down; for example, in Spain I was told that buildings of more than two storeys are rather frowned-upon – there seem, however, to be plenty of exceptions, like Santo Tomás at Jaén (here an oddly sloping site made a lower building impracticable) or a couple of rather striking five- or six-storey buildings I recently saw at Palma de Mallorca.

Spain is devoting much thought to school buildings: an article in *Vida Escolar* (November/December 1972) by Señor Jaime Acebrón of the Inspectorate draws heavily on a conference held the year before at Elche to discuss the new EGB and its building requirements. Señor Acebrón lays down his basic principles with flexibility and generosity, and then considers actual plans for a school of sixteen classes (two in each year of the eight-year course), for which he envisages a total of twenty-one teaching-spaces. Thirteen will be classrooms in the old sense, two are designated as areas for individual work, and the remaining six are appropriated respectively as laboratory space, multiple activities room, audio-visual room, resources room, gymnasium and library. The total accommodation of this school, on the Spanish norm of forty pupils to a class, will be 640. The writer points out that to those who still think on the old lines there are two contradictions in this plan: first, that there are more rooms than there are classes (twenty-one as against sixteen); and second, that not every class has its own classroom, as there are only thirteen ordinary classrooms. These contradictions can be reconciled either on traditional lines, by letting three of the classes use specialist rooms as their class base, or on entirely new lines by reorganizing in 'cycles', each with one section of the school building. Thus the first cycle (years 1–3) would have six classrooms, an individual-study area and a share of the ancillary rooms such as interview-rooms, toilets, etc.; cycle 2 (years 4–5) will have two classrooms and an individual-study area; and cycle 3 (years 6–8) will have five classrooms and the resources area. Again, each of these cycles will have its share of the ancillary rooms. The library, audio-visual room, laboratory area and so on will be shared in common by all pupils. Of course, even with this cyclic division, there is in a sense dual use of the individual study and resources areas, but, as I understand it, the idea is that the individual class as such will more or less disappear, the pupils simply moving up from cycle to cycle at the appropriate time; thus, no one group of pupils 'owns' one classroom space, but each cycle owns a group of rooms. It is suggested that in the first 'initiation cycle', the first-year pupils should have a room entirely to themselves, because of their special problems, but the rest of the cycle will use its share of the space flexibly. In the 'intermediate cycle' it is suggested that pupils be grouped differently for different activities, according to their level. In the 'final cycle' an arrangement of rooms or spaces by subject is suggested: rooms may be allocated to Spanish, the foreign language, mathematics, religion, social studies and science, this last, of course, having the laboratory area.

In Appendix IX I give the suggested dimensions of a Spanish school for 640 pupils, taken from the Ministry booklet *La Reforma Educativa en Marcha* (Madrid, 1973). For a country which has a great deal of building to do, and is not among the richest in Europe, the provision is not ungenerous, and it is worth noting that the small but essential rooms for administration and pastoral activities have not been forgotten.

I have used Spain as my first example in this chapter because I felt it was there that most effort had been made to re-examine the traditional pattern of 'cells and bells' – the schools where pupils spend most of their time in boxes shut off from everyone else, and with their time equally uncompromisingly sawn into chunks of identical length. It is a time-honoured system, and generally fairly effective, but it is not necessarily the only, or the best, way of doing things, and it is well that it should receive some critical examination.

I also felt that many of the newer Spanish schools were, both externally and internally, pleasing to the eye. So were those of Italy (where, incidentally, I was told that the architect of one new school was so proud of it that he saw to it that it received a fresh coat of paint every year!) and of Germany, though their layout and planning were usually quite orthodox and traditional. In particular, I felt German schools compared very favourably with our own in the generosity of their planning; here, economy often demands a ruthless paring of all non-essential space, leaving us with cramped corridors, inadequate staircases, and a skimping of such necessities as storage space. Not so in these German schools; one's first impression was that one might stage a full-scale symphony concert in the foyer of such a school as the Treckfahrtstief Gymnasium in Emden. Consequently, there is ample room for the thousand and more pupils to move around at break-time without any sense that they are a crowd – even though, by and large, German pupils are even less given than most youngsters to sedate and orderly movement when they are assembled in quantity. The schools are spacious, and they are often also very handsome internally (externally perhaps less so, the repetition inescapable in school architecture being sometimes too emphatic for my taste). Treckfahrtstief has a huge window of coloured glass in the modern idiom; the Früchteburg Grundschule's corridors and staircases are embellished with attractive tiled designs; and many schools are liberally supplied with display-cases in which pupils' own art and craft work can be exhibited. There is much beauty in the modern German school, and because there is space one can enjoy it undisturbed.

Only once in Germany was I slightly disappointed by a modern building. This was at the Hindenburg-Gymnasium at Trier, a grammar school of 900 pupils, almost all boys, in the centre of Trier. The exterior of the school is promising, with four or five storeys of corridors whose gentle curve follows that of the street in which the school stands. But the promise is scarcely fulfilled, aesthetically at least, when one enters the building, the appearance of those long corridors, with their uniformly drab colouring, being rather depressing. When a building is so large and so repetitive as this one, a little adventurousness is surely called-for in decorating it. Lest I be misunderstood I would add that the atmosphere of the school seemed lively and vigorous enough despite its institutional appearance, and it has some enterprising features, including an arrangement with the local *lycée français*, involving some exchange of staff, and the teaching of some subjects through the medium of French.

Buildings and equipment

But I think it was in France that I felt most uneasy about the design of school buildings. The primary schools were often pleasing with one- or two-storey buildings along one or two sides of an attractive playing area; externally, the secondary schools were often rather striking too, but internally, they really are sometimes horrifying. There the concept of the cell comes uppermost: one finds long grey-painted corridors, with, at regular intervals, plain grey-painted doors leading into square grey-painted class-rooms. Thank heaven, the pupils no longer all wear grey *blouses* as well, or the prison atmosphere would be complete! Stand outside one of these buildings, housing perhaps between 1,500 and 2,000 pupils, and you can imagine yourself in a science-fiction nightmare – in every one of those rooms, you feel, are identical people doing identical things in identical ways. Happily, it is not so: the French are as individualistic a nation as any in the world, and you may be sure that no two teachers, no two classes, will be alike. But the nightmare is still there: you imagine that a boy might leave one of those classes in the middle of a lesson to go to the dentist and return half an hour later to the wrong room, without either noticing it or being noticed. Why the authorities cannot order a few pots of differently coloured paint, so that at least some rooms could be blue, some green, some yellow, I can't imagine; it would cost no more, and it would do away with that appallingly claustrophobic feeling I get inside the big French school. Better still, let the pupils themselves turn each room into something different and individual, as they so readily will at the primary stage. One school I saw had even been reduced to erecting 'street names' in each corridor: 'Avenue Lavoisier' led to the chemistry laboratories, and 'Couloir Pasteur' to the biology department.

The somewhat prison-like atmosphere of some French schools is made stronger by the tendency to lock the big iron playground gates against intruders throughout the school session; it was, however, Spain which most often introduced me to the locked classroom, and I recall one school which had Yale-type locks on all the doors, so that a pupil given permission to leave the room couldn't get back again without knocking to request his re-admission. I also recall waiting with a form outside a school library while people flew hither and thither in search of a key that nobody could remember having seen. Germany, too, often has formidably massive classroom doors, on which one's timid knuckles made no impression, but I don't think these were actually locked.

A much pleasanter idea was that of the Ramon Calatayud school at Jaén, where each classroom door had painted on it a symbol to give it a special identity of its own – various animals, a house, a shoe; some of these, I was told, made punning reference to the teacher's name. This was a *colegio nacional*, with pupils from six to fourteen, in the suburb of Peñamefecit; there were some 1,200 boys and girls, with a staff of thirty permanent teachers and a number of students; nearby are two other schools, making a very large campus which serves a wide and expanding residential area. One classroom at Ramon Calatayud had a delightful mural of a comic steam train puffing across an entire wall: each coach belonged to one of the work-groups of the class, and displayed its activities and achievements. Other schools with similar murals were La Inmaculada at Gerona, and La Barbière in Avignon (which seemed to specialize in jungle animals).

Such frivolities are surely worth the little they cost; so, too, were the aviary and display of plants at Virgilio in Cremona, where also the gardens contained a pleasant piece of modern sculpture; but a girl pupil was pleading in the school magazine for better planting in this garden, and I hope her pleas were heard. A different, but equally laudable, feature was the retention of an interesting medieval tower in the grounds of Santo Tomás at Jaén.

But sometimes, alas, there *are* no grounds to speak of; even modern schools are sometimes built up to the street line, so that lower windows must be fitted with frosted glass or with close wire meshes, to stop passers-by from enjoying a free view of the lessons. Such rooms are also, of course, subject to much extraneous noise.

Two main layouts seem to be most popular. First, there is the square or rectangle built round a central courtyard. Sometimes this plan takes the more modest form of a single block, or an L-shaped building, occupying only one or two of the four sides of the patio. Second, there is the building which comprises a series of wings which radiate from one corner or from some central point; again, this may be varied to take the form of an irregular series of linked buildings. The classrooms almost always open off corridors: in the case of the CES J. B. Pellerin at Beauvais, very narrow corridors. Only in the newer open-plan buildings of Spain has this concept been shelved.

It is one of my pet creeds that human beings cannot help being influenced by their environment: children cannot be fully happy in drab surroundings or well-behaved in a school that has been allowed to become dilapidated and grubby. Conversely, even the most selfish or thoughtless will think twice before putting a boot through the panels in a room which has been built and adorned with love and care. I am not even dissuaded from this belief by the knowledge that there is, somewhere, a mindless idiot capable of scratching a political slogan on the Cambridge Rubens. Therefore I find drabness offensive, whether in the grey paint, the cement walls or the dusty playground. Most countries' schools can at times sink pretty low, not least our own. Even my much-admired little village school at Porcellasco is scarcely uplifting as architecture, despite the vast improvements wrought by the paintbrushes of the parents. Often it is sheer poverty that perpetuates this drabness; undoubtedly the worst schools I have seen are some in southern Italy – dirty and dismal dens. The ultimate nadir is possibly a certain type of Spanish railway-station – happily becoming rarer, either through the closure of the more poverty-stricken lines or with the coming of prosperity to some others. There remain, however, many grey, cement-rendered structures, unpainted for generations, their floors littered with peanut-shells and cigarette-ends which the sweeper's listless brush never reaches, their walls adorned with tattered remnants of crookedly pasted posters proclaiming that as from the first of May 1964 the 8.35 train will leave at 8.26. Some of this dismal atmosphere at times afflicts other Spanish buildings, not excepting the schools; even some of the modern ones can be discouragingly rectangular, and their walls excessively prone to eruptions of wire-netting on chipped-looking concrete posts.

For most schools in Europe suffer, just as ours do, from certain deprivations of financial origin. Even wealthy Germany has its problems: there are few, if any, school libraries; textbooks are liable to become unavailable at critical moments; staffing is a major problem; and some schools are very short of space. The figure of 28 per cent deficiency has already been quoted for staff; as for rooms, I could instance the *Realschule* at Emden, where some five classes have no permanent room of their own but must wander about the school having their lessons in whatever room has temporarily been vacated by some other class who are working, say, in the gymnasium or the laboratories. (What with this, and the provisional timetable changing from day to day, and the absence of numbers on the doors of many of the rooms, and the construction of the doors themselves being so solid that from outside one could gain no clue, it was decidedly difficult to find the class you wanted in this school; the authorities had done their best by trying to group forms of the same year together in the corridors, but those peripatetic classes defeated one every time!)

If Germany suffers in this way, other countries are often far worse off. In parts of southern Italy the same building has to be used for two quite distinct groups of children, one attending in the morning and one in the afternoon or evening. Indeed, I have even come across a place where *three* shifts had to be worked each day. The Venetian newspaper *Il Gazzettino* for 28 May 1974 reported that parents were becoming concerned, and were seeking interviews with the authorities, because they feared that when the new school year started in October many children would be unable to find school places. The specific case which the newspaper quoted was that of the Scuola Media Forni at Zelarino, whose 569 pupils are already distributed over five different buildings, mostly quite inadequate, and with a further increase in numbers expected in the coming year. Some of these buildings were described as 'old and dangerous', others as 'insanitary and unsuitable'; only three or four classrooms out of twenty-two are considered to be even barely adequate, and the pupils have to sit elbow to elbow, and scramble over the desks to get to and from their places. There is no gynmasium, no sports hall, no playing-field. A further five classrooms will be needed merely to keep pace with the increased number of pupils (and if there *is* any more potential classroom space in existence at Zelarino, one guesses that it is likely to be even worse than that which is already in use!). The parents end their manifesto with the firm statement that they are 'no longer prepared to accept this state of things'. I confess that I rather doubt their chances of moving anyone in authority to action, when I think of the time that some departments have taken to reply to my own modest requests. The present parlous state of the Italian economy in any case seems to make a permanent solution to the woes of Zelarino rather problematical. However, the same newspaper did report a day or two later that the opening of some new schools in the region would ease the position a little by making possible some rearrangement of catchment areas.

In Spain also local newspapers have been expressing concern over similar situations; the Alicante paper *Información* devoted about a page and a half of its issue of 23 April 1974 to a detailed review of the situation in fourteen localities in the area. The actual position clearly varied from village to village, and the problem seemed at least in part to be that vacant places were not always where the surplus children were. Pre-school education was particularly deficient in this area, said the article. It also commented that the vast majority of the schools in the fourteen localities were state schools, with the private sector playing little part, whereas in Alicante city the situation was exactly the opposite. It may therefore be justifiable to assume that where relatively few state school places are available, parents who cannot afford, or do not wish, to send their children to the church schools simply do not send them to school at all. (Now that the principle of providing at least the basic education free of charge in all schools has been approved, however, this situation should cure itself.)

Despite these pockets of privation, Spain has very many excellent new schools, clean in their architectural lines and bright in colour. I greatly liked the new La Inmaculada College of the Marist Brothers in Gerona, a fascinating series of pale clustered hexagons, with silvery roofs; I thought this a very commendable building, beautiful in its sense of lightness and space. On the island of Mallorca, at Palma and Inca, I saw fine big schools already open, and more under construction, some of them using a plan of external staircases leading to open balconies from which the classrooms were entered, an arrangement very well-suited to the gentle climate of Mallorca. Though smaller and simpler, a building like the Colegio Nacional Santo Tomás at Jaén is nevertheless most attractive, with its warm buff colour and its diversified balconies; Martin Noguera, also at Jaén, is rather similar; while Menendez Pidal, at Salt near Gerona, is in a bright deep brown and cream, with windows which, though obviously of standard modules, are interestingly varied in style and placing; a big complex of schools in the Peñamefecit suburb of Jaén shows some agreeable contrasts in its use of dark brick and concrete, and a bold, simple handling of both materials. The Evora Technical School in Portugal uses buildings of varying heights and roofs of differing pitch to interesting effect, and has not disdained to add ornamental sculptured panels to some outer walls.

This last-named school, though recent, is already substantially outgrown – a common feature, alas, of schools everywhere! Its campus includes several linked blocks, of one, two or three storeys, some built on a plan using open galleries round a courtyard roofed with transparent material; this is a pleasant plan, and very practical except perhaps for brief periods during the day when everybody is moving at once, when it becomes rather noisy.

Good as some of these buildings are, I do not think we need be ashamed of the comparison with our own modern schools; I saw only a few which were as architecturally striking as the best of British school buildings. Externally, some of the French ones had long, airy perspectives that were visually very stimulating, whatever their interiors were like, but perhaps La Inmaculada was in a class of its own among large schools in that it was as good inside as outside. Some of the small schools, however, not least those in the villages, can be very satisfying to the eye. In some respects, though, I think we must concede that we are often badly beaten: the solidity of construction and quality of workmanship often seemed to me greatly superior to that of modern British schools, so often the victims of misplaced economies that cut down first costs at the price of vastly higher maintenance costs later; and some items of equipment and classroom fittings also have much to teach us.

Once inside the classroom, what then? One of the few ways in which one room can be made different from another similar little box, is by finding a new arrangement of the desks, and this will largely depend on the methods preferred by the teacher. An older building may often have rather larger rooms, but if, as frequently occurs, the furniture is also older, its greater bulk and immobility cancels out the advantage of larger floor-area. If the teacher's main preoccupation is with mass instruction, he will probably prefer the formal arrangement of desks in rows and/or columns; if he is more concerned with his pupils' individual work he will arrange the desks in little groups. My photographs show me that the former arrangement is much the more common in secondary schools; at the primary school, although the less formal layout is

Buildings and equipment

more likely to occur, there are still at least two 'rows-and-columns' rooms to one 'little-groups' room. The shape of the room also partly controls the layout of desks; it was sometimes necessary to have as many as four desks placed together in order to cram in sufficient seating for a large class, and this, of course, drastically reduced the children's mobility. One or two of the oldest schools even had stepped floors in the classrooms, raising the rear rows above the ones in front to give better visibility. And the oddest arrangement of all was in a Portuguese primary school where one teacher, having to teach two classes in one room, had first ranged a line of desks *diagonally* from corner to corner, and then had put rows of gradually-decreasing numbers of desks into each of the two triangular halves. This arrangement probably wins the all-time prize for inconvenience; moving about the room became an adventure not to be undertaken without careful preliminary planning. However, this was in one of the odder schools I came across.

Where the 'interest-group' arrangement was in use, the furniture was usually fairly light and movable, but another Portuguese school had made a gallant attempt to introduce this arrangement despite the handicap of enormously heavy wooden desks of great age; the expedient was not entirely successful, but I admired the teacher's refusal to accept defeat at the hands of his furniture.

Sometimes, especially in Germany, layouts seemed to have been dictated rather by the size and shape of the room or by the number of pupils to be accommodated, rather than by any educational philosophy; thus, at the Früchteburg School, Emden, one second-year class had three continuous rows of desks arranged round the walls in a U-formation, providing seats for twenty-two pupils, while the remaining fourteen occupied a block of desks in the centre of the U; but a fourth form had continuous desks only along the two side walls, while about twenty pupils sat in pairs of desks placed at right angles to the two rows and projecting from them like the teeth of a comb. The *Realschule* also used this plan in some rooms; and the Gymnasium am Treckfahrtstief produced a class which had two shorter continuous rows of desks down the sides, while the space between was filled with other separated rows of differing lengths.

The less formal the layout, as a rule, the greater the sense of vitality in the air; but a far bigger part in giving the room a lively 'feel' is provided by the use of wall space. Not every school perhaps would feel able to provide as much sheer gaiety as the Maternelle Jean Moulin, which not only displayed an almost infinite series of art-forms created by the small pupils, but also had live pets such as a pigeon and a large guinea-pig to divert the children. But with the exception of Portugal, where art education is still fairly elementary, most primary school walls were a riot of colour, using posters and coloured pictures as well as the children's own work. In the secondary school, walls more often tended to be blank, save where an individual teacher had stuck up one or two travel-posters or the like. Certainly, this was not always the fault of teacher or class; sometimes classroom walls were tiled, making it much harder to affix any decorative material to them, and in other cases a freshly-painted wall probably inhibited people from trying to pin or sellotape material to it. There seemed to be a great need for at least some large panels of softboard or cork, to which pictures could easily be pinned. But a commoner reason for this lack of classroom adornment is the fact that so often secondary school classes move from room to room at the change of lessons, and so have no fixed base to which they can begin to attach some pride of ownership. All sense of 'belonging' is lost, and I wonder how much of the restlessness of the adolescent school student may be due to this everlasting shifting of scene?

Germany was something of an exception to this last situation; there, if the schools I visited are typical, it seems to be more usual for the teacher to move than the class. Consequently, the group does have a fixed base and some attempt is therefore made to make it their own. It is true that almost all the rooms where this had been done were adorned with a quantity of large coloured photographs of pop singers, and I cannot claim any great educational or even aesthetic merit in such displays; nevertheless, they are better than bare walls, and if, as I assume, they are chosen and displayed by the pupils themselves, this at least argues some concern for the appearance of the room and some desire to make it congenial.

Where the class must move to the specialist teacher several times a day, there seems little point in inducing the class to put up decorative material, for the only person who will spend any great amount of time with it is the teacher, and he will probably

Buildings and equipment

grudge devoting wall-space to material not concerned with his own specialist subject; thus it becomes very much his responsibility to try to prevent specialization from automatically producing drabness.

Of course, the needs of the specialist teacher and the pastoral side of education are bound to conflict to some extent, but we may be leaning too heavily on the former in our secondary schools. If our training colleges could produce more teachers who, while still well-qualified to teach their main subject, were able to turn their hands to one or two subsidiary subjects, we should have some very useful form-masters and form-mistresses, who could teach their classes for, say, a third of the whole teaching week, so building up with them a close rapport which would help the children to feel that they belonged to some person and some place.

After this mild attack on specialization, I nevertheless turn briefly to consider some of the special teaching-rooms: laboratory, gymnasium, workshop and the like.

Readers will realize by now that the lavish provision of science laboratories found in English schools is rare in Europe. Teaching methods are different and syllabuses less directed towards practical work. For all that, I thought that many of the laboratories which I did see were distinctly good. On my 1973 tour, I saw fourteen schools which possessed laboratories: five of them had one only (for biology or natural science) and three others only two. But there was compensation in the comprehensive way in which those which did exist were laid out and equipped: I think, for example, of the laboratory of the J. Vicens Vives School in Gerona, described in chapter 4. Others with notably good equipment were the Lycée Frédéric Mistral at Avignon; the Collège d'Enseignement Technique at Beauvais; the La Salle College at Gerona; the Instituto Virgen del Carmen at Jaén; and the Evora Technical School. It will be noted, however, that almost all these are schools catering only for *advanced* secondary pupils; those dealing with the younger teenagers, the French CES or the Spanish *colegio nacional*, usually have less generous provision; and as far as I saw, there is virtually none in Italy, where the only laboratory I heard of was one in the as-yet-unbuilt new school at Soresina.

Since these laboratories are mainly used for biology and some elementary physics, they do not usually carry much apparatus, and those typical English rows of glass-stoppered bottles of Conc.

and Dil. H_2SO_4 are not to be seen. Still, I think we can learn something from them when it comes to the construction of the workbenches: many of these are covered in white glazed tiles, attractive in appearance and very easy to keep clean, while one or two had instead a hard-looking plastic surface of shiny black. The La Salle College at Gerona had what *looked* like marble, though it was no doubt a synthetic substitute. I was less envious of the open-plan laboratory at Salt, being frankly at a loss to see how one man can supervise three groups of pupils carrying out experiments in different sciences without risk of either mishap to the pupils or insanity to the teacher.

The absence of a specific room for practical work in science does not necessarily mean that experiment is impossible: and it does not have to be experiment on the melancholy scale which I saw in Portugal and have described already. In Spain at least, and no doubt elsewhere, 'experimental kits' are supplied for use in ordinary classrooms, with which the children can do a variety of experiments in mechanics, heat, electricity and optics, as well as quite a lot of chemistry provided that some sort of small sink or water-basin is available.

An article in the Spanish magazine *Vida Escolar* described a *colegio nacional* of possibly 1,500 pupils, at Elche near Alicante, which possesses one physics/chemistry laboratory, plus weather-station and photographic laboratory; one biology laboratory, plus geology laboratory and natural science museum; an experimental farm and a field for agricultural experiments; a mathematical laboratory and a data-processing room. The school has made some enterprising links with industry, with scientific installations outside the school, with the local authority's programming and data-processing sections, with conservation societies, etc., and a considerable stock of teaching material of many kinds has been built up. I mention this as proof that when it really tries, a school at this level can produce a quite impressive programme of science teaching.

I have already referred briefly to the provision for science in German schools; here I should only add that, as a layman, I was greatly impressed by the standards of layout and design in the laboratories, and the high quality of the equipment provided. At the Grundschule–Hauptschule at Zewen near Trier, for example, the laboratory was a beautiful room with clinically white tiling,

Buildings and equipment

and meticulously-kept equipment; this was a fairly new building, but the far older Wallschule at Emden could also show some very well-designed laboratories, with service and power points most conveniently arranged for the pupils' use and a central control for the teacher. It must be even more of a pleasure to work in the laboratories at the Treckfahrtstief Gymnasium, and in this last school (as also at Zewen) I was very envious of the well-equipped photographic laboratories which were available for use by the pupils studying this subject as part of their 'options'. I saw some of the work produced in these rooms (to call them merely 'darkrooms' gives a quite wrong impression) and it was of a very good quality.

One can rely more confidently on finding a decent gymnasium and/or sports hall than perhaps one can on finding a good laboratory. With only fifty pupils, one could not expect the little village school at Porcellasco to have one, but all the other Italian schools I saw might have been expected to provide something of the kind. In fact, two were primary schools and were not equipped with gymnasia, and a third was occupying a very old building where it would have been virtually impossible to contrive anything suitable. One school would come into possession of a fine gymnasium when its new buildings were completed; and the other two already had excellent and well-equipped provision. The antiquated buildings of the Juan Bruguera school in Gerona, Spain, were not provided with a gymnasium; nor was the old building of La Inmaculada College in the same city; here some very lively, if rather formal, PE was taking place in the outdoor patio. But the new buildings of La Inmaculada include good provision, and so did all the other Spanish schools I visited, the Instituto J. V. Vives in Gerona having two gymnasia, one for each sex. In France, one modern CES appeared to have no gymnasium, which surprised me; on the other hand, two primary schools which I saw had exceptionally good ones, and the two schools of the *lycée* category each possessed two. There was quite good provision in the Portuguese *liceus*, but no such luxuries were to be found in their primary schools, where indeed the only physical education teaching I saw was a little rhythmical clapping and stamping to accompany a singing session!

The link between music and physical education is, in fact, a feature of both the Portuguese and the Spanish programmes, and since a good sense of rhythm is essential to both, their coupling is less eccentric than may at first sight be thought.

Undoubtedly the most impressive gymnasium I saw was that possessed by the Zewen school at Trier. This was a lofty room, 33 metres (about 108 feet) long. It could be divided into two unequal sections by means of an electrically lowered screen. Along one side ran store-rooms, whose garage-type lifting doors were also operated automatically at the touch of a button. All fittings such as door-handles were flush, to avoid any possibility of injury to pupils, and the plentiful apparatus was easily handled on castors. The floor surface was admirable: smooth, springy, yet firm. This hall is also used, I gather, by outside organizations. I do not recall seeing a spectator gallery here, but many Continental school gymnasia do have them.

I actually watched two or three physical education lessons, of very different kinds. I have already mentioned the 'physical jerks' in a Spanish school patio; this lesson took me shudderingly back to early morning sessions with an army corporal in 1940, though the boys apparently enjoyed it. A French primary school lesson consisted mainly of rather mild relay races and outdoor games. More varied was the one I saw at Zewen, where Herr Günther told me – in impeccable French, the only language we had in common – that his lesson was aimed at increasing the creativity and the coordination of his seven-year-old pupils. After a few minutes just running, walking or crawling about, the children watched with excitement while the teacher prepared a sort of obstacle course from benches, mattresses and other apparatus. Two pupils having demonstrated, under the teacher's direction, the class divided into two teams, boys *v.* girls, and competed over the course. To my amusement, the girls won this one hands down; Herr Günther then made them repeat the race in slow motion and in dead silence, and, believe it or not, this time the boys won! After one or two more races of the same kind, the lesson ended with a few minutes of deliberate chaos, in which the children ran amok with wild war-whoops, which they then had to stop instantly on a clap of the hands. Incidentally, the children were mostly dressed in black vests and shorts, which looked rather strange to my eyes, accustomed to white.

Many of the schools in France and Spain were fortunate enough to have their own heated indoor swimming-pools. The pool at the Lycée Technique at Beauvais was, in fact, right in the heart of the building among the science laboratories, possibly as a matter of convenience in providing the necessary plumbing to both. Where there was no pool, lessons were often taken in a public swimming-bath.

Of other specialist teaching-rooms, we may next briefly look at those used for teaching art, handicraft and the various technical subjects. Art, I am afraid, by no means always *has* a specially equipped room in European schools; it very seldom does so at the primary level, and at the secondary stage the room often seemed to have less in the way of special facilities than we should expect in this country; it differs from an ordinary classroom only by being larger, and perhaps by having somewhat different furniture. Frequently, however, even the secondary schools have to make do with an ordinary classroom for teaching art and, for that matter, with an ordinary teacher too, with relatively little artistic training or aptitude. This would certainly account for the stiff and unimaginative quality of much art work in Portugal especially; and the understandable reluctance of teachers to splash paint about in an ordinary classroom also no doubt explained the widespread use of pallid crayons or lurid felt-pens to produce coloured drawings.

But where a proper room existed, or an imaginative teacher, some remarkable work was to be found. At the Institution du Saint-Esprit in Beauvais I saw an exhibition of work by the pupils of all ages; at the end of the display, the work was to be sold off to parents to raise funds for buying more materials. It included some really beautiful painted plates, some interesting work in coloured glass, a collection of lively plaster masks, and some charming soft toys as well as the usual paintings and drawings. The Collége d'Enseignement Technique in the same city also has some very gifted teachers, and its art room displayed a fascinating variety of work: delicate paper-cuttings, fierce coloured masks, a charming family of owls mounted on a hanging bar, butterflies and other insects made out of fine string pinned to shape, patterns formed by coloured paper wound into tight spirals which produced most interesting textures, and designs made of plastic yoghourt pots of various shapes and sizes stuck in patterns on a board. The delicacy of much of this work was all the more striking because this is a school which specializes in building technology and the pupils spend much of their time on far coarser work, laying bricks, mixing concrete and so on.

Yet another school to show me a very impressive exhibition of pupils' art work was the *liceu nacional* at Evora in Portugal; and the technical school in the same city was encouraging the arts in several ways – its walls and staircases were made beautiful with some excellent handicrafts, and one room was given over to a small, but quite choice, museum and art gallery, the paintings being either by people associated with the school or by local artists. It would be good to see this far-sighted and imaginative idea widely practised elsewhere.

In schools of a great many types one can enjoy imaginative techniques in art and handicraft: tiny children at the *maternelle* (nursery school) which I visited in Beauvais had produced vivid paintings, sand-sculptures, mosaics, coloured perspex patterns, glazed clay models, needlework (by boys as well as girls) and pictures made by taking impressions from inked glass sheets; at the J. H. Fabre school in Avignon I saw an interesting lesson on the use of 'drawing-gum' (you paint, as it were, with this gum, and then cover the paper with Indian ink; afterwards, the gum can be rubbed off, bringing the ink with it, and leaving the design in white against a black background); La Barbière, also in Avignon, produced some delightful work in coloured glass, and also a technique of drawing with a blunt point on metal foil, which is afterwards covered with ink, the ink then being wiped off before it can dry, so that it remains only in the depressed parts of the picture.

Hard as it may be to do good art in an ordinary classroom, it is far harder to do satisfactory handicraft, unless one confines one's ambitions to such gentle pastimes as making paper flowers. But even where special craft rooms existed, they were seldom really satisfactory except in one French CES. Cellars and basements seemed to be favourite places – as at Virgilio in Cremona, and at two German schools. Apparatus was often lacking; despite this, quite young pupils at the Marist College in Jaén were doing varied and creative work; a class at Zewen, Trier, was experimenting with simple pottery, while others in the same school had made delightful ceramic tiles and had concocted metal plaques out of old fruit-tins and pieces of wire. One must not forget Porcellasco, too, with its remarkable variety of crafts and the almost limitless

Buildings and equipment

ingenuity of its teachers. In Germany girls as well as boys may do woodwork and metalwork (and the boys can, and do, choose cookery if they wish); at the Wallschule in Emden a lady teacher, Frau Schultze, was in charge of woodwork, and brought both an artistic and a practical sense to her teaching.

True technical schools, of course, can offer really remarkable facilities. At Ecija, the Sagrada Familia school had a large workshop wholly devoted to motor-engineering; and the CET at Beauvais had every gadget one can think of for teaching building crafts, whether gas-fitting, roofing, water-heating or electrical wiring. This school could also turn out excellent blueprints and plans from its own resources. In a quite different field of technical education, the Evora technical school in Portugal could teach every aspect of commercial and office routine, from the intricacies of a filing-system to the mounting of a full-scale advertising campaign.

I think only the Gymnasium am Treckfahrtstief, at Emden, could show me a separate music room, suitably furnished and equipped. Elsewhere, music was another subject that usually took pot-luck in an ordinary classroom. Treckfahrtstief also had about the best domestic science room that I saw, with batteries of gleaming appliances looking like something out of the Ideal Home Exhibition. Owing to its earlier service as a school for girls only, this school has a stronger domestic science side than most of its type; very properly, now that there are also boys in the school, they too may take the subject if they wish. Outside Germany, I think the only other school catering really well for domestic science was the CES J. B. Pellerin.

Continental schools seldom assemble their pupils for any kind of ceremony to begin the day; it is quite a common practice for classes to line up in the courtyard outside and be led into school in orderly files by the teachers responsible for the following lesson. (This also happens after break and before afternoon school.) There is therefore perhaps little need for a large assembly hall. At Treckfahrtstief, the headmaster told me that he planned to cut off part of his hall (an attractive room with comfortable blue tip-up seats) to augment his language-laboratory space. J. B. Pellerin School at Beauvais also had what looked uncannily like an English assembly hall, and didn't seem quite sure what to do with it. Elsewhere, however, one might often find some sort of large room available for the staging of plays or concerts, for holding parents' meetings, for teaching activities involving very large groups, or for those odd purposes, like private study for older pupils, for which no other provision existed. In Spain, such a room is called the *salón de actos*. They are often very well-furnished with cinema-type seats, nicely upholstered; I saw excellent examples at the Colegio La Salle at Gerona and the Instituto Virgen del Carmen in Jaén. Such halls often provide facilities for the projection of films, and these often seemed well up to professional standard in their equipment.

It was at the CES J. B. Pellerin again that I saw a most ingenious arrangement for converting the dining-hall into an auditorium for the showing of films. The tables were hinged down the middle and one half folded down to form a bench; at the same time, the chairs on that side of the table could be swivelled to face the screen. The operation could be done quite quickly, and this convertibility had been achieved without in the least marring the appearance of the room or its usefulness for its primary function as a refectory.

Although school prayers as a compulsory daily activity do not happen in European schools, several of those I visited had small chapels. That at the Evora *liceu* was very small – more of a place to drop into for a moment of private devotion than for public worship – and perhaps even our secular society might have a use for such a place, as I believe some Leicestershire schools have found. Larger chapels were not by any means confined to Church-owned schools; one of the pleasantest was at the Instituto J. Vicens Vives at Gerona. The windows in the small oratory at Saint-Esprit, Beauvais, had been designed by some of the older pupils, I gathered; and their taste was certainly better than that in one or two other chapels I saw, with deplorable stained glass and even neon tubes circling the head of the Virgin!

Libraries were less common than in this country, though quite often individual classes had small collections of books available for borrowing. Often, too, collections of pedagogical works were available for the use of teachers. But as far as true school libraries were concerned, they were mainly confined to schools of the *lycée* type. The technical school at Evora had an excellent, if rather small, collection of general books, and a full-time librarian to look after them; the *liceu* in Evora, and the *lycée technique* at Beau-

Buildings and equipment

vais also had quite good collections, as did one ordinary secondary school, J. B. Pellerin at Beauvais. In most of these schools, the library also provided a service of indexing magazine articles and pamphlets which might be useful to the pupils in their work. With the exception of that at the Evora technical school, most of these seemed to be austerely limited to books of reference, technical works and so on, with little recognition of the role that purely recreational reading of high quality can play in children's development; the same outlook can perhaps be detected in the almost total lack of library provision at the primary level. In theory, Spain is an exception here, with provision for libraries in her new all-age *colegios nacionales*, but in practice most of these are at present very short of actual books. The situation in Germany puzzles me; certainly the regulations for *Gymnasien* in Rhineland-Palatinate even says that pupils have a positive right of access to the school library, and of working there outside school hours, but the rule goes on to say that the school controls the use of the library according to the availability of rooms and personnel, and I must report that in fact I did not see or hear of a single school library in my tour there, except for some collections of reference books solely for the use of teachers.

I was, however, pleased to find in most schools a generous provision of small rooms capable of holding anything from two or three up to about twenty people, for club meetings, interviews with parents or pupils, or preparing teaching material: only the practising teacher knows how much more effective his work can be where such rooms exist, and how hampered where they do not.

Germany was well-supplied with language laboratories: in one school the installation overwhelmed me, indeed, with a panel of instruments like that in the cabin of a jumbo jet. Language laboratories, however, were not always effectively used; some of the lessons I saw taking place in them would have been more profitable in an ordinary classroom where greater freedom of movement and discussion would have been possible. Outside Germany, I also saw an excellent language laboratory in use for the training of teachers at the Centre Départementale de Documentation Pédagogique in Beauvais; but as far as schools were concerned, a small and only partially equipped one at Saint-Esprit in Beauvais, and the prospect of one for the new *scuola media* at Soresina in Italy, were the only two language laboratories which came my way.

To complete this round-up of the 'miscellaneous' rooms, there remain such oddments as the 'usual offices' and the catering facilities.

It is not usual to find special cloakrooms provided for pupils to hang their outdoor clothing, the more usual practice being the eminently sensible one of providing a row of pegs either in the corridor outside each room, or at the back of the room itself. When I was in Germany, these pegs did not seem to be used very much, pupils preferring to take their anoraks into the classroom with them, and drape them over the backs of their chairs.

Every school, of course, has some form of WC – or the more earthy equivalent, in the case of the village school I visited in Portugal – and sometimes these are fairly primitive, particularly in the older French schools, where some distinctly nasty little sheds often lurk in corners of the playground; but the only one calling for special mention, I think, was at the São Vitor primary school at Braga in Portugal, where access could only be gained after the lady custodian had unlocked some fairly forbidding-looking iron grilles. The cleanliness and decency of these particular toilets was unusually good; but one Italian school solemnly includes in its printed rules the following:

> The toilets must be used cleanly, using the special urinals and not soiling the floors or walls. This is as much a matter of hygiene as of decency and good manners.

Evidently boys will be boys: let us pass on to sweeter-smelling topics.

Several schools had an interesting equivalent of the British tuckshop: a room officially designated 'Café' or even 'Bar'. At J. Vicens Vives and the two Portuguese *liceus* these were fully equipped café-shops serving light refreshments (indeed, in the first-named, full meals could be bought); small items of stationery were also obtainable. Pupils who had reached the statutory age could sometimes obtain alcoholic refreshment. The concept was sometimes simply that of authorizing somebody to open a shop on the school premises, which was then run much as a village café or bar might be – and indeed a large school could provide quite as much business as many a village. At the technical school in Evora the café profits are used to subsidize the meals serviced in the refectory – a sensible way of making it possible to provide more varied and appetizing meals at a reasonable price, and one which our own administrators might well consider. Some schools also had coffee-machines available for pupils to use during their breaks; and in Germany there was usually a stall set up in some convenient point during the first break to sell rolls and a curious drink called *Kakaotrunk* – a sort of chocolate-flavoured milk.

Having thus arrived on the periphery of the subject of food, we may next consider school dining-rooms and the meals served in them.

Opportunity came to me to sample a number of school meals in different countries, and, even if none of them could exactly be described as a gastronomic experience, all were adequate and wholesome.

Normally, of course, Italian schools meet only in the morning, and so need no provision for meals; but the village school at Porcellasco is a *scuola a tempo pieno* and necessarily provides lunch. Some of the children sat at my table, and I was delighted by their good manners and friendliness. Most of the serving was done by two jolly ladies, who had also done the cooking, but some of the older children also helped. The teachers shared the meal, and the whole atmosphere was that of a large and happy family. We ate a splendid meal of gnocchi, roast chicken and salad. As dessert there was a delicious fruit-tart, sprinkled with chocolate, which I was told had been made in honour of the English visitor. I learned that the menu is a well-varied one, with such dishes as ham, meat-stews, rissoles, eggs, tunny-fish, omelettes or cheese, with a variety of vegetables, followed by fresh or cooked fruit or other puddings. The children have mineral water, milk or fruit-juice to drink. It was very apparent that they were greatly enjoying their meal, as I did. The actual arrangements for dining were somewhat improvised – which is understandable, since the building is an old one not really adapted to modern educational practice.

In France I ate a number of meals at schools; one or two of these were in rather untypical circumstances, one of them being as a guest of the headmaster in his little private dining-room annexed to the refectory, and another being a truly memorable banquet – it is the only word – provided by the school kitchen for a special party of visitors, and served in the staffroom. Both were notably good meals, and the second indeed would be thought exceptionally good even by French standards; but they can hardly be taken as representative of school catering as a whole! Two meals which I had at the CES J. B. Pellerin in Beauvais may be more representative. Each commenced with a small portion of fish, in one case sardine, and in the other maquereau au vin blanc; the main course of one meal was ham and fried potatoes, and of the other meat-balls served with a rather dull sauce and a kind of pasta; one meal ended with a pot of some kind of factory-made chocolate mousse, and the other with an orange. The pupils are also served with a beverage, which is included in the price of the meal, and for the staff the choice includes beer or wine. A self-service system is used, admission being by ticket, and the staff queue for their meals with the pupils, though they afterwards take them to their own small private dining-room, as is usual in France. I regret to say that piped music was provided during the meal in the pupils' refectory. As one might expect in so modern a school, the kitchens were splendidly equipped.

Some of the other French schools I saw also had very fine dining arrangements: the Lycée Technique at Beauvais has a big circular dining-room with kitchens in the centre and small individual rooms such as the staff dining-room opening off the periphery; and another school I remember especially was the La Barbière primary school at Avignon, for its airy and attractive dining-room in spring-like pastel colours which were echoed in the actual tableware. Male chefs are quite common in French schools, and sometimes they have a very big staff to cope not only with meals for their own school but also with those served to pupils in other nearby schools.

The long Spanish lunch-hour has something of the same effect as the Italian mornings-only system, in that relatively small numbers of children will actually stay to lunch, most either going home or being able to obtain meals outside the school. At Virgen del Carmen in Jaén, I was told that as few as forty out of 1,000 pupils stayed, though a quite good meal was supplied for only 15 pesetas (say 12p). Sometimes, as at J. V. Vives school in Gerona, the provision of the meal is left to the school café, run by people unconnected with the school. As Spain has in recent years come closer to the modern welfare state, the provision of school meals has greatly increased; a few years ago I saw some jolly children in a small Andalusian town queuing outside what looked like a soup-kitchen for their midday meal, but now there is probably a smart and up-to-date school with its own kitchen and refectory there. I ate two Spanish school meals and watched the preparation of a third, and if none was brilliant they were excellent value for the small sum the pupils paid. At Juan Bruguera school in Gerona, about 300 of the school's 740 boys took lunch, in three sittings. Inevitably, there was a lot of noise, but behaviour was good. Boys acted as waiters at the staff table, and I was told there was keen competition for the privilege. We had first a dish of haricot beans and boiled potatoes; then some very tasty meat-balls; finally, a compote of peaches served with wafer-biscuits. Sometimes, I was told, chicken or fish replaces the meat course. A year later, at Menendez Pidal, Salt, the charge was 30 pesetas (about 23p); here only about 130 pupils regularly take the meal. We ate a good dish of rice with meat, followed by fried fish and lettuce, and an apple as dessert; pupils had a chocolate-milk drink provided, and there was wine and/or mineral-water for the staff. The children sat at small square tables seating four, older and younger children of the same family often sitting together. Service was slow, and the meal was again rather noisy; those of the staff who were on duty had their own separate meal first to enable them to supervise the children with greater fortitude. Finally, at Miguel de Cervantes in Ecija, the male cook was preparing lentil stew, followed by junket and fruit with biscuits as the dessert; here the charge (1975) was also a maximum of 30 pesetas, but pupils paid on a sliding scale according to family circumstances, some receiving their meal entirely free.

None of the Portuguese primary schools I visited provided a midday meal; the break lasts at least two hours, and each school serves a neighbourhood area, so it is probably unnecessary. But the two *liceus* both provided meals, and at one of these, the Evora *liceu*, I had an excellent meal in the beautiful old refectory of the former university, with its grand marble tables. Here, for a modest cost, the pupils ate a meal comprising a tasty soup, a delicious chicken stew with a variety of vegetables, and a sweet of the custard family, topped with nuts. I was told that charges are on a sliding scale according to means, but that nobody paid more than 7.50 escudos (then about 12½p); as the school at present works on a two-shift system owing to lack of space, not many actually take the meal, for those working in the morning can eat when they get home, while those on the afternoon shift have lunch before leaving home. When I was there, however, the attendance was higher, as it was almost the end of term, and pupils then have the pleasant custom of inviting their teachers to eat with them in the refectory in something of a 'party' atmosphere.

If the internal equipment of Continental schools is often excellent, the surrounding terrain may sometimes leave much to be desired. English schools tend to be set well back from the road, with lawns or shrubbery separating them from the outer world, and acres of grass, sacred to football and cricket, all around. Something of the same atmosphere prevails in the newer schools of Emden, a spacious town with many open spaces. The Treckfahrtstief school is particularly attractively situated in a quiet backwater of a road right on one edge of the town, close to a small harbour for little pleasure-boats, and the school itself has plenty of grass as well as its more everyday hard-playing areas. Compared with this, the average French or Spanish school can sometimes appear bleak. But not always: I know of few more dramatically situated schools than the Martin Noguera and Santo Tomás in Jaén, from both of which, but especially the former, one sees a prospect of magnificent mountains on all sides, with the superb Renaissance Cathedral of the Assumption lifting its towers into the sky. Even these two, like so many others, are not very well endowed with playing-areas of their own: the former has an athletics-track and a football-pitch, and a certain amount of hard playing-area, but the latter has only the hard area and not very much of it. Many schools stand directly on the line of the street – Juan Bruguera and the La Salle College in Gerona, for example, and the Marist College at Jaén; the same is true of the Scuola Media San Paolo in Perugia, and a great many French schools. Often there is only a small scrap of playground, which may be rough and dusty as at Juan Bruguera or the São Vitor school in Braga; or there is a central asphalted or cemented courtyard round which the school buildings stand. Even in some of the big new French schools there is little grass or greenery, save perhaps for a few rather institutionalized trees growing out of small circles which the asphalt has spared.

This lack of grass is most felt during the lunch-hour in France: it seems to be quite unheard-of for the children to be allowed the use of any rooms in the school during this period – indeed, rooms are often carefully locked by the teacher every time he goes out –

Buildings and equipment

and so they must find somewhere outside to play. There is a limit to the attraction of just standing about talking, or chasing one another up and down the playground; there is seldom enough room to organize with any real hope of enjoyment a game of football in the playground (as the Spanish would certainly do) so one sees groups of boys and girls squatting or sitting on the asphalt in the shade of the building, checking a piece of work together or chatting. They often look forlorn and uncomfortable, and merely on the principle of not letting Satan find any work for their idle hands to do, some more positive provision of usable space would seem desirable.

I noticed that the new La Inmaculada College at Gerona had provided such space, and the Wallschule at Emden also has plans to provide at least some covered play accommodation; a school like the Treckfahrtstief has amply wide covered passageways which at least partially solve the problem. The difficulty is less felt at the primary stage; when you are about eight, it is pleasure enough just to rush around being an aeroplane, or flinging yourself in an amiable way upon your friends; or you can always play marbles, which the French child enjoys as much as his father enjoys the adult version of the game which is played with what look and sound like cannonballs.

The furniture and equipment found in the schools often show interesting differences from our own patterns: desks, for example, which were in all but special rooms and laboratories. English schools seem incurably addicted to the locker-type desk, which is always inconvenient in one way or another, for if you give the pupil enough storage-space you restrict his leg-room, and vice-versa. But the typical European desk simply does not have a locker; it usually has a commodious shelf below the desk top, or a deep trough at one side, but these are not expected to contain all the pupil's books; they are simply a convenient place to put what he is not immediately using. Often he has a small locker provided elsewhere, and anyway he will usually keep fewer books and other articles at school than his British counterpart. The arrangement has something to commend it, not least the fact that it discourages the pupil from keeping all sorts of noisome-smelling rubbish about the place.

Often, too, the desk is provided with a stout bracket at one side to hold a brief-case or satchel. The good old-fashioned school satchel is by no means extinct on the Continent, where it is generally of that excellent pattern which is worn high on the shoulders like a rucksack; but many pupils nowadays prefer to lug around a brief-case or one of those American-army-type haversacks (almost invariably lettered in English, too). Whichever article is used, it becomes a peril to life and limb if left about in the gangways between desks; hence the admirable little bracket, from which it hangs conveniently out of harm's way. Incidentally, many French schools also provide stout metal racks attached to the walls for pupils to park their bags while they play, or eat their lunch.

My third approved feature of the European school desk is that it is nowadays usually provided with a top surface of some hard plastic like formica, often of a pleasant pale-green colour (though I did once or twice see that repulsive material, plastic simulating wood, I'm afraid!) These surfaces are hard, smooth and ideal for working on, and unless the child is a very dedicated vandal he cannot carve his name on them. Childish ruderies are easily wiped off with a damp cloth, and indeed one Italian school even allowed the pupils to write with chalk on the actual desk surface when doing casual tests, or doing 'rough working' in arithmetic ... and why not, for it saved paper and did no harm to the desk!

Perhaps the very pleasantest of all these desks were those of the new school of La Inmaculada at Gerona. These were white, approximately square, and usually used in groups of four with the children sitting on the four sides of a large square to facilitate group work. These very pleasing desks were, I was told, made in the Marist Brothers' own workshops.

German school desks seemed to be all of much the same pattern: a rectangle with slightly rounded corners, quite often surfaced with formica, and large enough to hold two pupils side by side, seated on separate chairs, which are often of rotating pattern.

Desk frames are usually of metal; those at La Inmaculada were of a very light tubular alloy, making them delightfully easy to move, whereas one of the Ecija schools had heavy steel desks which clattered alarmingly on the tiled floors if they were moved. One advantage which the Ecija desks possessed, however, was a rubber-covered bar on which the pupil could rest his feet.

Both single and double desks are found – often the same school will have a mixture of each – except in Germany, where I do not

Buildings and equipment

think I ever saw a single-seater desk. Occasionally I came across examples of the combined desk-and-seat, but usually separate chairs are preferred. Older schools commonly have older furniture, and in Spain and Portugal I was sometimes jolted back in memory about forty-five years to a small kindergarten I briefly attended, whose standards even then were considered old-fashioned.

Other classroom furniture is pretty predictable: a teacher's desk, often rather venerable, sometimes on a raised dais, perhaps placed in a corner rather than centrally; one or more cupboards; a row of pegs to take pupils' outdoor clothing or their school smocks; a chair for the teacher (seldom used, and rarely comfortable, though I did once or twice see leather-upholstered ones). In Spain and Portugal, and in the Catholic areas of Germany, one can usually count on finding a crucifix or religious picture. Portugal sometimes produced a picture of the national leader (then Caetano); but the austere gaze of Generalissimo Franco more often dignified the headmaster's study than the classrooms of Spanish schools.

Until I came to Germany, I thought it safe to say that an absolutely constant feature of every classroom was a chalkboard, but at the Emden Wallschule some rooms in fact had none, the overhead projector being used instead – rather misguidedly, I thought. While I concede all the virtues of the projector in itself, there are situations in which the older and simpler apparatus is better: for example, one can hardly set two pupils competitively writing on the acetate sheet as one can on the chalkboard. And I found the projector somewhat difficult to read from the back of the room, where the chalkboard would probably have been legible.

It will be noted that I use the term 'chalkboard' rather than 'blackboard', though as a matter of fact they very often are literally black. To my mind the ideal chalkboard is the kind you can move up and down on rollers, but I never came across this type on the Continent. The invariable pattern in Germany is the triptych, with wings that can be folded over a central section; the whole board moves up and down very easily to adjust it to the height of the person using it; this, too, seemed to me an excellent tool. Sometimes the various sections are ruled in different ways – plain, lined and squared. Quite often there is also a supplementary board on one of the side walls. France also uses the triptych board quite often. La Inmaculada, in Spain, had some very handsome boards in metal frames, free-standing on wheels instead of being fixed to the wall; these were adjustable to any convenient angle, which is a useful provision in a country where the sunlight is sometimes dazzling. The pleasant surface was a dark bluish-green in colour. But often, alas, a school would have only plain boards fixed to the classroom walls, and those sadly in need of maintenance; sometimes there might be a pair side by side, but if there was only one, the situation was rather desperate, for far too little working-space would then be available. It is strange that this deficiency should be so common, seeing how often European teachers and their pupils use a chalkboard, and how artistically; for sheer perfection in this line, I have seen nothing to touch the blackboard-art of Porcellasco in Italy.

To clean these chalkboards, a large square sponge was the usual implement, though sometimes a simple damp cloth was used. As for chalk, it does not admit of very much variety, though some Italian schools used large sticks of square section which were very effective for shading diagrams and also could produce thick or thin lines at will.

A feature peculiar to German classrooms is that a substantial washbasin, with running water, is provided in every classroom. The initial installation may be expensive, but the idea is none the less an excellent one, for it has so many uses, from washing inky fingers to staunching a nosebleed, to say nothing of the value it must have when the room has to be used for art or science lessons. Clocks, however, are comparatively rare in German classrooms; indeed, I could not remember seeing one until a careful search through my photographs proved that I had done so, once at any rate.

Except in Portugal, audio-visual materials seemed abundant; German schools especially seemed to have just about everything – for example, the Wallschule at Emden cheerfully admitted owning three colour television receivers and a further one for black and white programmes only. The official Spanish recommendation (whether fully implemented or not, I cannot say) is that every school should own two slide projectors, one sound film projector, one 16 mm. film projector with magnetic sound, one episcope, one back-projector, one television receiver, one FM radio receiver and two different types of recording apparatus. The Italian

Scuola Media Virgilio and the La Salle College at Gerona in Spain both had installations enabling announcements to be made to all parts of the school from the headmaster's study, and the headmaster to 'listen-in' to each room. At La Inmaculada, the new complex of buildings provides closed-circuit TV and – of all things – constant piped music throughout the school. The Hermano Director was proud of this last feature, and said it was very popular with the boys. I was relieved to see that there was a merciful switch in each room enabling the teacher to cut off the supply of melody at will! A similar system existed at the Miguel de Cervantes school, Ecija, and here one classroom had a gramophone on which the teacher played soft background music of a 'pop' or 'folk' type while his eight-year-old pupils worked at their *fichas*.

Most schools make some use of broadcast or televised lessons; here the Germans undoubtedly score because broadcast programmes can be easily planned to fit their highly standardized timetable; not for them those infuriating problems of trying to use a programme which runs from 11.30 to 11.50 in a lesson which ends at 11.40.

But, of course, books are any school's principal tools. In Italy pupils of the *scuola media* and above must supply their own textbooks and stationery; in the primary school they are theoretically free, but there is a shortage of textbooks, and some pupils buy their own to make up the deficiencies. Portuguese schools too have a chronic book-shortage; there I often saw two or even three pupils sharing a copy, and sometimes only the teacher had one and the pupils had to copy out their exercises before they could do them. At São Vitor School, Braga, even routine test-papers were laboriously written out by hand, presumably for lack of duplicating facilities.

In France, Spain and many areas of Germany, the rule is that the school prescribes the books and the pupils buy them from local shops, so there is seldom any actual shortage. Books are quite expensive – one used in an Italian *scuola media*, for example, cost about £1·50, but it covered a three-year course and would last at least that length of time if treated decently. There is some traffic in second-hand books; for example, the Emden Wallschule advertised in its news-letter the holding of a 'bazaar' of second-hand books, but a later issue reported that the response had been small.

There is, in fact, quite a good case for this method of supplying textbooks. Pupils can be very careless and irresponsible in their treatment of public property, but might be less so if the books were in fact their own. The possession of a shelf of one's own school textbooks may just possibly start the book-buying habit and the annual purchase of new ones ensure that it continues. It must be this system that accounts for the appearance in quite small Continental towns of larger and better bookshops than the average English provincial city can offer: I especially recall with wonder the day when I took refuge from a sharp shower in a bookshop in the small Italian town of Bassano del Grappa (population perhaps 35,000) and found its stock to compare favourably with any I have seen outside of a university town or a really big city – and later I found a second shop every bit as good! If we assume that the average English secondary school pupil has in his possession books bought at the public expense amounting in value to some ten or twenty pounds, say, and multiply this figure by our total number of pupils, it becomes clear that there is a substantial sum of money involved, which might be devoted to other educational needs. True, it might mean that fewer pupils could afford a new tape-recorder, electric guitar or motor-bicycle, but I don't know that I should weep too much over that. Financial help would, of course, be available, as it is on the Continent, to really deserving cases.

The quality of the textbooks seemed to be generally good; they were substantially produced, on good paper and plentifully illustrated. Since they differed little from the corresponding English article, no more need be said, except to refer briefly to one category which will, I think, be almost unknown to English teachers: the 'all-purpose' book, containing within its covers all, in theory at least, that the primary school pupil needs to know of his own language, of mathematics and of general knowledge.

In Germany, the choice of textbooks appears not to be a matter for the individual school, as it is here, but for state schools acting as a whole. A committee of school heads decides on the books to be used and submits its list to the Education Minister of the state concerned. Once a book has been authorized in this way, it may not be changed until a year's notice of the change has been given, and in practice books will remain in use for some years, as obviously a number of interests – publishers, book-sellers and

Buildings and equipment

parents – are concerned to ensure that changes are not made too often. English teachers will see the disadvantages of this system; certainly, I prefer to have some say in choosing the books from which I am to teach, rather than having them picked for me by a committee to which I may not have very easy access. It is, however, interesting to note that teachers at the Colegio Nacional Juan Bruguera at Gerona in Spain quoted exactly this same desire to have freedom to choose their textbooks for themselves as a justification for operating the system of having all books bought by the pupils from the bookshops; they felt that if the educational authorities were responsible for providing the books free of charge, as in England, this must necessarily mean governmental interference in the actual choice of books. They did not appear to be convinced by my assurances that we have been able to devise a system under which that doesn't happen!

It is, however, fair to say that the German system of standardization has the very obvious advantage of making transfer between schools much easier.

German textbooks were generally quite good to look at, but the actual text often struck me as looking decidedly stodgy, though I know too little German to be a competent judge. However, since some teachers were supplementing the official textbook with photocopied extracts from other works, I am perhaps justified in thinking that not every teacher was happy with what his committee had given him.

Some recent Spanish textbooks are exceptionally good: I have a very handsome mathematics course for 13-year-olds, and the literature course for the same age-group which includes such unexpected writers as Joyce, Brecht and Sartre!

Pupils normally must provide their own exercise-books and most other stationery; this may explain why a few schools seemed almost to be undergoing a paper famine, with work done on all sorts of odd scraps. The school café sometimes sells ball-pens, rulers and exercise-books, but more often a small shop near the school augments its modest trade by supplying these necessities. Before the start of the school year, however, most big stores devote a large section to the sale of school stationery, mathematical instruments etc.

In Italy and Spain pupils often possess a little 'educational diary' rather like the 'schoolboys' diary' which I recall affectionately from my own schooldays. The Italian one is published by the children's newspaper *Corriere dei Ragazzi* and I have a Spanish one most improbably presented by the Barcelona Office for Old Age Pensions and Savings. There are, incidentally, many other small ways in which commercial firms show some interest in educational matters: for example, I have some German class timetables printed on quite attractive forms issued by the milk industry and by a local savings-bank.

Continental exercise-paper is almost always *squared*, with faint vertical lines about the same distance apart as are the horizontal ones. This is a most helpful guide in producing regular and even handwriting, and I warmly recommend it to English teachers also. The paper generally seems to come in the form of a double sheet about 8" × 6" when folded; the guide-lines are about $\frac{1}{5}$" apart, but the children write on alternate lines and leave a space of one additional line between paragraphs.

European teachers seldom hump around piles of exercise-books for marking; just as we did at my own English grammar-school in the nineteen-thirties, the pupils do homework and class tests on separate sheets of paper. It is often the practice for all this material, when marked, to be meticulously filed away for the whole of the current year, for reference by teachers, parents, inspectors or anyone else concerned. This may take up space, and consume some time and effort, but it may well pay dividends to have the material available when discussing the pupil's progress or prescribing remedial action. German schools similarly keep the work on which periodical assessments are based, and these are retained for at least two years, I believe; one school devoted the whole of its upper storey to housing the considerable amount of paper involved, and one hopes that no school ever suffers the fate that befell the British Parliament in 1834 as a result of a similar accumulation of ancient records.

Where exercise-books are in use – for note-taking, for example – it seems to be usually left to the pupils to choose the pattern they find most convenient. In Germany, however, one type seemed very prevalent: this was a rather small, slim book, often with squared pages, and always with rather wide white margins on both sides of the page. I should imagine that pupils get through a considerable number of these in the course of the year; however, their compactness and lightness is certainly a convenience.

8
Away from the classroom

Those who would argue that Britain won the Battle of Waterloo upon her playing-fields could doubtless argue that France lost it upon hers, and it is certainly true that no other countries have ever exalted sport to quite the same place in the educational pantheon as have the English-speaking peoples (for we must surely count the USA among the ball-worshipping nations). Nevertheless, sport is by no means wholly ignored in European schools.

School magazines often provide some clues about the sporting activities of the schools which publish them. An Italian magazine such as *Il Formicaio* contains no reference to sport except the occasional youthful article on some favourite professional player or popular team; but of course the half-day basis of Italian schooling is bound to operate against any kind of out-of-school activity. In *La Farga*, the magazine of the Menendez Pidal school at Salt, results frequently appear of weekly or fortnightly games of football, handball and basketball at various levels against other schools. *Feder*, published by the Zewen Hauptschule, Trier, reports both internal tournaments and occasional inter-school championships in football, swimming and athletics.

Some quite young pupils at Miguel de Cervantes school, Ecija, had a football league, with the four teams named with titles taken from local history. A French CES had a variety of games running on a voluntary 'club' basis. In Portugal I was several times shown trophies and pennants gained by school teams or by individuals in competitive games or athletics, and this was at both primary and secondary level. La Inmaculada college at Gerona had a large notice in its patio announcing the result of a recent volleyball match against a rival school. The Emden *Realschule* had a basketball team, but I was told that there was at present no football team as there was no teacher able or willing to run one.

From these brief comments it may be gathered that there is seldom quite as highly-organized a sporting side to European schools as ours generally have; but everywhere (least, perhaps, in France) there is plenty of informal sport. If anything kickable is to be had, and there is a reasonable space in which to kick it, one may be sure that a game of football will be contrived within moments. Some schools also thoughtfully provide a certain number of indoor games to occupy their pupils in leisure periods; for example, La Inmaculada had a sort of table-football, played by cut-out players moved by rods, which was immensely popular (and perhaps more acceptable than the real thing on a grilling Spanish summer's day).

This may be as good a moment as any to remark that I was somewhat upset when a Spanish class innocently asked me whether football was played in England. I pointed out with asperity that we had, after all, invented the game: I forebore to add that nowadays there may be some reason to wish we hadn't. Another moment I prefer not to think of was when another group of Spanish boys asked me to tell them how the game of cricket is played; I did my best, but the resources of the Spanish language are not quite adequate to the task.

Apart from games, there is a fair variety of out-of-school activities to be found in most European schools. The range is narrower than here; for example, I saw no evidence that such activities as Scouting are practised in the schools, though I met a number of individual boys and girls who belonged to Scout or Guide organizations or the like. Nor is there any parallel to the Cadet

Corps which sometimes exist at the secondary level in England: indeed, I think this particular type of activity might be rather frowned on in some of the countries.

In Germany, out-of-school activities are not in a very strong position. The Zewen school at Trier apparently does something in the way of concerts and plays, mainly as a part of its 'AG' *Arbeitsgemeinschaft*) programme. This school also, as already mentioned, has a fair amount of sport taking place. Elsewhere in Germany, there was not very much doing. The lively headmaster of the Treckfahrtstief Gymnasium at Emden, Herr Wittneben, said he regretted this very much and was trying hard to stimulate something of the kind; he would like to have large numbers of pupils returning in the afternoons for voluntary activities such as clubs, games, theatre and music. His problem is to find enthusiastic staff to run these things, however. The choir has been restarted after a hiatus, and some drama. Other schools reported very little.

It is not for me to cast stones in any direction, but it was my impression that the German teacher is not going to be easy to move in this particular direction. His teaching programme is limited to a specific number of teaching periods; when he has done these, he is free to go home, and he generally does so; consequently, it is rare to find more than the odd individual in a German staff-room during teaching hours. Obviously this tradition of watching the clock carefully leaves little room for rehearsing plays, coaching football teams or running school clubs.

In France, things are somewhat brighter. A feature often found is the 'Foyer Socio-Culturel': I have before me the duplicated rules and organization of one such in the CES J. B. Pellerin at Beauvais. The object of the *Foyer* is there stated to be 'the promotion, co-ordination and encouragement of all the school's extra-scholastic activities – intellectual, artistic, social, sporting or outdoor'. The *Foyer* is run by the pupils themselves, with some adult participation. It must not be used to propagate any political or religious attitudes. Membership is open to all students of the school, to all staff, and to anyone else approved by the management committee; it embraces not only clubs with special interests such as the theatre, cinema, music or photography, but also sections which are affiliated to other associations, such as, presumably, sporting clubs or Scouts, which would also have their own governing bodies. Each section or club has its own pupil-representative, and also what is called an *animateur technique*; this last official may be a senior pupil, a teacher or *surveillant*, or an approved person from outside the school. The other statutes of the *Foyer* deal with its committees, funds and so on; as they are very precisely and legally worded, it appears that the whole thing is on a much more formal basis than would normally be found in an English school.

Here, as in sport, Italy is probably almost a non-starter, though I heard of a voluntary gardening group in one school, and also heard one or two choirs practising. I also know of a *scuola media* in Bari where about two-thirds of the pupils return in the afternoon for voluntary activities of many kinds. Italian schoolchildren do seem, however, to be very good at mobilizing practical help for those who need it; the press has reported instances of classes 'adopting' a school-mate whose family has met with misfortune, and a school near Pisa recently raised about £700 to buy a Tibetan bear which was in danger of being killed for its skin to pay its owner's debts!

I heard a very pleasant-sounding choir rehearsing at the *liceu* in Evora, Portugal, and the technical school there also stages plays and concerts from time to time. In Spain, too, there was much evidence that plays and concerts occur, and this must imply the existence of groups which meet out of school hours to rehearse. The Instituto J. V. Vives at Gerona told me of their recent production of a Catalan version of Aristophanes' 'The Clouds' (they assured me that it goes far better into Catalan than Spanish, and I'd love to know why!). Schools with boarders took trouble to provide spare-time activities for them, including handicrafts; and there was even a small play-park for the very youngest children at the Marist College, Jaén. I had evidence that photography was flourishing in one or two Spanish schools, and at the Colegio Santo Tomás in Jaén, I saw pupils making titles for a film they had produced.

One year's issues of the school magazine of Menendez Pidal School at Salt, in Catalonia, shed some interesting light on the extra-curricular activities of this quite modest-sized school: they had set up teachers' committees to deal with sport, cinema, handicraft, music and drama, and the initial plan envisaged, *inter alia*, a Christmas play and a choral recital in the same season. Later we

Away from the classroom

read of a four-weekly cycle of activities taking place, all on Saturday mornings, with a festival of all the groups to round off the series; and each term thereafter the magazine carries brief notices of concerts, plays and art exhibitions as well as a wide range of sporting activities. One event which will strike an exotic note to English teachers is the 'Floral Games' announced for the spring term; prizes were to be awarded under five headings: the best floral arrangement; the best performance of songs, original or otherwise, sung either as solo or group items, and in either Spanish or Catalan; the best Catalan poem on a set subject; the best recitation of poetry in either Spanish or Catalan on a regional theme; the best essay in either language on 'Books and the Media'.

This use of Saturday mornings for extra-curricular activities is becoming the regular thing in Spain, and one may see a variety of groups going about their tasks on that day; one lovely spring morning, for example, I walked along the main avenue in Gerona and passed twenty or thirty boys aged about ten, all utterly absorbed in transferring to their sketching-blocks their notions of the handsome old houses lining the side of the street. The drawings were perhaps a little stiff and solemn; but one could not miss the enjoyment the children were obviously deriving from the activity, or help admiring the seriousness with which they were doing it.

School outings and excursions take place in every country. The Scuola Media Virgilio frequently reports in its magazine school trips to other cities: for example, 2A and 2F went to Florence one day in April, visiting the Cathedral, the Palazzo Pitti, and other places; and some of them, apparently, had their first-ever experience of a self-service restaurant there. A more recent issue of the same magazine mentions another visit to Florence (and prints its report, somewhat oddly, in German); there is also a long list of more local visits carried out by various classes over about six months, the places included ranging from museums and places of architectural interest to the workshop of a distinguished maker of musical instruments. One rather off-beat expedition was a tour of shop-window displays specializing in household goods; possibly this was part of a domestic science course. Day trips to Rome and to Bolzano are mentioned; and two third forms spent four days in Rome towards the end of the spring term. Other Italian schools

F

also mentioned similar visits; and in the São Vitor primary school at Braga in Portugal I found that the class timetable actually included a regular period for such visits, on one of which I was privileged to accompany a class of lively, but very well-behaved, youngsters on a conducted tour of the remarkable city library and archives.

In a rather different category are the special schools set up all over France, to which whole classes go for a week or two at a time with their teacher. These visits take place during term-time, and as well as special activities appropriate to the place, the children do a fairly full programme of ordinary work with their own teacher. There are *écoles de neige*, held in winter in the mountains, where the children can learn winter sports; *écoles de campagne* and *écoles de montagne*, where they take part in country and mountain activities respectively; and *écoles de mer*, held by the sea. They are not to be confused with the *colonies de vacances*, which are quite independent of the schools, though the latter often co-operate closely with them; these are simply children's holiday-camps.

Another flourishing activity in many schools is the production of a school magazine. Three different Italian schools provided me with copies of some kind of printed or duplicated magazine, of which the most ambitious is *Il Formicaio*, produced by the Scuola Media Virgilio at Cremona; I have referred to this incidentally several times already. It is a long-standing publication; the latest issue I have is headed '24th Year, no 1'. My copies were edited by various different sets of pupils, but all seem to belong to forms 2E or 3E, which leads me to think that 'E' denotes the initial of a particular teacher and that she uses the pupils of her own class as editors. Issues sell at 150 lire a copy, for which one gets eight or twelve pages of quite good-quality paper, about $10'' \times 13''$, printed in double columns and with plenty of illustrations. It seems to appear twice a year, once in December and once in the spring or early summer. The editors are always boys, but whether this means that only boys are considered to have editorial talent and/or business acumen, or whether the class consists only of boys, I cannot say. Contributions, however, come from both boys and girls, and they are always well-written. They include such varied items as a proposal for the reorganization of the school timetable, an obituary of Picasso, short book reviews, articles about individual or group journeys, a thoughtful little article on the colour problem and a passionate plea for the conservation of wild life, some reflections on the effects of the petrol-famine, and a good deal of direct and sincere poetry.

One feature of *Il Formicaio* which we may find rather unusual is its 'Roll of Honour', which prints, at great length, the names of all pupils who gain an average mark of 70 per cent or better in the terminal examinations: the end-of-year list for 1972–3 included the names of sixty-five boys and sixty-eight girls.

Il Formicaio is professionally printed; but *Il Lanternino*, published by the small village school of Porcellasco, is entirely home-produced. Issue no. 3, of 1972–3, is devoted to the theme of 'Winter', and almost every child seems to have contributed something, even if it is only one line of big, childish handwriting. There are just over twenty foolscap pages, bound into a blue cover; about half of them are printed by the children on their own small hand-press, and the rest are cyclostyled. Almost every page has some coloured decoration, either a coloured lino-cut or a spray-painted background suggesting snowflakes or some other wintry feature; the whole effect is distinctly pretty. Again, a good deal of the work is in verse.

The two Spanish magazines I have seen are both duplicated productions. The Colegio Martin Noguera at Jaén launched its magazine in 1973, and at present it runs to only about four pages per issue. It includes an editorial by the headmaster or director of studies, some cartoons, one or two brief articles on general topics, some short letters from pupils and rather a lot of earnest moral exhortation such as 'A good pupil is a credit to his school: what are *you*?' or 'To do our duty is the highest form of self-fulfilment'. The pupils' letters are interesting: a twelve-year-old pleads for the setting-up of a school branch of the Rescue Service; another asks for some organized chess; a third wants a school excursion, mysteriously adding the proviso 'but *not* to Ubeda' (which seems an unjust slight on a very delightful town!). Others call attention to the need for repairs to the basketball courts or to the shortage of coat-pegs; classes in karate and an end-of-term dance are proposed; and the twelve-year-olds complain that they need a mid-morning break, even if it is only a few minutes to eat a sandwich. The staff hit back, too: some pupils have been loafing about on the premises at week-ends; others are unpunctual, or their language is indelicate; there is a lack of sportsmanship on the games-field. . . . Back again come the pupils: can't we have a choir, a dramatic production, handball and basketball matches against other schools or among ourselves? It is a different concept of a school magazine, no doubt; but this kind of dialogue surely has some value, at the very least?

The other Spanish magazine is the product of Menendez Pidal school at Salt. Again, it is a recent innovation, issue no. 1 being dated October 1973; but by March 1974 four issues had already appeared, making it one of the most frequently published of such magazines. It is bilingual, some pages being in Catalan, others in Spanish, and it is a lively little production, despite its simple cyclostyled format. There are sketches and cartoons in plenty; puzzle-pages; items of school news; reports of sporting and other activities; some quite interesting articles on the history and life of the little town of Salt, now to be swallowed-up by its big neighbour Gerona; and articles both by teachers and pupils. In the first issue, a fourteen-year-old writes in warm praise of his new school building – which must, indeed, seem a paradise compared with its grim predecessor – but is also prepared to offer some critical comment: the playground needs to be levelled so that pupils do not ruin their trousers on the sharp stones if they happen to fall over; the wall of the neighbouring convent should be fitted with netting to avoid the loss of footballs (or presumably aerial bombardment of the Sisterhood, though this is not mentioned); and there is one great lack still – a swimming-pool. By the time issues 3 and 4 appear, the flood of poetry has begun, and will doubtless flow for a very long time; there are also accounts of school visits, to a bakery, a butchery, a sheep farm, a power-station. . . .

I have not seen any school magazine from France, other than some produced as part of the *Pédagogie Freinet* mentioned in an earlier chapter. A group of these have come into my possession from various schools in the Département de l'Oise: first, there is the *Journal de la Joie* from a school in Bonvilliers, with some most attractive coloured decorations; then *Gerbe*, which covers schools from four places in the Canton de Breteuil, and in fact reprints one or two of the Bonvilliers pages; next, *Le Petit Oiseau Bleu*, produced by some very young pupils of a school at Méru; and finally, a less colourful but more literary production called *Bonjour*, from a CES in Beauvais. All these are home-produced, like the

Away from the classroom

Porcellasco magazine already described, and in their various ways they are quite attractive.

As far as Portugal is concerned, I have not come across any school magazines; but I cannot resist mentioning here Maria Rosa Colaço's little book *A Criança e a Vida* with its remarkable collection of children's verse. While it is obviously difficult to evaluate poetry in a language one does not know really well, I would risk saying that the quality of some of the verses in this book is as high as that of any children's writing that has ever come my way. I may not quote extensively from it here, but I will allow myself just one poem, by a little boy of nine, Victor Barroca Moreira, whose wistfully poignant verse can sometimes turn a thought in a way that perhaps Andrew Marvell might have done if he had written verse at the age of nine:

> In this happy school,
> with poems on the walls,
> little children painting,
> and flowers in vases,
> everything's fine.
>   But I'm writing this poem,
> which comes from my heart
> in this hour of peace.
> I hope some time to go
> to the mourning blackboard
> to do some addition sums,
> and in that simple moment
> to draw on the pink wall
> a new sea with white foam
> and little boats,
> and sail into that joyful morning.

Lastly, Germany. Here, with characteristic insistence on having everything organized, the regulations for the Gymnasien of Rhineland-Palatinate actually lay it down that pupils have the legal right to produce a school newspaper, and that the regulations for so doing will be found stated in 'Orders for School Newspapers'. I have not actually seen the resulting publication, though I was told at the Hindenburg-Gymnasium, Trier, that a newspaper called *Pons* is published, officially once a month but in practice rather less often.

But a Hauptschule at Zewen did provide me with several copies of its magazine, *Feder*. This periodical is issued about three times a year as a product of the *Arbeitsgemeinschaft* periods, and the pupils have their own printing-shop where it is produced. One of the staff, I gather, was a printer before switching to teaching, and under his direction a very workmanlike set-up is installed in a basement room. To take one issue as typical of all, there are eight printed pages and a further sixteen of duplicated material, either typed or hand-written. Coloured inks are used quite effectively, and many pages are enlivened with small drawings, but attempts at reproducing photographs are not always very successful. The content of the magazine is fairly serious, though there are usually one or two lighter features; however, the rather earnest prevailing tone is illustrated by articles on modern maths (addressed to parents), notes from the cookery class, a brief study of the French educational system and a discussion on a proposed change of name for the school. There are usually a number of items of official information such as lists of the parents' committee members, dates of the main school holidays and details of school visits.

I conclude this chapter on extra-curricular activities with a brief reference to the purely social events which the pupils sometimes arrange to mark the end of term or of the school year. At the CES J. B. Pellerin in Beauvais I was invited to an end-of-term party put on by a first-year class. They had invited all their class teachers; the room was decorated, a pleasant little exhibition of art and craft work was laid out, and refreshment of home-made cakes, cherries, cider and soft drinks was offered. The children had also prepared a programme of entertainment including music, poetry-reading and the presentation of some very beautiful projects they had carried out in connection with their set reader, *Lettres de mon Moulin*. These included such varied ideas as hand-drawn slides illustrating episodes from the book, an ingenious cardboard 'television set' whose 'screen' showed pictures which were wound past on rollers on the principle of the destination-indicator on a bus; and, best of all, one of the girls presented a quite remarkable medieval-style illuminated manuscript – a folio-sized volume with every word exquisitely hand-lettered in Gothic script: a labour of love if ever I saw one. Children really have the most astonishing skill and patience when they are sufficiently motivated! The leading spirits in this delightful party were the girls: the boys seemed cheerfully content to tag along as hewers of wood and drawers of water. I believe that end-of-term gatherings of this kind are found elsewhere, too; unfortunately I could only be in one place at a time, and so I have no other first-hand experience of one.

Two newspaper reports from Portugal describe rather more formal end-of-term events at Oliveira de Aziméis, a little industrial town of a few thousand inhabitants south of Oporto. The pupils of the *liceu*, the *escola preparatoria* and the technical school started the day's festivities with a gymnastic display, followed by basketball and handball tournaments; there then followed a celebration lunch attended by both teachers and pupils, followed by what was coyly termed a 'cultural session', and then an 'exhibition of school activities undertaken throughout the year, a magnificent display'. The day ended with more sports. As well as the teachers and pupils, all the local educational bigwigs were present, and, to quote once more, 'they did not conceal their satisfaction with everything which was presented to them'. Undoubtedly, a good time was had by all.

The second report described the individual festivities of one of these schools, the *escola preparatoria* (the school filling the gap between primary and upper school). This event took place in the local cinema, and the newspaper prints at some length the names and official styles of the various dignitaries whose presence graced the occasion. The entertainment presented included regional dances, poetry, choral singing and the performance of a play of which the newspaper weightily remarks '. . . set in an agreeable setting, and entirely rewarding to the efforts of the young pupils'. This same report, by the way, speaks of the first appearance of a magazine edited by the pupils of this school, which it describes as 'well-produced, with good graphical presentation and a foreword by the Director'. This is the only actual reference to a Portuguese school magazine which I have come across, but no doubt there are others.

9
Pastoral care and welfare

Increasingly today almost the most important part of a school's responsibility to its pupils is seen to be the provision of advice and guidance, help with choice of careers, remedial work where necessary for those who have fallen behind in their studies, and making sure that physical handicap or lack of material resources does not mean loss of opportunities to achieve a full and useful life. Good teachers have always known this, and have acted in their own way to supply their pupils' needs; but private enterprise in such matters can be selective in its application, and so today most good schools have some more or less organized way of ensuring pastoral care for their pupils, while the State itself, through its welfare services, deals with financial or physical needs.

Schools can still differ greatly, however, in their willingness to tackle these problems; in some the teacher is still not very interested to know about his pupils' home circumstances, regarding his function as ending at the classroom door, and as simply that of imparting a specific quantity of physics or English to his class; in another school, the teacher may well find himself acting as welfare officer, marriage-guidance counsellor, home-help or psychiatric social-worker, according to the nature of the latest problem posed him by the latest problem child. It is possible that in the kind of towns I visited, and in countries like Spain and Italy where the unity of family life is still immensely strong, the more harrowing problems arise more rarely than they would in the large cities and in the unnatural and inhuman conditions of our industrialized societies; still, they do arise now and then, and the school may be expected to provide for them.

In all these situations, the key-figure is the form-master or form-mistress, the one person who in primary and lower-secondary classes sees the pupil for all or nearly all his school hours; and even in the more specialized organization of the upper-secondary school, this teacher will still have a special, and very personal, responsibility. His greatest asset will be his ability to form a bond of understanding, even of affection, with his pupils; but however far he succeeds or fails in this, there are two other things which, if it can be contrived, he ought to have. One is an adequate system of records, to provide him fully and quickly with the information he requires – Has the child lost his father? Has he a number of brothers or sisters? What is his home like? Has he bad eyesight? Is he left-handed? – and any other similar information which may be available. The other need is some means of meeting the child's parents to talk with them comfortably about his problems; and this means having a room available and some time available at which he is known to be free from all other duties and at liberty to meet parents.

I have already, I hope, made it clear that I came back from Europe full of respect and admiration for the decency and dedication of the average teacher; but the ways in which school organization supported their efforts demand rather more comment.

In a number of schools there were rooms provided in which staff and parents could meet in reasonable comfort and privacy. One school, the A. Fabretti primary school at Perugia, required every member of staff to be available once a month for seeing any parent who wished to come, though I was told that only a limited number of parents availed themselves of the opportunity. In the Virgilio middle school, at Cremona, every teacher was allotted a free hour each week in his timetable for the same purpose, and this also happened at several of the Spanish schools; and there was similar provision for counselling individual pupils, both there and in some of the French schools. I did form the perhaps unfair impression that parents were somewhat less warmly welcomed in certain French schools than elsewhere; and as for Portugal, one head told me that there was little tradition of involving parents there, because, he thought, the average Portuguese works hard and works late, and therefore is less amenable to the idea of turning out again for evening meetings and interviews.

But I certainly found many Portuguese teachers to be just as well-informed and concerned about their pupils as others, so that the relative lack of contact is less of a handicap than one might imagine; perhaps small provincial communities, where everyone knows everyone else, provide efficient informal ways of acquiring information. But there are other ways too; and in the Colegio Menendez Pidal at Salt (Spain) I was interested to see the walls of the staff room covered with 'sociograms' carefully prepared by the class teachers. If any of my readers don't know what a sociogram is (and I didn't) it is a diagram showing the linking of pupil with pupil in friendship groups; and the object of this particular survey at Salt was to enable teachers to arrange the pupils in the most effective groups for their work, in accordance with the approved modern practice of Spanish schools. Natural group leaders emerged very clearly in this diagrammatic form, as did also the 'loners' who would need help to integrate them into the work-pattern of the class.

As well as meetings with parents, staff meetings are of course highly desirable, and I found the concept of the 'class council' to be widely developed. At the Scuola Media Virgilio, for instance, the class teacher must convene once a month all his colleagues who teach the form – probably not a very large number of people – and preside over a discussion with them about the pupils and their progress; minutes are kept and sent to the headmaster for his information. There is a similar system, though only operating about twice a term, at the Saint-Esprit college at Beauvais in France; and at the Porcellasco primary school the staff meet each Saturday morning (when the pupils have no school) to discuss the past week and prepare for the coming one. Parents sometimes come in on their discussions also. This is an excellent idea, which could be adapted to many schools; would it really be so very terrible if, say, the children were every so often dismissed an hour early and the time spent on such mental stocktaking?

A similar solution had been found to a slightly different problem in Gerona, where on the Saturday of my visit the local schools had abandoned their usual morning's activities to allow a district teachers' meeting to take place, addressed by the Inspector of Schools.

In French secondary schools, the class council have a wider counterpart in the *conseil d'éducation*, which discusses certain aspects of school policy; on this body, parents may be represented either statutorily or exceptionally.

This is also as good a place as any to mention a curious German institution, that of the *Verbindungslehrer*. Whether one should translate this term as 'liaison teacher', or, bearing in mind that the dictionary translation of *Verbindung* is 'union', call him the 'shop steward', I don't quite know. His function is apparently to represent the interests of the pupils in staff discussions, and he is chosen either by the pupil-representatives or by the school assembly. An English teacher who had just completed a year's service in Germany gave me to understand that the functions of this official can at times be productive of a little staff-room friction!

Few teachers probably enjoy the keeping of records, but they undoubtedly can help us to do our jobs a little better. I felt that European schools emerged very well out of a comparison with our own in this aspect of their work, even if the strong European tradition of bureaucracy occasionally makes the documentation a little excessive. For example, in Spain one was constantly confronted with a creation known as an *organigrama*, a sort of flow-diagram or chart showing the organization of the school or its individual departments. Like an impending hanging, it no doubt concentrates the mind wonderfully, though I doubt whether it in fact achieves any greater efficiency. A sporting attempt to produce one for my own school, indeed, only taught me something about the different national characteristics of Spain and England, for whereas a Spanish *organigrama* is beautifully neat, mine resembled an octopus's knitting, with strange curves doubling back on themselves or passing through one another. For what other nations would refer through stages of an ordered hierarchy to a final decision by the appropriate committee, is often decided here over a cup of tea in the staff-room.

The first really comprehensive set of school archives I saw was in the fine modern building of the Scuola Media Virgilio, in Cremona. Here I was shown a large room fitted with sets of shelves from floor almost to ceiling, which could be smoothly rolled back to reveal more, and still more, shelves. On these were kept all the information one could reasonably demand concerning the pupils. To my surprise, however, the actual records themselves were kept by a method more suited to the days of quill-pens and clerks on high stools than to an age which has invented the computer: they were in vast, hand-written ledgers, with three pupils' particulars on each double page. Full and careful as the records were, the system seemed to me highly inconvenient; to find any one pupil's data involved taking down an enormously heavy tome and turning the pages until one arrived at the desired name; and of course, the order in which names appeared was inflexible. Another school with very extensive records kept in absolutely apple-pie order was the La Salle College at Gerona; the male secretary here took particular pride in his work, and I can well understand this.

A rather unusual way of keeping records was that used at the *liceu* in Evora, Portugal. Here a big loose-leaf file was kept in each classroom, with a single sheet devoted to each pupil in the class; on the front of the sheet were entered the personal details – name, address, family background, physical characteristics; on the back were columns for recording all the test-marks as soon as they were given; thus the book served both as a class record-file and as a continuous register of marks.

To my surprise, the record documents used in some German schools seemed rather primitive. One, for example, was headed with the word *Beobachtungsbogen*, which certainly sounds impressive (literally it means 'Observation Sheet') but it was no more than a foolscap-sized sheet of paper bearing a duplicated *pro forma* calling for the pupil's name, date of birth, parents' names, position in family, a note of such factors as left-handedness, dyslexia or asthma, and then a series of ruled lines under the headings Class / Date / Remarks / Teachers' initials. There was nothing to indicate *what* remarks the teacher was supposed to make, and no attempt to divide up the sheet so that different types of observation could be kept separate. If other German schools have other systems – and one would hope they did – I can only say that I was not shown any.

Pastoral care and welfare

However, in the Früchteburg Schule and in the Treckfahrtstief Gymnasium, I spent some time browsing through the classroom log-books which partly fulfil the purpose of record-books also. They were substantially bound volumes, about foolscap-sized; most of the book was taken up with the work logs, on the basis of one day to a page, but the volume also incorporated the class mark register, the attendance-record, details of the teachers who take the class and of the class timetable, and such information as the names of the class prefect and its representative on the school committee, plus space for recording medical and psychological data about the pupils. It was all very comprehensive, but the effect was marred when one teacher remarked 'Not many of us bother to fill all that up!' In any case, personal data about the pupils is not best kept in a book which lies all day on the teacher's desk and can be looked at by the pupils themselves, if they are so minded, during the breaks between lessons.

I acquired specimens of record documents from a number of Spanish schools. One of these was the Colegio Juan Bruguera at Gerona, whose documents are typical of those used in Spanish state schools. The *Registro Personal del Alumno* ('Pupil's Personal Record-Card') is a formal and highly important document, which begins as soon as the pupil starts school and goes with him thereafter, unless he changes school, in which case only a copy of relevant extracts is sent to the new school. The card contains details of the pupil's home and background, health record, results of 'evaluation', classified as 'basic knowledge', 'aptitudes and personality', 'social behaviour', 'habits of work and study' and 'interests and plans for the future'.

Secondly, there is a handy-sized card colloquially called the ERPA (an acronym for *Extracto del Registro Personal del Alumno*) which is the normal working document. This card is very carefully completed at stated intervals during the year; it serves for only one year at a time, and is a white card measuring about 8" × 6" on which are entered all the details a teacher might wish to keep. My one reservation about this admirable card is that the space allowed for some entries is rather limited: one square inch, for example, for an assessment of 'behaviour and sociability'. More space for such data could be made, perhaps, by omitting some of the more bureaucratic details such as the pupil's place of birth and his father's age; perhaps also the recording of vaccinations on this card is rather superfluous, since they must surely be recorded elsewhere.

The back of the ERPA provides space for recording the pupil's scores, subject by subject, in the five annual 'evaluations', as well as space for final decisions on promotions, recommendations for remedial work and so on. One bureaucratic touch is that the card carries space for the signatures of both class teacher and head teacher: one pities the latter if he has to sign personally for a thousand pupils each year!

A third document from the Juan Bruguera school is a large yellow card folder; when opened up, this measures about $14\frac{1}{2}"$ $\times$ $9\frac{3}{4}"$, with its fold slightly off-centre to allow the part bearing the pupil's name to stand up clearly when filed. What then becomes the outer side carries a summary of the pupil's history, including full family details and medical data; the back carries twelve columns covering a possible four years of nursery school and eight of EGB, with spaces to record gradings in conduct, punctuality, application, attendance and what is cryptically called 'self-correction', which is probably the capacity to learn from one's errors; there are also spaces for numerical assessments, remedial work etc. The standards corresponding to marks gained are given as 'Very Unsatisfactory' (below 3); 'Unsatisfactory' (3–4); 'Satisfactory' (5–6); 'Good' (6–7); 'Commendable' (7–$8\frac{1}{2}$) and 'Outstanding' ($8\frac{1}{2}$–10).

Inside the folder is space for a photograph and a great deal more personal information. Most of the space provided is for recording, four times in the pupil's career, at 'nursery age', six, ten and fourteen, an analysis of his physical and intellectual development, temperament, aptitudes, etc. For many of these, the 'opposites' method is used, classifying the pupil as approximating more nearly to, say, active/passive, initiative/routine, intuitive/reasoning and sporting/sedentary. There are also spaces for careers guidance and for recording the pupil's relations with the school after leaving.

This is an excellent record-system, adequate for all normal needs if properly used. About equally good, though with somewhat different virtues and weaknesses, is the record-booklet which I acquired from a French primary school, which is also, I think, a fairly standard one. It has eight pages, in a green card cover, about $13\frac{1}{2}"$ $\times$ $8"$; it is sent from one school to another if

Pastoral care and welfare 167

the pupil moves, and a prominent note says that it should not be shown to the class-teacher until he has had the pupil a full term, so that he can first form his own honest opinion of the child – a wise provision so long as the head does pass on facts that the class-teacher really ought to know, such as that the child is hard of hearing or subject to epileptic seizures. Another wise comment on this booklet is that children are developing creatures, liable to periods of advance and periods of stagnation, so that one must be careful not to let one year's comment influence the next.

Page 1 records data passed on from the infant school, and also the pupil's medical record, with some interesting and rather unusual comments on his capacity for physical activities: 'Individual: daring/fearful/active/indifferent' and 'Group: self-effacing/shows initiative/competitive/shows team-spirit'.

Page 2, as well as the information on the Spanish card relating to family background, records the parents' own level of education, the child's relations with the rest of his family, the length of his daily journey to school, the suitability of his home conditions for working and the family's degree of contact with the school – all useful to the conscientious class-teacher. Page 3 records results of standard tests or psychological tests of aptitude; page 4 is used for annual assessments of the pupil's attentiveness, comprehension, memory, effort, rhythm of work, discipline, general attitude to school and manual or artistic abilities; all except the last are recorded on a three-point scale in which A represents the most desirable attitude and C the least: for example, under 'Discipline' we find 'A: capable of self-discipline; B: disciplined through passivity or fear of sanctions; C: undisciplined or disorderly'. Shades of meaning can be indicated by underlining any part of the explanatory rubric.

Pages 5 and 6 record, on a similar three-point scale, the assessments in individual school subjects, and also record whether at the end of his five years of primary school the pupil has adequately mastered the techniques of reading and arithmetic, both manipulative and reasoning; these pages are mainly used in connection with the transfer to secondary school. Pages 7 and 8 contain other transfer data, including the comments of the Inspector of Primary Education and the decision of the committee as to whether the pupil should be admitted forthwith to the CES, required to sit an examination, or otherwise dealt with. Two pages are required for this in case the pupil has to repeat his final year of primary school.

The Spanish and French documents are not quite parallel in fact; the former is a continuous record for a pupil whose school life is normally spent in the same school, while the latter is at any rate partly a diagnostic document used to enable the pupil to be placed in the most suitable secondary course. The Spanish card folder is more convenient to use than the French booklet, but the range of information in the French is more useful than that of the Spanish, good as the latter is.

French parents are also apparently sent a questionnaire early in the child's school career, and from this much of the information in the booklet must derive. The questions are very detailed, and one would imagine that the building up of such information must be of very great value to the teacher, provided that the parent does not misunderstand, and therefore resent, their being asked.

I also have a French secondary school dossier before me, from the CES J. B. Pellerin, and relating to pupils in the *premier cycle* of the course. It is a large buff-coloured card folder, about 13" × 9½". There is not very much information actually entered on the folder itself, which mainly serves as a cover in which to keep separate sheets; my specimen contains three of these: the first, printed in red, is simply divided into sections, one for each year of the course, without headings, for the insertion of any relevant data concerning the pupil's character; the second sheet, printed in orange, is the 'Medico-pedagogic' record (one must enter a mild protest against these jargoniferous words: I have a rich collection, including such gems as 'Psycho-motor Aptitudes' and 'Psychosomatic Factors'); I take it that this term anyway only means 'School Medical Record'. This is a rather more useful form, actually, providing for six tests covering vision, hearing, constitution ('robust/good/mediocre' – no decent French child will have a 'poor' constitution, evidently), growth ('rapid/normal/slow'), group for physical education (I–IV), tiredness (normal or excessive), and school difficulties. The third sheet is headed 'Socio-Familial' – I despair of translating that, but the message comes through clearly enough – and on this are entered the answers to a variety of questions similar to those on the corresponding part of the primary school dossier. This third sheet is printed in blue.

I do not think so highly of this form of dossier as I do of the

Pastoral care and welfare 169

other two; it is adequate enough, but it leaves a vague impression, compared with the precise and well-chosen headings of the primary-school booklet, and calls perhaps for more thought and invention than a busy teacher will always be able to spare for it. One does not quite see why the admirable primary school dossier has not simply been adapted for use at the secondary level, keeping, however, the loose-leaf format of the secondary dossier, which is probably rather more flexible in use than a booklet.

So much for personal records. But many other records are kept: was not the old-time English teacher told that it didn't matter what he did so long as he kept his register correctly? I observed that in some schools – the Evora *liceu* in Portugal was one – every teacher was required to note at the start of his lesson the names (or rather, in this case, the class-numbers) of those pupils who were not present; we hear much today about the over-large schools where nobody knows exactly who should be anywhere at any time, and pupils turn up for the morning roll-call and then quietly disappear about their own business for the rest of the day, but surely this European system would go far to prevent such truancy, for with the class log-book testifying against them, few miscreants could get away with their truancy for long. At Evora the log-book in due course finds its way to the headmaster, so he has the best possible means of knowing if any of his pupils are absenting themselves frequently. Evora, indeed, even has the answer to the teacher, if such there be, who doesn't know who *ought* to be in his lesson, for outside each room is a glazed frame containing a neat typewritten list of the pupils in that class, together with a condensed summary of their timetable and the names of the teachers in charge of each subject.

Two forms of documentation which are perhaps unfamiliar to English teachers must now be considered. One of these is the record of minutes of the class council, whose periodical meetings have already been mentioned; these minutes also are submitted to the headmaster for his information. The second important document is the official log-book of work done.

Most countries use these; they are generally kept in quite considerable detail, teachers being expected to enter a summary of the work covered in each lesson, together with homework set, notes of absentees, and so on. Often there is a further space in which the teacher can later add additional comments. Again, the log-books go to the headmaster for his inspection; in one French school, the log-books were kept in racks outside the headmaster's office; but usually they seem to live more or less permanently in the teacher's classroom. The value of such a record is obvious enough; from it the teacher himself, his head of department, his headmaster and all the world can see whether he is filling the unforgiving minute with sixty seconds' worth of distance run, and no doubt suitable action is taken if he persistently doesn't. Such a system should effectively dispose of certain recurrent curses – the parent who complains, with little justice, that his son is not being given enough work; the pupil who justifies his score of 8 per cent in the terminal exam with the plea that 'Mr Jones never taught us that, sir!' – and possibly the teacher who spends half of every lesson telling the class what he did in the Navy in 1942...

Many English schools (I beat my own breast...) adopt a very hit-or-miss approach to the keeping of proper records of work done, and it might do us good to have this particular discipline imposed on us. However, honesty compels me to admit that there was much difference between the meticulous care with which the best log-books were kept and the more casual and condensed entries I saw elsewhere. I think the Italian schools usually came out best from this particular test.

Even the actual tests done by the pupils often find their way into the archives. Two schools, the Scuola Media Virgilio and the Instituto J. Vicens Vives, carefully filed away all such tests for subsequent reference, indexing them by forms and subjects. Without necessarily feeling that I should wish every scrap of paper to be kept in this way in our own schools, I can nevertheless think of times when it could be useful; those awkward post-report interviews with parents who feel that the staff's strictures on their son's efforts are totally unfounded might well be profitably shortened if they could be confronted with the ignominious results of sonny-boy's last six chemistry tests!

That seems to bring us to the topic of marks and assessments. In general, the giving of specific marks for ordinary routine work is somewhat less prevalent than it is in this country, where a pupil sometimes seems aggrieved if the ritual $\frac{7}{10}$ is not appended to his work. Especially in the primary schools, a word or two of praise or comment is usually regarded as sufficient, though one Italian primary school did give marks exceptionally if parents requested

Pastoral care and welfare

them. For more formal tests, however, there is usually a recognized system of marks, often standardized on a national basis.

For example, in the 'passing-up' tests at Leonida Bissolati school in Cremona, the child must obtain at least 6 marks in each subject to obtain promotion. Theoretically a range of marks from 0 to 10 is available, but the class-register showed that in practice only the marks from 5 to 10 are used, any mark lower than 5 being regarded as 'too discouraging'. There is some logic in this; since 5 means that you have failed, it merely rubs your nose in the dirt to award anything lower. As well as for academic subjects, marks are also given for physical education and for conduct; for the latter, I was told, nothing lower than 9 is normally given! The most curious feature is that marks have to be entered in words (*sette* or *otto*, not 7 or 8), presumably to guard against some infant forger skilfully altering a 5 to an 8. Perhaps it is not surprising to learn that there is a move to have all marks abolished!

The *liceu nacional* at Evora in Portugal uses a simpler system. Simpler, yes; but I can think of less confusing ones, for work is given one of five grades, which are MB (*muito bom*, very good), B (*bom*, good), S (*suficiente*, satisfactory), m (*mediocre*, not very good), and M (*mau*, bad). The principle is a simple and an admirable one, but the mind boggles at a system which, with a couple of dozen letters in the Portuguese alphabet, contrives to use M three times and B twice in a total of only six symbols; of course, it's unfortunate that the Portuguese for 'very' and 'moderate' and 'bad' all happen to begin with M, but still . . .

Incidentally, I saw a teacher in one school recording marks for a test twice over, once in the usual way and once, listing the marks by the pupil's class-numbers instead of their names, on a special list which, I was given to understand, would in due course be sent up to the Ministry in Lisbon for some unspecified statistical purpose. My mind did another quick boggle.

The Spanish system has six grades, four above the median line and two below it; but here the actual numerical marks are shown on the lists, any comment ('outstanding', say, or 'most unsatisfactory') being merely a gloss on the figures. Another system I saw in Spain, at the La Salle College, was useful in connection with the individual work-sheet method teaching mixed-ability classes: work was marked, say, in blue when it was returned to the pupil, the code being Sf (satisfactory), B (good), N (noteworthy, very good) or S (outstanding); but work not meriting any of these was marked in *red* with R (meaning that it was to be repeated as 'recuperation' work). If it was satisfactory on being presented a second time, it received the appropriate blue mark.

One French school showed me how parents were kept informed of their child's marks: each pupil had a book, like an ordinary exercise book, in which he had to enter all marks gained, with space for the teacher to add his comments and signature. In a primary school I saw a similar system, but here the book was in fact a folder in which the actual tests were kept, along with a mark-sheet on which the teacher also added signed comments. Both methods provided useful ways of keeping parents 'in the picture'.

Another document relating to assessment was the summary of teachers' opinions used at the *Realschule*, Emden, after the periodical *Zensurenkonferenz* (assessment meeting); it was a simple duplicated sheet with columns for summarizing the views of subject teachers and form teacher, and entering the final decision about the pupil's future.

A clutch of other miscellaneous documents which I acquired included two curiously similar letters of inquiry about pupils' absence, from Spain and from France; a duplicated form from France certifying that the pupil had attended school for a given period (used, presumably, to facilitate transfer to another school or to employment) and a detailed form completed by parents of children seeking admission to a Spanish school. This seems to have been devised on the principle of 'put down everything you can think of and then double it', for it requests, *inter alia*, the place and date of the child's baptism and first communion, details of seven different inoculations and personal data of all his family. The bottom section is detachable, and if the child is accepted this portion is returned to the applicant. If it is not received, the parents are told to assume that the child has not been accepted, an arrangement which suggests a deep faith in the reliability of the postal services. The child re-presents the detached portion on the day of his arrival, with a whole fistful of civil documents, medical certificates, etc.

Quite a different sort of form was the coloured card used by La Inmaculada College to record the pupil's 'inscription on the Roll of Honour', and awarded as 'testimony of his good behaviour and application to his studies during the month'. Such certificates are not at all uncommon, and I believe small medals are sometimes awarded for good work at the end of the year. This may also be the point to record that *Il Formicaio* lists the names of thirty-odd pupils awarded book prizes for their year's work; half a dozen also won bursaries of value ranging from 30,000 to 66,000 lire (say £30–£60), and some others had smaller monetary prizes, mostly of about 20,000 lire.

Rather amusing is the elegantly printed card from a Spanish school asking that parents 'be punctual in fetching their children, as the teachers have to employ their time in lessons, marking, etc'. Certainly, there is a widespread tendency in Mediterranean countries for parents to accompany their children to and from school; in Italy especially one finds crowds of mothers, and sometimes fathers, at the gates just before lessons end. Often, too, teachers have to supervise their pupils' departure; the children line up at the door, after collecting their raincoats, anoraks, etc., and are then led in crocodile to the gate, whether the teacher watches over their dispersal, escorting them across the road if necessary.

In Italy it seems to be a commendable standard policy for a uniformed police-officer to be on duty in the neighbourhood of the school for about twenty minutes before and after school to ensure that pupils cross the roads safely. It may be reasonable to ask if the police in Italy are really so much more lavishly staffed than our own that they can provide this service when we merely issue a white raincoat and a 'lollipop' to some devoted housewife or old-age pensioner? In Germany, senior pupils commonly perform these patrol duties, and very efficiently too; they wear a distinguishing cap, belt and gloves to make them recognizable. I believe that younger German children sometimes have to wear a distinctive cap to make them identifiable to motorists. But this is a digression from the theme of school documents, I fear.

The most important of all documents, to the pupil, must be the end-of-term report. One Italian school said they issued no reports, which must make it almost the pupil's idea of a perfect school.

Two otherwise very different French secondary schools used an identical system of reports: each class had a big folder of report forms, in a large rectangular format divided into three by vertical perforations. The three sections thus created corresponded with the three terms of the year. One section of each page was sent to parents each term, a carbon copy being retained in the folder. The teachers' comments had to be kept to the minimum, for each report has only two columns, the first for an assessment-letter on a five-point A–E scale, and the other for a terse comment. With respect, I thought these comments were almost all totally useless, since they were almost invariably just a verbalization of the assessment-letter. 'A' is surely enough without adding 'Good pupil', and 'C' makes its point without any need to comment 'Fairly good'. The one positively useful feature of this report-form was that it provided a space at the foot of the page for the insertion of suggested remedial work for the pupil to carry out during his holidays. There was also a sentence – to be deleted if not applicable – inviting the parents to make an appointment with the headmaster to discuss the pupil's progress.

I also have a copy of the *carnet de correspondance*, or report-book, of a French primary school; this is apparently a commercial product sold in bulk to schools, which must insert their name on the cover by hand; the back cover has some extraordinarily fussy 'school rules' printed thereon, with such items as 'It is forbidden to drink from the fountain. It is forbidden to remain without movement in strong sun or in cold weather'. One wonders what kind of school will consider buying its rules ready-made in this way!

This report-book gives a rather amusing key to the mark-scheme, which I quote as a delicious example of stating the obvious:

0 . . . Nothing	1 . . . Very bad.	2 . . . Bad
3 . . . Very mediocre	4 . . . Mediocre	5 . . . Passable
6 . . . Quite good	7/8 . . . Good	9 . . . Very good
	10 . . . Perfect.	

I wonder how long it took the deviser of this note to decide regretfully that 'Good' would have to do both for 7 and for 8? I don't think he was really trying; if he could perpetrate 'Very mediocre', he might have tried 'Very quite good', possibly?

The inside of this report-book provides a column for each of the nine months from October to June, with a tenth column for the year's average; there are also wider columns to contain a monthly comment by the teacher and the headmaster's signature, as well as a space for the parent to sign as evidence that the report

Pastoral care and welfare

really does find its way home. Marks are awarded for every conceivable subject and activity, and with spaces also for a monthly order of merit and for calculating every month the average of marks gained, as well as a yearly average in each subject, the thing is a statistician's delight. I should say its educational value was absolutely minimal; someone seems to have agreed with me, for the specimen I have contains a duplicated insert replacing the tables of marks by a monthly assessment on a graph, the lines of the graph being entered in red for French, blue for mathematics and green for other subjects. There is also a separate graph for 'Pupil's General Standard', but I am not clear how this is arrived at, as my copy has not been fully completed. The subject-graphs, however, are plotted on a 0–20 scale.

I have also before me two German school report-forms. The first comes from a *Volkschule* (elementary school) with extension-course; it is a single sheet headed with the pupil's name and age, and details of his absences, classified as 'with excuse' and 'without excuse'. There follows a small space for stating the pupil's overall standing in the school, followed by a list of subjects studied, each with a space of about 1½" for entering an assessment. At the foot of the page are three lines for 'Remarks', and then come the signatures of the class teacher and the head of the school. On the back is a brief statement of the purpose of the 'extension-course' covering classes 5 and 6, and a declaration that successful pupils in this course may enter without further examination into class 7 of the *Realschule* or *Gymnasium*.

The other German report, from a secondary school, is much the same in its layout, except that it provides about three times as much space for the 'Remarks', and lists the subjects in categories: basic subjects, set subjects, options and study groups. On the back of this form is an explanation of the basis of these four categories, taken from the official government edict; and there is also a list of the grades used, which are: 1 (very good), 2 (good), 3 (satisfactory), 4 (adequate), 5 (unsatisfactory) and 6 (insufficient). I am afraid that my vocabulary is both unsatisfactory and insufficient when it comes to differentiating between these subtle shades of meaning: the German scholar had better be informed that in the original the words are 3 (*befriedigend*), 4 (*ausreichend*), 5 (*mangelhaft*) and 6 (*ungenügend*). An example, perhaps, of contemporary reluctance to discourage an inadequate pupil – or just of refusal to tell an unpalatable truth, as when the newspaper-reporter calls a footballer 'tough' or 'physical', when we all know he really means 'brutal' or 'dirty'?

My final example of a school report is that issued by the Colegio Juan Bruguera at Gerona. This is a green-covered booklet, about $5\frac{1}{2}'' \times 8\frac{1}{4}''$, containing pages to provide for five evaluations – that is, to last for one year, the assessments normally taking place in November, January, March, May and June. The 'Notes to Parents' ask for parental support, offering to discuss with parents any cases of disagreement; they remind them that the marks are also entered in the all-important 'ERPA'; and they offer verbal equivalents ('good', 'satisfactory' and the like) for the plain numerical marks.

The five pages which follow carry a simple layout for entering a mark for every subject. As well as the normal subjects of the curriculum, marks are also given to all pupils for conduct ('order, respect, good habits and courtesy'); punctuality ('regularity in arrival'); application ('the child's effort and interest, irrespective of results'); attendance ('number of absences from morning and afternoon sessions'). Finally, and perhaps most interestingly in view of modern trends in the same direction which are appearing here and there in our own schools, there is, as well as the traditional space at the bottom for the observations of form tutor and headmaster, another one for 'observations of the family', to be signed by the parent. The very last entry of all in the book, on a page of its own, is a formal statement of the level attained by the pupil in his year's work, with a note of any 'recuperation' to be carried out, and a supplementary certificate to be completed after this has been acceptably performed.

Without claiming anything like perfection for this book, I find it much more acceptable than the others which I have here described; it makes at least some effort to provide encouragement for the child who has worked hard without achieving much success; it offers the parents an opportunity to make any observations they may think proper; and it is positive, in that it enables the teacher to state quite explicitly what remedial work has to be done. Its main fault is that it does not give the teacher much scope to clothe with flesh the bare bones of a numerical mark; its format, also, is a trifle cramped, though this may matter less in that the teacher's comment only needs to be brief when the report is taken home as often as five times in the year – probably twice as often as in most English schools. Once again, it is interesting to find that it is Spain which shows most awareness of modern educational trends.

Our examination of this Spanish report-book again brings us close to one of the great talking-points of European education, 'recuperation'. The system does have certain virtues: the able but idle pupil, not having worked during the year, receives a salutary shock from his results, is forced to work hard during his holiday period, and almost certainly does better in September; the teacher takes over at the start of a new year a class in which he can feel fairly sure that every pupil has reached an acceptable standard of knowledge; and no pupil falls so far behind the rest of the class that his results grow steadily more and more abysmal.

But it is not as simple as that. What of the willing but not very bright pupil who already *has* worked hard, and works hard again during the holidays, and still fails in September? What of the pupil who has already repeated one year and finds himself repeating yet another? Remember those dismal figures quoted by the Barbiana pupils: over 500 thirteen-year-old Italian children still hopelessly bogged-down in the first-year primary course, alongside the six-year-olds! Clearly, no system which allows this to happen to even a tiny percentage of children can be right; hence the recent developments in several countries which replace the old system with the theory of 'continuous recuperation'. This system requires more careful pastoral guidance, more thorough documentation, more ingenious and imaginative preparation of teaching material than the old one did.

To my mind, as much school indiscipline has its roots in academic failure as in any other cause. Most children start their school careers with good intentions and high hopes, but if they find themselves falling behind, they become so discouraged that they no longer make any serious effort – or they try to fortify their faltering pride with a 'don't-care' attitude. The first time they take an examination, their mark may be an undistinguished 40 per cent; the next time perhaps it is 25 per cent; 15 per cent the time after that. But if only somebody had taken hold of the child after that first 40 per cent, and had given him some sensibly graded remedial work directed to enabling him by his own efforts to raise his poor 40 to a respectable 50 or even a good 60, that child might be so raised in his own self-esteem as to become an enthusiast for his work rather than a drop-out. As Maria Rosa Colaço so movingly and inspiringly shows us in *A Criança e a Vida*, what the deprived child wants is that somebody shall love him. In terms of the classroom, that means showing that we think he matters and is worth a bit of our trouble. This is what the 'continuous recuperation' system at least *tries* to do, and many articles in *Vida Escolar* are devoted to examining the ways and means. One especially good article, by Señor Antonio Blanco Rodríguez of Madrid, reminds us that the key to the teacher's success is his knowledge of the child's personality and capacities; he further says that in any case the pursuit of homogeneity in a group of pupils is a myth; a gap of three years between mental and physical age, either way, is possible, so that a class of twelve-year-olds could have a mental range from nine to fifteen years, and this will be constantly changing as the pupils' personalities evolve. So, if recuperation is not going on all the time, it makes no sense at all. He utterly demolishes the idea of making any pupil repeat an entire year's course: to do so is equivalent to saying that no progress whatever has been made during a year, which is manifestly absurd.

An article I read in a later issue seemed to me much less convincing: in it, the writer postulated the totally unstreamed school, in which flexible interest-groups replaced ordinary classes, 'groups of pupils less complex, less fixed, appearing or disappearing at any given time according to the interests and activities of each individual pupil'. Intellectually, one may acquiesce: but in practice, it seems rather like running a railway without a timetable and with the passengers doing their own driving.

To be fair to the author of the article, this somewhat Protean school is only one of a number of possibilities put forward for discussion.

Pursuit of these stimulating, if not always down-to-earth, topics has taken us some way from what is actually happening on the pastoral side in European education; without too much reluctance, therefore, I turn back to offer a brief comment on some aspects of educational welfare which have come my way.

Some of the countries I visited have a good many problems of sheer poverty to overcome. It is true that all have made some progress: the tourist boom in Spain, membership of the EEC for Italy, Portugal's rich overseas possessions, have all increased the national prosperity in recent years. But the spoils are very unevenly shared and, especially in Portugal, one can see people living very near the bare minimum level of subsistence. This poverty inevitably is reflected in the extent to which people can take advantage of educational opportunities; therefore, all have at least some provision for helping parents of children who are in need.

It must be remembered that in some of these countries, education is only free at the elementary level, and that in all it is often necessary to pay for books and equipment. Where fees are charged, they are normally quite low as far as the state schools are concerned; obviously, however, a boarding school run by an independent body must charge according to the amenities and quality of education which it can offer.

By way of example, let me quote from the prospectus of La Inmaculada, the College of the Marist Brothers at Gerona. The actual fees are not stated, the prospectus merely remarking that directives from the Ministry of Education and Science are awaited; but prospective parents are told that fees are payable monthly. Special concessions are available in certain cases; for example, there is a reduction of 10 per cent for a younger brother, or of 15 per cent for the third brother of the family. In the event of there being four brothers in the school, the fees of the youngest will be waived altogether.

As well as the fees, there is an entrance payment to cover a variety of incidental expenses; this payment is of 1,000 pesetas (about £7·50) for pupils in the infant and junior sections, of 1,500 pesetas for older pupils, and of 2,500 pesetas for boarders. The expenses covered by these payments are listed in the prospectus as:

Medical inspections	Parents' Association
Teaching material	Upkeep of equipment
Examination material	Sport
Psycho-technical tests	Pupils' insurance
School assistance	Swimming-pool
Information bulletin	Teaching practice

More modestly, the Wallschule at Emden informs its parents in one issue of their occasional newsletter that, owing to the increased use of duplicating materials, a charge of one mark per pupil (say about 15p) will be made from the start of the new school-year!

Higher secondary education often involves payment of fees. The *liceu nacional* at Evora in Portugal charges a fee of about 150 escudos per term – no great sum, say about £3, but wages in Portugal are not high and this fee could exclude children of the poorest parents, though most, I imagine, would consider it a very modest sum to pay for the very high quality of the education which this school actually offers. An Italian handbook I own quotes fees for the various *scuole medie superiori*; these vary from 7,400 lire in the first year and 5,900 lire thereafter at the *istituto magistrale* (teachers' training school) up to 18,000 lire (first year), 16,000 lire (second year) and 25,000–32,000 lire (subsequent years) at the *istituto tecnico industriale*, or technical college. The orthodox *liceo classico* charges 8,800 lire in the first year and 7,300 lire in later years.

Grants are available in most countries to assist the poorer parents. For example, the 1972/3 booklet of the Spanish Ministry of Education quotes the following maxima: education 9,000 pesetas; transport 4,000; meals 5,000; boarding and further education, various amounts ranging from 15,000 to 45,000 pesetas, depending on the type of school; grants for special and miscellaneous items, EGB 500 pesetas, *bachillerato* and professional 2,000, university 4,000. Students are eligible from the age of eleven upwards. At present exchange rates of about 135 pesetas to the pound, these do not appear to be bad grants, bearing in mind that costs are generally lower in Spain than in most western countries. In Jaén I was told that a school meal cost 15 pesetas, so that a parent who received the maximum grant of 5,000 pesetas for meals would be receiving enough to pay for 333 meals, but as the school year only contains about two-thirds of this number of days, I doubt whether many parents in Jaén receive the full grant!

One problem, of course, which concerns the Spanish parent very little is the cost of school uniform; either his son or daughter has no special uniform at all, or it is simply a *bata*, which is an inexpensive overall or pinafore. This point is dealt with more fully in the next chapter.

While I have little specific information concerning grants in other countries, it is safe to assume that similar provision does exist. One aspect of the welfare services, however, which I saw much more of was that of medical care; school after school showed me lavishly equipped medical-inspection rooms, often with regular attendance two or three times a week by a doctor – daily, indeed, in one Spanish school. Routine medical inspection of pupils is also more frequent than it often appears to be in this country, though I was told of local difficulties in one or two places. The children everywhere looked sturdy and well-nourished, but it is otherwise difficult to tell just how much actual medical care children may have received; perhaps the one common external indication is the wearing of spectacles, and on this rather uncertain basis, I would deduce a pretty high standard of medical welfare, since a study of my own photographs suggests that between 8 and 12 per cent of schoolchildren wear glasses.

Rather to my surprise, my inquiries about the provision of medical services in German schools produced little response. It is possible that my questions simply were not understood, of course, but I did try several times, and none of the replies suggested any very frequent medical examination of the pupils; nor did I see, as in the other countries, any provision of medical facilities in the schools, except for one school which arranged for children feeling ill to lie down on a couch in a small all-purposes room which also housed the staff library.

Spanish children have the right to school insurance as part of the system of social security; they are protected against family misfortunes, accidents, sickness and other contingencies which could affect the course of their studies. It does not seem that this is so in France, where one school's rule-book strongly advises parents to take out their own insurance against accidents, etc.

The last aspect of pastoral care to which I want to refer is that of parental involvement in education. In Portugal, I was told, there is little tradition of such involvement; in Italy, I saw the shining example of the admirable work done by the Porcellasco parents, but this was then quite untypical. All this may soon change, however, for Italy is moving towards greater parental involvement, and the magazine *Oggi* of 12 June 1974 has the bold headlines 'In October, parents and children will sit at the desks together'. This is good journalistic over-simplification, of course, but it does seem that new laws are setting up groups of parents, outside experts and interested bodies like trades unions, to help solve the problems of the schools. To quote two sentences from *Oggi*: 'in place of the centralized or "Napoleonic" school system, there emerges the new concept of a decentralized "community" school, the active instrument of a real and individual "social service".' These are indeed fine words; but a later article of February 1975 suggests that there is still some way to go before they are universally translated into deeds.

Teachers, it seems, approached the new order with some hesitation: would politics be brought into the classroom? would comfortable old attitudes have to be rudely disturbed? Sometimes they seem to have mistaken the purpose of the consultations with parents, attempting to use them, for example, to bring about the removal from the class of a troublesome pupil, or to complain about the poverty of their pupils' cultural backgrounds (one parent seems to have replied with the sharp observation that a teacher can hardly expect a parent whose own vocabulary is necessarily limited by his lack of education to do much about increasing that of his children: that is precisely what the school is there to do!). Occasionally, a dictatorial headmaster has done his best to sabotage the whole idea of parental consultation.

Parents, for their part, have also had their problems. Italian women especially have been reluctant to open their mouths on public occasions; there has been a predictable falling-off in attendance at parents' meetings on evenings when a popular football match or film could be seen on TV; many have felt that however good their will there was in practice little they could really do to help. Others, however, have erred on the side of trying to do too much, coming up with grandiose schemes for spending vast sums of money which there was no hope of obtaining; but their efforts have at least underlined the deep concern many Italian parents feel about the lack of classrooms, the absence of gymnasia or sports grounds, the often appalling toilet facilities and so on. Sometimes they have voiced criticism of the way the schools are run, demanding an end to marks or reports, or (more justifiably, perhaps) criticizing a teacher who had publicly humiliated some of his pupils – the comments of the parents on this person were of an impressive decency and dignity. It appears that the meetings have, as one might perhaps expect, tended to be dominated by professional people – lawyers and other teachers particularly; it seems that teachers have an extraordinary capacity for getting themselves elected as parent-representatives in the councils of the schools their own children attend! Leftists have in some cases dominated the councils, and in any case a limited

Pastoral care and welfare

number of highly articulate types can easily take over a whole meeting.

Despite these teething troubles, the feeling of most teachers seems to have been that up to a point the new order has been a success; attendance at meetings has been steadily increasing, and the usefulness of the discussions has followed suit. They do, however, point out that good heads and good teachers have been having this kind of contact with parents long before it was made a statutory requirement. Perhaps the people who have come out worst from the reform have been the school caretakers, accustomed to a leisurely life once their pupils have gone home at midday, but now faced with meetings at all hours of the day and night; some of them, it seems, have actually mutinied and downed their brooms.

Proof that parent–teacher associations could flourish before the new law is in a report of the *comitato scuola-famiglia* of the village of Chirignago, contained in *Il Gazzettino* of 28 May 1974. A full programme of activities had taken place, including meetings to discuss such topics as 'Religion in the school' and 'Schools of tomorrow'; there had also been meetings of teachers in primary and secondary schools to ease the transition of children from one to the other, an excellent idea that might be more widely copied; and parents had also assisted teachers in school outings.

France, I felt, still seemed to feel that the place of parents is well outside the school gates; I saw little positive indication of parental involvement. Germany does more: the Emden Wallschule issues regular newsletters to parents, and the Zewen School includes pages of interest to parents in its termly magazine. German practice is to elect one parent to represent each class on the parents' committee (*Elternbeirat*); these seem to involve parents both at class level and at that of the school as a whole. I was told at one school that the committee may not raise funds, but has considerable influence on school policy.

The Zewen magazine also reports an *Elternsprechtag*, or Parents' Consultation Day, held from 8.30 to 12 noon one Thursday. The parents discussed with the teachers such problems as curriculum, syllabus, pupils' progress and future prospects; it was the first such occasion, which accounts for the large amount of space devoted to what will doubtless soon be a routine event, and the percentage of parents taking advantage of the opportunity ranged from 50 to 80 per cent in the various classes.

In Spain, both the private colleges I visited in Gerona had parents' associations, and one of them gave me a copy of its rules. The booklet deals mainly with constitutional and legal matters, but it also says that one object is 'to defend the rights of the College and its pupils in case of need against any organization or authorities', which is fine fighting talk! In this school (La Salle College) some special rooms are actually set aside for parents' committee meetings and the like. An article in *Vida Escolar* seemed to me to strike a rather nervous tone, constantly assuring its readers that this or the other act, decree or law made everything quite in order, so nobody need get alarmed; I suppose it may well be rather a delicate matter in an authoritarian country for any group of the citizenry to organize themselves into a kind of pressure-group! However, the head of Sagrada Familia at Ecija was very enthusiastic about the role of his school's parents' association which, incidentally, runs the school shop for the sale of stationery and other small articles each day.

As well as such organized support, one also reads of individual gestures; *Il Formicaio*, for example, reports the gift of a fine set of encyclopedias by the parents of a pupil who had just left after a successful school career, and this is hardly likely to be a unique instance. I saw enough myself to feel sure that many pupils and their parents must have good reason to feel grateful, and perhaps a little affectionate, towards their schools.

10
Rules and regulations

Indiscipline in our schools is all too often in the news, and I was naturally concerned to know whether teachers in Europe faced similar problems to those which apparently confront the staffs of some London schools today. That there *are* such problems is indicated by the article quoted in an earlier chapter from an Italian periodical; but I am bound to say that the schools which I myself saw seemed to be pretty peaceful places. It is true that a teacher in one Spanish school shook her head sadly and said that the older pupils were very unruly, but such things are, after all, relative, and the behaviour of the pupils in that school seemed to me in fact fairly decorous. An Italian teacher has told me a delightful story of a class who rigged up a radio loudspeaker in their classroom and told a very raw young teacher that she must not begin the lesson as the headmaster was intending to make an important announcement through it, until which time, music would be played; they were thus enabled to enjoy an uninterrupted pop concert throughout the hour, and went on their way rejoicing at the end – and if that story is true, I have high hopes of that particular group of youngsters, and would certainly not see them as any menace to the future of civilization! But of grievous ill discipline – loutish rudeness, threatening of teachers, vicious vandalism – I should guess there is comparatively little, and that confined to the squalid urban areas where such things breed.

In thinking of school discipline, indeed, it is doubtful whether we should be more exasperated by the over-authoritarianism of the headmaster who tries to lay down a precise uniform length for his pupils' hair, or by the over-permissiveness of the media which delight in building up the occasional rebellious child into a much-wronged martyr. Certainly, many English schools in the past have imposed arbitrary regulations on their pupils, forgetting that whereas most reasonable human beings will accept reasonable rules, it is not unusual (or even undesirable) for heels to be dug in when the rules are unreasonable ones. Surely, for school rules as for any others, the criteria should be: first, is the rule necessary? second, is it workable and enforceable? third, is it clearly stated? And then, having established one's minimum of necessary, enforceable and intelligible rules, one must be quite clear about what one is going to do if they are contravened.

In a school, there are likely to be two main areas where some kind of sanctions will be required: the area of work, and the area of school society in general. In the first of these, misdemeanours would take the form of failure to do tasks set, or failure to do them acceptably; and the sanctions will normally be devised so as to meet these conditions. Most schools will include in their regulations some cautionary sentence to the effect that pupils are expected to work hard during the school year (and even outside it: La Inmaculada College at Gerona says firmly: 'We think it proper that pupils should have something to do during the holidays in connection with the assignments of work they have followed during the year, and therefore they will be supplied with various holiday-tasks at the end of the year; parents are asked to make sure their sons perform them and hand them in to their teachers in September. Education is a team effort!'). But as a rule necessary corrective measures when work is ill-done are left to the individual teacher, the emphasis rightly being on remedial action rather than on punishment. It is the second area of offences which can produce problems, and can lead a school to draw up

Rules and regulations

codes of rules which are sometimes necessary, and occasionally also enforceable and intelligible.

I have talked to a number of European teachers about the code of conduct operative in their schools, and in fact acquired copies of the printed rules of several schools. Here and there I found schools with no rules at all – such as the École Primaire La Barbière in Avignon, a happy and sensible little community which found that the only regulations it needed were a few commonsense safety precautions in the playground. Printed rules varied from the usual Spanish formula, a very generalized statement of duties, rights and responsibilities, to extremely pernickety and detailed lists of do's and dont's. Some of them make rather entertaining reading, and I should have liked to quote extensively, because they shed much light on what I most want to reveal, that is, what it is really like to be a teacher or a pupil in these schools; but space restrictions compel me to be selective. It may be taken as read, therefore, that nearly all school rules cover such obvious matters as opening hours, absences for previously foreseen causes, entry to certain parts of the premises, individual or class movement about the building, orderly behaviour in classroom or corridors, care of property and the like. The extracts which I quote, therefore, are selected either for some unusual feature they may possess, or just because I find them entertaining or even absurd.

I begin with one of the most splendid documents of all, the *Règlement Intérieur de l'École*, published by a body with the nobly sonorous title of 'Association Départementale Autonome du Personnel de l'Enseignement Public du Département de l'Oise', and subscribed with the mark of approval of the Inspecteur d'Academie of the *département*. I assume that the ADA du P de l'EP du D de l'O (if that is how it abbreviates itself) is a teacher's organization which has drawn up the document and secured its acceptance by the local authorities. It seems to me, for all that, to be a shining example of how *not* to draw up rules, because, unless the spirit of the French Revolution is quite dead, its pedantic insistence on dotting every i and crossing every t must surely lead every decently enterprising pupil to see just what he *can* get away with that is not provided for in the 23 'articles' of the document, from which I quote some of the more remarkable passages:

1. Children must not carry in their pockets, satchels or

bags any objects other than those needed for school work.
2. In particular, the following are forbidden: objects dangerous to handle (such as knives, scissors, bottles, glass tubes, guns, caps, cartridges, catapults, spinning-tops etc.), books, booklets, printed papers or manuscripts of a non-educational nature whose use has not been authorized by the teacher . . .
8. So as to avoid accidents which may arise during pupils' movements, penholders, pencils and rulers must be put down as soon as finished with, or on order of the teacher.
11. Pupils are enjoined not to put into their mouths any pens, pins, needles, marbles, counters, coins or pen-holders; they must not put pens or pencils into their ears.
12. Pupils must not throw pens or paper. They must avoid throwing any object whatever at their friends. It is specifically forbidden to spit on the ground.
13. When playing, games must be restrained. Violent or dangerous games, excessively violent arguments, quarrels or disputes are strictly forbidden. It is also strictly forbidden to roll in the dust; play with taps; throw stones, dust or paper arrows, and indeed any kind of projectile; run at high speed; pull one another about; tear one another's clothes; jostle or hit one another etc.
16. Children must go one at a time to the toilets; they are warned not to stand in front of the doors of the compartments and not to soil the interior.
18. Pupils must show themselves tractable and hardworking; at all times they must show deference to the teacher. In case of manifest misbehaviour or persistent indiscipline, the child will be sentenced to exclusion from the school under departmental regulations.

One wonders how strictly all this is observed. Some of the rules seem to be there only so that the school can disclaim responsibility for any child who is conveyed home with his pen-holder irremovably wedged in his ear, or after being jostled, pelted with stones, spat upon and barricaded in the toilets. Yet even this awe-inspiring document omits some things we might have expected to find; for example, there are no dress regulations, or anything about the care of property.

I would far rather run a school on the lines of the rules drawn up for themselves by the juniors of Porcellasco in Italy:

OUR RULES

In school you may not . . .

  run in the classroom, along corridors or on the stairs.
  jump about
  spit on the ground or in the faces of other children
  slide down the banisters
  push one another
  kick one another
  make a disturbance
  interrupt somebody who is talking
  mess or tear someone else's books
  shout during break
  take other children's belongings
  lean out of the windows
  be ill-mannered towards the teachers, the other children, the headmaster, or people who come into the classroom
  tell lies
  behave like a pig at the table
  misuse the handicraft tools
  waste material
  use bad language
  be disobedient

THE GROUP OF JUNIORS

After all the huffing and puffing of our friends of the ADA and all that, are not the Porcellasco children's rules refreshingly simple, clear and direct? They obviously spring from actual situations, and no bureaucrat's hand has touched them.

To follow these two very different examples of primary school rules, I quote some from a very good French secondary school, the J. B. Pellerin at Beauvais. A preamble emphasizes that the rules are to be seen as necessary restrictions imposed on everyone for the greater freedom of all, and they are interesting as including rules for the staff here and there, which perhaps makes the point to pupils that any social contract must have two sides. Some extracts follow:

1. Parents are asked to note very carefully the 'allocation of time' inserted at the top of each pupil's notebook at the start of the school year.
5/6. On returning from absence, a pupil must obtain a re-entry form from the office; without this the teacher may not accept him back into the class; similarly, a pupil arriving late must obtain a re-entry form from the *Surveillant-Général* after he has explained his lateness.
8. Day-boys must not arrive before their first effective lesson, and may only leave after the final lesson of the half-day; they may, however, on production of their 'leaving-card', be allowed to leave earlier if their teacher should be absent at the end of a half-day. They must remain on the premises between two non-consecutive classes in the same half-day.
16. During the change of lessons at 9.30 and 14.30, forms which do not need to change rooms may stay in their room while awaiting the new teacher, under control of the class prefect.
18. Groups of pupils may be permitted to stay in a classroom for private study, for putting up decorations, for making tape-recordings, listening to records, etc., under the responsibility of the teacher concerned, and under the control of one of the pupils in the group. In all such cases, the teacher concerned should inform the *Surveillant-Général*.
20. Class prefects may assemble their forms under their own authority in a room allotted to them on request to the *Surveillant-Général*.
21. Correct, sober and decent dress, conforming to the rules of cleanliness and safety, is expected of all.
22. To protect clothing from chalk, ink-splashes and the accidental spilling of chemicals, the wearing of a smock is obligatory.

Rules and regulations

24. All political and religious propaganda, and the introduction of immoral publications, is forbidden.
25. Pupils may not smoke on the premises or in the immediate neighbourhood.
26. Teachers and supervisors are required not to smoke in class.
28. Pupils must look after and keep in good condition the walls, tables, chairs and books. They may contribute towards the adornment of their classroom.
29. Any pupil who accidentally causes damage to any fitting is asked to report it at once; he will not then be punished. If the damage is wilful, or results from negligence, total or partial repayment for the damage will be expected, without prejudice to any other punishment that may be imposed.
32. When damage is caused to the premises without its being possible to determine the guilty party or parties, it is evident that there has been some administrative failure, and the school alone will assume responsibility for the cost.
36. Because of the increasing number of accidents, the use of bicycles between home and school will only be allowed in cases where there are special reasons of health, distance etc.
43. For all routine correspondence, or requests for official documents such as attendance certificates, signatures on grant forms, bus passes, etc., pupils will use the *enveloppe-navette** which is collected each day from the office and returned by the class prefect.
44. The class prefect will also collect each morning and afternoon, in time for the first lesson, all lesson-registers and notes, as well as the attendance-return on which every teacher lists the absent pupils and appends his signature.
45. At any time, except during lesson-hours, parents may have information from the lesson-registers of their child's class.
47. The first sanctions imposed on an offending pupil will be

*A *navette* is, for example, a train or bus which operates a shuttle-service up and down a short route at regular intervals; the translation of the phrase *enveloppe-navette* may therefore be difficult, but the meaning is obvious enough.

pieces of extra work, to be signed by the parents, which are done in the Wednesday detention.
48. Pupils absenting themselves from detention when required to attend will not be readmitted to the course.
49. For any grave offence, the class council will require the offender to appear before the Disciplinary Council in accordance with the Act in force (Decree 68.698 and *Arreté* of 8 November 1968).

This is a town school of about 1,000 pupils, and obviously its rules are more extensive than those for a little village school like Porcellasco. Yet (despite Decree 68.698) they have, to me, the same feeling of being sensibly framed to meet actual needs of a community; they admit that the school itself may sometimes be at fault; they show pupils that the staff also are expected to accept some restrictions on their liberty; they attempt to explain *why* things have to be done in certain ways; and they do not attempt the impossible.

The rules of another French CES I saw were generally fairly similar to these, but one startling difference was the inclusion of this paragraph:

At the end of each term, parents receive in a letter, the results obtained by each pupil. The decisions of the Class Council, taken in the interests of pupils and their families, are irrevocable, and no subsequent representations will be of any avail.

Surely that last sentence, printed in heavy black type, is needlessly arrogant? If it represents this school's general approach, I can see why this was one of the few schools where the atmosphere seemed to be rather sultry at times.

The Italian Scuola Media Virgilio, about the same size as J. B. Pellerin, is decidedly more detailed and pernickety in its rules. Here are some extracts:

1. Pupils must be outside the school entrance not more than five minutes before the start of lessons. . . . Boys wait outside the main gate, girls on the pavement footpath. The entrance must be left clear. It is strictly forbidden to hit one another with satchels. School discipline also extends to behaviour outside the school, which must be of

Rules and regulations

the most decorous and correct kind, such as will do credit to the pupils' families and to their own status as students.

6. Pupils must come to school provided with everything necessary for lessons or other classwork; it is absolutely forbidden to telephone home for things forgotten.
9. During the 10.30 break, pupils must make use of the toilets, a few at a time. They must not do so at other times, except in case of illness supported by a medical certificate.
10. Any alterations in correspondence or written material sent between school and home will be considered a grave offence, and deserving of punishment.
11. Any defect of manners or respect towards a superior will be severely punished.
12. In and out of school, pupils have a duty to greet the Headmaster and all staff, including those of other departments of the school.
13. In school, girls must wear a blue pinafore with white collar.
14. Every pupil must occupy the seat allotted at the start of the year; no change may be made save with the teacher's permission. Every pupil is responsible for the condition of his desk.
18. If a pupil's absences reach a number likely to compromise the successful completion of his course, they may lead to his exclusion from the final assessments.
24. The Collective Salute of the class, properly offered whenever the teacher enters or leaves the room, is given by rising in an orderly manner, and thus remaining until the teacher gives his permission to sit again.
26. . . . both in and out of class, pupils will avoid the use of slang words or vulgar gestures.
27. Pupils may not distract their attention during a lesson by studying work of another lesson; even less may they do homework which they have failed to do at home.
28. Pupils will be excluded from the mark-list if they obtain fewer than 8 marks out of 10 for conduct; those who obtain fewer than 6 out of 10 will not be permitted to take the *riparazione* tests (the second series of examinations for those not qualifying on the first).

It may well be felt that these rules are somewhat old-fashioned and heavy-handed. Be that as it may, I enjoyed my visit to Virgilio very much, and thought it a good, and a happy, school. I should hazard the guess that the rules are interpreted in the spirit rather than to the precise letter; the pupils were as delightful and carefree as Italian children generally are.

But there are interesting points in those rules: why, for example, is there uniform for the girls but not for the boys? How can the very first rule possibly be observed, since, if it were, it would require 900 children (and their parents, very often) to converge on the gates in the space of five minutes? How does the teacher, under rule 24, give the class permission to sit down after he has left the room? And if he does not, how can they rise to give the collective salute to the next teacher who comes in? Most intriguing of all, what are those 'vulgar gestures' which rule 26 forbids so sternly? Certainly, these rules do sound a little authoritarian; yet the Director, Signor Cecarini, was in fact a very humane person, and had obviously established an excellent atmosphere in his school. That he was flexible in his approach was perhaps apparent from his answer to my question about Rule 13: he said he would have preferred to have the boys in smocks also, but as they themselves didn't much care for them, and the girls were more tractable in this respect, he accepted the situation as it was. And in fact his boys used their freedom very responsibly: they wore nothing that the most censorious person could deny to be 'of the most decorous and correct kind . . .' Were I required at pistol-point, to adopt as they stood the rules of either Virgilio or J. B. Pellerin, I should unhesitatingly choose the latter; but for all that there was nothing to choose between the two schools in pleasantness of atmosphere and educational efficiency, and in neither was the rule-book oppressively in evidence in everyday life.

The sets of French *lycée* rules which I acquired were, perhaps predictably, less entertaining, since they contained less detail. Here, however, is an interesting extract from the rules of the Lycée Frédéric-Mistral at Avignon:

> Besides more usual methods such as oral reproof, extra work, direct correspondence with parents, etc., there is at the base of the system of sanctions the 'Written Observation'.

This must be initialled by one of the Chief Counsellors, signed by the parents, and returned to the *lycée*, where it is filed. The number of such written warnings which entail the summoning of the parents to the school and the issuing of a *solemn warning* by the Principal is:
in the first cycle, four for a day-pupil; five for a pupil who stays through the lunch-hour; seven for a boarder;
in the second cycle, three, four and six respectively as above.
After this, the Emergency Council will be convened in the event of a further three written warnings being issued to a pupil of the first cycle, or two to a second cycle pupil.

The rules explain that the Emergency Council is a disciplinary body composed, according to circumstances, of the school principal, two teachers from the division of the pupil involved (or one teacher and a supervisor or 'agent') and two responsible pupils from the same division, or their deputies. The punishments which it awards may be either a 'solemn warning'; one or two days' suspension from school; or appearance before the disciplinary council, which is a higher body comprising the permanent administrative committee of the *lycée* sitting as a disiplinary committee.

This all sounds formidably legalistic, and in fact the headmaster told me that the atmosphere in his school was good (as I saw for myself, too) so that he had no need ever to call in this last authority of the disciplinary council, which in any case, he felt, would quite possibly exacerbate whatever situation had already arisen. His other sanctions, he said, were quite sufficient.

One other extract from this *lycée*'s rules may also be of some slight interest: 'All pupils are forbidden to smoke inside the buildings; the use of tobacco in the grounds is, however, permitted to pupils of the second cycle. It is strictly forbidden to those of the first cycle'. Those of the second cycle will probably be about sixteen years of age and upwards. Similar concessions are made to older pupils in some Spanish schools, and in one, Virgen del Carmen at Jaén, I found the oldest pupils were authorized to smoke in class if the individual teacher agreed.

The *lycée* at Beauvais had rather similar rules to those at Avignon, though they paid less attention, on paper, to sanctions, and instead of the emergency council it appeared that serious offences were dealt with by the ordinary class council, modified in composition to provide representation of pupils, parents, supervisors and so on, as necessary. The imposition of extra work was the first line of sanctions; more serious, or too frequent, offences might involve detention on Saturdays or on the mid-week half-holiday, or appearance before the class council. Again, the disciplinary council looms in the background as the Ultimate Deterrent.

The Beauvais *lycée* takes much the same line as the Frédéric-Mistral about smoking, but it is more explicit on dress. There is no uniform as such, but every pupil is required to have a smock for practical work and it is firmly stated that for safety reasons this must not be of nylon. Now, since about 95 per cent of all smocks on sale in France seem to be of nylon or of some substance indistinguishable from it, and that this prohibition does not appear in the rules of any other school I have seen, I have no idea why greater perils lurk in synthetic fabrics for the boys and girls of Beauvais than for others; surely they can't be hoping to revive the defunct Beauvais tapestry industry in a new form to provide hand-woven overalls for the *lycéens*? There are also some jolly rules about games kit: girls must have an all-black outfit, comprising (and here I use the original French, my powers of translation being wholly unequal to the struggle) 'une paire de baskets, une paire de chaussons de rythmique, une culotte ou short, une chemisette, un ras de cou, et un sac de sport'. Boys are attired more splendidly in red and black, and their somewhat simpler requirements are 'une paire de baskets, un short, un maillot, et un sac de sport'. Predictably, each article must be clearly marked with the owner's name, as also must the smock.

One commendable feature of the Beauvais rules is that they contain a whole section on 'self-discipline', emphasizing that older pupils are allowed to supervise themselves in private study. The cautionary, and no doubt necessary, rider is added that any pupil who shows himself unworthy of such trust must go to a supervised room for his private study. That strikes a familiar note to English ears.

The generalized nature of most Spanish rule-books makes quotation unnecessary, but I liked these three extracts from the brief rules of the Colegio Juan Bruguera at Gerona:

Rules and regulations

It is the pupil's duty to participate attentively not only in his studies but also in the complementary activities of the school...

He must observe the affectionate respect due to his teachers and companions...

The headmaster and staff use no kind of humiliating or corporal punishments. The pupil's fulfilment of his standards and duties must be secured through persuasion and the authority of the teacher...

There is a pleasant humanity about these extracts, though one can hardly imagine an English school being so demonstrative as to put on paper a plea for 'affectionate respect'. Yet is this not precisely what every teacher would like his pupils to feel towards him, and what very many do in fact receive? So, is it really unthinkable that we might sometimes indicate that it is pleasant to receive it? One great failing of the present day is precisely this reluctance to admit to the more heart-warming emotions.

The reference to the absence of corporal punishment is also of some interest. Nowhere did I come across any sign that it is practised, officially or otherwise, though if Miguel Delibes' novel *El Camino*, written in 1950, is in any degree autobiographical, erring Spanish children were at one time liable to the rather trying punishment of being made to kneel for long periods holding a heavy book at arm's length, as well as being caned on the palms of the hands. But in 1973 it was rather humbling to find that a number of pupils asked me in a horrified way if it was really true that in English schools the pupils were sometimes beaten by the teachers. I tried to convince them that our corridors do not in fact ring to the sounds of the birch and the howls of the afflicted, but some of them, I thought, looked a little sceptical.

Spanish school rules are usually brief and fairly earnest in tone; it seems to be felt that most points not covered by national education laws can be left to common sense. For example, La Inmaculada College, after sternly reminding parents that they must send written explanations of lateness or absence, abstain from asking for exceptional leave of absence for their sons, and pay their fees promptly, prints precisely three rules for the boys themselves. The first admonishes them that it is their duty as Catholic Christians to attend Mass on the appointed days; the last enjoins them to 'present themselves punctually for lessons and all school activities, and be models of diligence and good behaviour to their companions'; and between these two is only a bright little reminder that they must wear proper kit in the gymnasium and regulation-pattern smocks in the classroom.

If I had to draw up rules for Spanish schoolchildren – a very pleasant and well-mannered community – I should add just one more: a stern prohibition of the chewing of gum in class, for all Spanish children seem addicted to this, and it is quite disconcerting when a beautiful little girl suddenly blows a huge and sticky gum-bubble in mid-lesson as though she were an over-excited camel.

In German schools there seem to be almost as many rules for the teachers as for the pupils. We are concerned with the latter, however, and the striking feature is their very positive wording: for example, '. . . at the first bell we form up, and on the teacher's command we go to our classroom without pushing or noise. Before we enter the building we wipe our shoes.' Or, 'we behave ourselves in the classroom, and get on with some sensible work before the lesson begins'. The approach is practical and sensible, though in places a little fussy, with much concern about not 'loitering' in certain places, or snowballing and throwing stones.

It was interesting to note that in the textbook for the subject known as *Sachunterricht* in the Früchteburg Schule, Emden, one of the passages for class study was a comparison of school rules 'then and now'. English teachers may be interested to compare these three samples:

Old Rules	*New Rules*
Every pupil must arrive punctually for lessons; repeated lateness will be punished.	We will always arrive punctually for lessons, because any late arrival disturbs the work.
Unnecessary talking during the lessons is forbidden. Any pupil needing to speak must raise his hand and wait for the teacher to call on him.	We will only speak when we have to give an answer, for when everybody speaks at once, nobody can understand anything.
Pupils must sit in their places quietly and attentively. It	We will follow the lessons quietly and attentively. Eat-

is forbidden to eat, move about, move the chairs, etc. during lessons. ing, moving about and chattering disturbs the class so that others cannot learn.

Certainly the tone of the second group of rules is more constructive, but I wonder also if it is not just a little priggish too? As for the relative efficacy of the two sets of rules, I obviously cannot judge; but I can report that in some schools there was quite a lot of eating, fidgeting and chattering, and in others there was very little. Which was probably also the case under the old rules too! Some of the noise was, anyway, good healthy *active* noise – German primary school children have an engaging habit of groaning and gasping with the intensity of their eager efforts to be the first to catch the teacher's eye and answer the question, and to this noise is added much snapping of fingers to attract attention. At the secondary level, much of the work involves classroom discussion, and this, though lively, was usually very orderly: it is a healthy classroom atmosphere indeed in which children can express their views as fluently, forcibly and frequently as these did, but can also listen with attention and respect to the views of others. Those classes which were at all rowdy or ill-behaved were, I thought, always those whose teacher had not taken control: either he had not provided enough for the pupils to do, or his lesson lacked point and direction, or he himself was guilty of wasting time. To this extent, at any rate, the disciplinary code in German schools appeared to be achieving its intentions. Not that it is always as sweetly reasonable, perhaps, as these extracts suggest: as well as the rules of the individual school, there are also the *Schulordnungen* of the provincial government, and these, if my copy of the Rhineland-Palatinate regulations is any guide, can be ponderously legalistic. They appear, indeed, to be drawn up with the object of letting all concerned – teachers, pupils and parents – know precisely what are their rights and their obligations, and one may question, perhaps, whether it is always wise to particularize too much. I have already, for example, mentioned the solemn assurance that pupils have the right to issue a school newspaper: is this really a matter for top-level legislation? Or again, an English headmaster might be surprised to find that it was not left to him to decide whether his pupils could leave the school premises during their free time: rule 1.2.3 takes the matter out of his hands and says plainly that pupils may do so only from Class 11 upwards.

All this is part of the intensive democratization of German institutions which has taken place since the dreadful traumas of the Nazi period, and I found myself wondering whether perhaps the trend had not gone a little far. Certainly, some teachers in Germany seemed a bit starry-eyed about democracy; one head, for example, became lyrical about the delights of living in a society in which, he said, his study door might suddenly be flung open by an eleven-year-old child demanding to know whether it was in order for Frau Schmidt to set so much homework tonight. I felt that this was a pleasure that would quickly pall for me. Nor did I much like the casual way children in some schools wandered in and out of the teachers' common-room; one boy aged about thirteen calmly drew up a chair and sat down, unbidden, to discuss his point with the teacher, who appeared to find nothing out of the ordinary in his behaviour. The boy may of course have been the *Klassensprecher* or the teacher the *Verbindungslehrer*, but I still thought the situation rather undesirable; teachers ought to have their privacy respected, and are entitled to a place where they can briefly escape from the demands of their pupils and talk freely. When I mentioned my feelings to a teacher in another German school afterwards, he said drily 'It wouldn't happen here!'

A friend with considerable experience of German schools has discussed with me his real disquiet about this overdoing of the democratic process; he mentioned a specific case which may illustrate the point. A certain class had a number of pupils whose insolent and disruptive attitude was proving very damaging to the class as a whole. When staff teaching the class raised the matter, the first step was to hold a preliminary *Klassenkonferenz* (meeting of teachers working with the class, with two representative pupils also present) to decide if the matter was serious enough to warrant a full *Klassenkonferenz* being held. It being agreed that it was so, this meeting took place a few days later, in school time, several classes having to be sent home early so that their teachers could be free to attend. A second meeting was then found necessary, in similar circumstances; and this led to a recommendation that the offenders be brought before a full staff meeting of some eighty or so people. This meeting, of course, necessitated closing the whole school early. After lengthy discussion, it was agreed that certain measures should be taken – nothing very awful; if I remember rightly, it was a matter of sending letters to the parents of some of the pupils, and suspending one of them from school for a few days. This, however, required to be ratified by yet another committee, which in turn required the re-convening of the full staff meeting to receive the ratification. Consequently, there was widespread interference with the education of a very large number of pupils in classes quite unconnected with the offence, the expenditure of a great deal of time by a body of busy professional men, a considerable amount of administrative work – all to produce the kind of punishment which surely ought to be within the discretion of a headmaster. The punishment was considerably delayed, too, which doubtless provided time for a good deal of student-politics to develop, and for the whole sorry business to get distorted and out of proportion. Nothing will convince me that this kind of thing is a sensible way of dealing with troublesome pupils, however noble the intentions behind it.

Asking in a *Hauptschule* what sanctions are available in cases of indiscipline, I was answered with rather rueful smiles. 'In the long run', they said, 'we can't do much. The *Gymnasium* or *Realschule* people are better off, because they can always get rid of a really difficult pupil, but we just have to do our best with him.' At the *Gymnasium*, naturally, I received rather a different answer: there, I was told, the mildest form of sanction was the recording of the offence in the *Klassenbuch*, the log-book which is kept in every classroom. Next might come a letter to the offender's parents, asking them to come and discuss the pupil with the teachers. The pupil might find his case referred to progressively higher authorities: his form-master, then the headmaster, then the various committees I have referred to. Ultimately, the final deterrent would be expulsion, but my informant hazarded the guess that perhaps there might be one pupil expelled in ten years.

The *Schulordnung* for Rhineland-Palatinate lists these sanctions in extended form. First it states firmly that all corporal punishment and collective punishments are forbidden: the German teacher cannot tell his class that they will all stay behind, or all be deprived of some privilege, until the culprits have owned up! Then come ten stages of action: verbal or written censure; temporary exclusion from the lesson; censure by the headmaster;

censure by the class conference; censure by the whole staff; suspension from school for up to a week; various written entries in the pupil's record; written warning of expulsion; expulsion itself; and finally, on the authority of the *Kultusministerium*, expulsion from all *Gymnasien* in the province. Readers may care to compare this list with the very similar Italian one quoted later: the curious thing, however, is that the Italian list dates from almost half a century back, while this German one is dated 1972.

There appears to be no German equivalent of our system of minor penalties like impositions or detentions (the latter would anyway be difficult to organize in a country where schools meet only in the mornings); nor was there, I think, any such practice as requiring offenders to do such socially-useful tasks as clearing up litter, the view being taken that such tasks are everyone's responsibility. One wonders, however, whether if a few such small penalties were permissible, it might not be possible to keep the more ebullient young in order without matters ever needing to come to the point of all those committees and conferences, which may even possibly make the teacher's task more difficult by increasing the disorderly pupil's sense of his own importance.

But this 'chain-of-command' approach is quite a general one in European schools, taking the question of discipline very largely out of the hands of the individual subject-teacher and referring it to statutory bodies of various levels. The idea is no doubt to ensure that 'justice is not only done, but is seen to be done', but as a means of dealing with an immature child or adolescent, liable to act before he thinks, and very rarely to have really evil intent, the establishment of this ponderous disciplinary code is rather like using a steam-roller to crack an egg: there is a decided lack of the delicate touch. While I do not doubt that most teachers are humane and reasonable in their interpretation of these codes, they might perhaps be even more so without them; and as for the chances such a system provides for the semi-professional student agitator, it is only necessary to refer to what the principal of the Avignon *lycée* told me: 'I never use my disciplinary council; to do so would simply risk making matters far worse.'

An article in the Italian magazine *Oggi*, which I read shortly before starting my tour, sheds further light on this matter. The article, by Cesare Marchi, is called 'I delitti e le pene tra i banchi di scuola', which may be rendered as 'Crime and punishment in

Rules and regulations

the classroom'. It first mentions some recent *causes célèbres* such as the suspension of a Milanese sixteen-year-old for calling his headmaster a 'miserable reactionary'. Signor Marchi says such cases bring into the light of publicity the whole problem of the Italian school disciplinary code. This code was laid down by a Royal Decree of 4 May 1925; that seems a very long time ago, and one would have thought that circumstances had perhaps changed sufficiently to warrant some revision of a Decree passed a couple of years after Mussolini had come to power.

I think it is safe to quote Signor Marchi as an authority on a factual matter which could be so easily challenged were it incorrect: he says that there are nine grades of punishment to which Italian pupils are liable, each with its own appropriate offences and administered by an appropriate individual or committee: (i) private or classroom admonition; (ii) exclusion from the classroom for one or two hours; (iii) exclusion from school for not more than five days; (iv) exclusion from school for up to fifteen days; (v) exclusion from promotion without examination, or from sitting the first examination; (vi) suspension until the end of the year's course; (vii) exclusion from final assessment and both sessions of examinations; (viii) expulsion from the school; (ix) exclusion from all schools in the Republic.

Most of these punishments carry with them additional penalties such as adverse entries in the pupil's record; and some of them, it will be realized, are bound to land the pupil in the unenviable situation of having to repeat a whole year's work because he has not passed the necessary promotion examinations.

It is a rigid code, and English teachers will think it odd that a *national* code exists at all; however, it is only fair to say that an Italian or German teacher might think it odd that the same offence committed in three different English schools can result, perhaps, in one pupil being caned, another losing free time or privileges, and the third pupil's parents being sent a stiff letter. But while there may be circumstances in which the just course is to treat all offences identically, rule-of-thumb justice can also sometimes be the very reverse of just. As the Barbiana school says in *Letter to a Teacher* – they are actually talking of the allocation of marks, but the principle is the same – 'Nothing is more unjust than to share equally among unequals'. And in *Un Anno a Pietralata*, Bernardini tells how some of his pupils were reported to him for misconduct outside the school, and after he had discussed the matter with the whole class, the children suggested that the offenders should be deprived of certain privileges, which he was happy to accept as a very sensible and appropriate punishment. Alas, news of his action reached the Director, who invoked the full splendour of the Royal Decree of 4 May 1925, section 3, and sentenced the two little boys solemnly to a period of suspension from school. One of the other children commented afterwards to Bernardini: 'It was no good suspending them, sir, because they'd only go out to play and not learn anything. When I got suspension last year I enjoyed it, 'cos I could spend all day mucking about.' Which is exactly the point: it is futile to suspend a pupil who possibly comes from a home which cares little about education anyway; an extra pair of hands is always useful for running errands or looking after the baby, and while those may at least be thought useful and even educational activities, running wild in the streets certainly isn't. And such punishments are not the only bad consequence resulting from the high-minded but wrong-headed policy of making the correction of erring pupils a matter of strict codes and committees.

Nevertheless, I will risk saying that I was very favourably impressed by the high standards of behaviour and courtesy among the pupils I met. I saw little sign of the surly, resentful and alienated youth which is the tragic inheritance of the over-affluent and acquisitive urban society. It may be that my choice of medium-sized, comfortably bourgeois towns did not give the Devil his fair chance; for all I know, I might have seen matters otherwise in Milan, Stuttgart or Lille, say, had I gone there rather than to Cremona, Trier and Beauvais. But I can only report on what I actually found, which was that the vast majority of the boys and girls I met were pleasant and sensible young people whom I very much liked and admired.

In one French secondary school I thought the pupils seemed rather sulky and discontented, and indeed my arrival there coincided with a bomb-hoax, which may have been significant; the head of another French school complained of periodical outbreaks of vandalism among pupils of a neighbouring CES; one or two of the German secondary schools produced isolated examples of rowdiness or insolence. Some of my visits were very near the end of the school year, when, I was told, a fairly high proportion of truancy is to be expected among older pupils. But apart from these few instances, the overall atmosphere was one of order and industry; pupils moved about the buildings in reasonable quiet, and played in the fields or yards with self-control; where dress regulations existed, they were generally observed both in letter and spirit, and teachers reciprocated by not fussing too much about the occasional non-conforming pupil; where no dress regulations existed, even my middle-aged eyes found the turnout of the pupils acceptable. One minor criticism I do make is that some schools seem to regard the chewing of gum as a way of life; and one or two classes in German schools indeed also had a number of compulsive eaters among their pupils. But there are worse sins!

What is much more important is that everywhere, and most of all in Spain and Portugal, I found a delightfully spontaneous friendship and welcome among the boys and girls of all ages. Nowhere have I been made more instantly at home than by the charming young ladies of Form 5c in the *liceu nacional* at Evora, and other Portuguese schools did not lag behind; the intelligent straightforwardness of Spanish pupils spoke eloquently for the standards of manners, morals and conduct in their schools (though the close-knit family life, strong church, and less-pressurized society of Spain also play their part). Italy, too, was most welcoming, though the ebullient and noisy Italian character sometimes left me feeling rather bruised and battered by so much sheer vitality emanating from thirty or so youngsters!

For a good school atmosphere, courtesy must prevail in both directions; the French school where things seemed to have gone a little sour was also the one where I saw the least well-planned lessons and the least considerate attitudes on the part of adults (such as the lady who kept her class standing out in the corridor for some six minutes while she wrote up her notes on the previous lesson). In shining contrast was the happy little village school at Porcellasco, where Rino Fracassi set such a high standard of quiet, gentle courtesy; or the A. Fabretti school at Perugia, where I heard no teacher snap or shout, and where virtually no punishment is ever used, but the pupils move about their work without any disorder; a slight hissing sound from the teacher brings immediate attention.

In some Spanish schools classroom discipline is still quite strict;

for example, pupils sit with their arms folded if they are not actually using them for any scholastic purpose; and I seldom saw a pupil lounging, as our own will sometimes do.

One common form of courtesy in Continental schools is the 'collective salute', by which pupils rise to their feet when any person enters or leaves the room; and when they have to address the teacher individually, they also generally stand. It is a pleasant custom, though I confess to having been trained to think that a good class is one that is so absorbed in its work that it doesn't notice that a stranger has come in. I was sometimes a little embarrassed by the 'collective salute' given in my honour; not realizing that in these circumstances it was I who should invite the pupils to resume their seats, I sometimes shamefully left them standing until the teacher took pity on them and asked me if they might sit down. I was, however, slightly cheered to find that occasionally the teachers themselves would forget that they had left a pupil standing; then the *status quo* was only restored if some bold spirit drew the teacher's attention to his lapse.

A question related to classroom courtesies is the form of address used by teacher to pupil and vice-versa. In general the tendency seems to be, as in England, for teachers to use the Christian names of younger pupils and the surnames of older ones, though sometimes Christian names are also used at the secondary level, and I met one French teacher who formally addressed her ten-year-olds by their surnames. One young woman teacher in Portugal punctiliously called the pupils in her English lesson 'Mr . . .' or 'Miss . . .' but I think she was simply adopting what she felt to be a proper English formality. Pupils generally addressed their teachers as 'Monsieur', 'Madame' or whatever the equivalent was in their own language, except in Germany, where the teacher's name ('Herr Zimmer', say) would be used, and in Italy where 'Maestro' or 'Maestra' was commonly used at the primary level, and 'Professore' at the secondary stage. Now and then a Spanish class also used 'Señor Profesor' – only one *s* this time! – and now and then I met the distinctively Spanish usage of 'Don José', or whatever the name might be. In church schools, too, one sometimes had to remember to address a priest-teacher by his correct ecclesiastical title.

One can often assess the degree of civilization in a school by looking at its desks and walls. Only in France, and occasionally

Germany, was there much evidence of graffiti and aimless scribblings, and even there it was confined to the secondary schools. Indeed, the cleanliness and tidiness of almost all the schools was remarkable not least in countries which the Anglo-Saxon has the temerity to consider less hygienic than his own litter-strewn and dog-befouled paradise. One Spanish headmaster told me with great pride that in the two terms since his new school had opened, damage to furniture and fittings, or soiling of the paintwork and walls, had been virtually nil. And one might go a very long way before finding a cleaner and brighter school than Zewen or Früchteburg in Germany.

The aspect of school discipline which has assumed quite disproportionate importance in English schools is that of uniform, largely because the matter is so greatly magnified by teachers themselves, not to mention governing bodies, old pupils' associations and other mouthpieces of public opinion. It is right, therefore, to give fairly extended treatment to the European approach to the question.

Leaving out Germany, where schools simply have no dress regulations at all, we may say that the European concept is that of requiring the pupil to wear a practical working-dress in the same way that, say, a carpenter or butcher will wear an apron, or a housewife a pinafore. Formal and elaborate uniforms on the English pattern are therefore very rare, though occasionally one finds girls in Spain wearing something of the kind.

School dress is not necessarily a uniform; this is particularly true of France, where many schools, both primary and secondary, prescribe the wearing of the *blouse* but leave the choice of style and colour to the individual, though some *lycées* do request a standard colour. Hence the normal French classroom presents a rather pleasing variety of colour. Boys perhaps will wear a plain overall in blue, grey, white, green or maroon, though many also opt for checked, patterned or striped ones, and each autumn brings to the shops a display of the latest styles *pour la Rentrée* – the 'in thing' of the year may be high Russian-style collars, or zip-fasteners down the side, or applied motifs of sporting or other badges. Nylon is the favourite material, being pretty well indestructible under normal usage. Girls tend to prefer softer or more feminine colours, or livelier patterns, but generally speaking their smocks do not show much difference from those of the boys.

If this attire is not what we normally think of as uniform, it is undeniably practical, quite inexpensive, and rather attractive: indeed, I thought a junior class at Saint-Esprit, Beauvais, with thirty-odd boys in thirty-odd different styles and colours of overall, and a mixed class of boys and girls at the CES J. B. Pellerin both looked as pleasing as anyone might wish.

Portugal comes rather closer to the idea of uniformity. In the primary schools both boys and girls wear pinafores; those of the girls are almost always white, and sometimes rather quaintly formal in style. The boys' pinafores are also often white, but plainer; they may also be of some shade of blue, and it is here that uniformity seems to break down, possibly because the pinafores are not normally on sale in shops but are either made at home or commissioned from a local dressmaker. In one single class at Braga I saw boys in white, ice-blue, sky-blue, a vivid kingfisher blue and navy; sometimes their pinafores buttoned down the back, sometimes at the front, sometimes down one side (not necessarily the 'male' right-hand side, either: possibly pinafores are sometimes handed down from an elder sister?). Portuguese teachers often also wear white smocks in the classroom or on playground duty, though, unlike their pupils, they do not also walk to and from school in them!

In the Portuguese secondary schools, the girls continue to wear some form of white overall; normally the boys wear no uniform at this stage, though one teacher told me that at his school boys also were nominally supposed to wear an overall, and at the Evora *liceu* a few boys, mainly younger ones, kept up the very curious traditional uniform (also seen at the universities) of a Victorian-looking black coat and a college-gown, often rather dilapidated. I assume that these boys, or their parents, were determined traditionalists.

Italy, too, usually has uniform for both boys and girls in the primary schools but for girls only at the secondary stage. The traditional school dress is a rather attractive one comprising a smock coming down to just above the knee, usually fastening behind, and often worn with a broad white collar and a big bow of ribbon called a *fiocco* or *nastro*, which may serve to differentiate between schools or sometimes between classes in the same school. Both boys' and girls' smocks are commonly black or blue; white is also used frequently for the girls, and occasionally for boys. The ribbons may be of almost any colour, but red and blue are common. Pupils sometimes wear a class badge, or the badge of their city, either on the breast or on one sleeve, and occasionally the pupil's name or initials will also be embroidered on the smock. A more modern type of uniform for boys, comprising a short jacket-type smock, is sometimes worn, with or without the collar and ribbon; in Perugia the pupils had small white bow-ties instead of the *fiocco*. In Venice I have seen a few boys in pale blue smocks quite unlike any others I have seen in Italy, and resembling the Spanish type to be described later. At the secondary level, boys occasionally wear the short smocks, but most often have no uniform; girls, however, often retain the black, blue or white pinafores, as we saw when glancing at the rules of the Virgilio school.

Spanish practice is rather variable. Older pupils – those of the *institutos* or the corresponding forms in private schools – do not wear uniform, but a uniform smock is commonly worn in the *colegios nacionales* and in the lower and middle forms of private schools by pupils from the nursery stage up to the school-leaving age of fourteen, though older pupils (as everywhere!) sometimes 'forget' to wear their uniform, and teachers tend to be tolerant about this. The most widespread form of this uniform, as far as boys are concerned, is a garment known as a *bata colegial*; one sees it all over the country and in all types of school. It is a coat-style overall, either of a cotton material or of a modern synthetic fabric; the main body of the garment is patterned with narrow stripes often of grey or blue, and the collar, cuffs, belt and a broad band along the top of the pocket is in a darker contrasting shade – usually navy blue, sometimes another shade of blue, or green, or brown. One may see identical *batas* on the pupils of the large, impressive, private La Salle college at Gerona and on those of a state school serving the poorest quarter of the city; at the Marist College of La Inmaculada, however, the basically similar smock is subtly varied by having a faint pinkish stripe between the blue and white ones, and a badge is sported on the left breast, sometimes with the pupil's school number embroidered below to safeguard against loss. In many schools pupils have their initials or their full name embroidered along the top pocket.

This semi-standard *bata colegial* is a completely classless uniform, but some schools do prefer their own patterns. In Barcelona and

Seville, I saw shop-counters stacked with several different styles, each pile being labelled with the name of the school to which it was appropriate. Besides the usual striped smocks there were some with blue or yellow checks, and others in plain colours. The Sagrada Familia School at Ecija has an attractive uniform of a bright blue smock, belted, with collar and cuffs edged with white; about half the boys were wearing the smocks, with a decided thinning-out the further up the school one went, and the headmaster said he and his staff saw no reason to enforce uniform rigidly.

My impression is that in Spain, as here, uniform is less common than it was for boys; but girls are usually required to wear pinafores, in white or pastel colours. At Jaén, for example, though one school had no pupils of either sex in uniform, another put its girls into decidedly Victorian white pinafores, while boys had no uniform at all; the girls seemed surprised when I said I thought this discrimination a little unfair! A third school, Ramón Calatayud, approximated to the Portuguese system; girls wore white pinafores, and boys either had a simpler white pinafore or a white jacket.

Different uniforms sometimes coexist in the same building; one school had older boys in plain navy smocks and younger ones in the standard striped *bata*, while another had no uniform for older boys, the striped *bata* for middle forms, and a dark blue pinafore with white collar for the smallest boys; in both these schools the girls all had pink pinafores. An Italian school where some children had the traditional black smock with large bow and others had the modern jacket-type garments, probably comes into a different category, however; I think this was a case of pupils from two different schools sharing parts of the same building, which often happens in Italy owing to the shortage of accommodation. More interesting, perhaps, was the situation at São Vitor school, Braga; here most of the boys' classes had a fair proportion of boys in pinafores, but in one class *every* boy was wearing one. On asking why this was, I was told that such matters are within the discretion of the class teacher, and this particular teacher liked to see all his boys in pinafores. Now, as in this school the class teacher moves up each year with his class, it follows that his pupils, 100 per cent pinafored, will soon be the top class of the school. Meditating on this, it struck me that perhaps we are illogical to impose, as we often do, dress regulations on the youngest pupils while exempting the older ones: inevitably, they see school uniform as a symbol of childishness, and lack of it as a mark of emancipation. Perhaps we should consider making a school uniform a mark of seniority and good standing in the school community?

As the Barbiana children point out (page 59 of the Penguin edition of *Letter to a Teacher*), we confidently assert that Education is a Good Thing, of which one can't have enough, and yet when we want to celebrate some national event the first thing we do is to award a day's holiday to the schoolchildren, thereby depriving them of what we have just told them they should value. Logically, Her Majesty should announce that she has been graciously pleased to award an extra day – even an extra week – of school to mark the great event. If we condition children to see school as a prison sentence from which they may be lucky enough to receive an occasional day's remission, of course they will believe us.

Applying this same reasoning to the question of school uniform may lead us to the conclusion that we should stop presenting it as an infliction which one gets rid of as soon as one gets a little older; to the child, eager to grow up, it simply does not make sense to tell him at the same time that he should be proud of his uniform. It would be better psychology to present it as a sort of distinction like the footballer's team jersey or the peer's robes – a mark of having qualified for a privileged and enviable status.

But I cannot help thinking that the European attitude is more sensible – not to associate any emotional ideas at all with the way one dresses for school. The blouse, the *bata*, and the Italian *grembiule* are not marks of any separation, but are worn by almost everybody; they are comfortable and quite attractive; they form a good working-dress with adequate protection for other clothing, and sufficient pockets; and – perhaps their greatest virtue – they are quite inexpensive. Since the pupil must in any case have other clothes to wear out of school, his school dress is always an 'extra', and an 'extra' which costs at most three or four pounds is a far better proposition than the very expensive English notion of uniform. Moreover, the overall is very adaptable to the child's growth, and even when outgrown will easily fit a younger brother or sister; it is easily maintained and kept clean. Now that we have closer links with Europe, we are learning the virtues of some kinds of Continental foods and household articles: is it so very unthinkable that we might also adopt this idea?

As I have already said, German schools do not require their pupils to wear any kind of uniform; and as far as I am aware, they have not done so for a long time. Being aware of this, I was curious to know whether I should find the appearance of a class of pupils impossibly outlandish. I did not; and indeed I rarely saw even the odd individual whose appearance offended my middle-aged eyes. To be truthful, some of their teachers looked far worse! I may have been fortunate, of course; neither Trier nor Emden is the kind of place one would expect to produce anything very subversive, but most of the pupils looked quite attractive. I admit that I did rather wonder why one cheerful thirteen-year-old was wearing a T-shirt inscribed with the one stark word BEAST but no doubt he knew his own business best. Some of the girls are still quite happy to wear such traditional attire as brightly coloured skirts with neat white aprons over them, and quite a number of boys look very comfortable in *lederhosen*, with or without the characteristic ornamental braces.

In discussing with a German class the differences between our schools and their own, I found them totally mystified by the idea of uniform. 'But what's the *point* of it?' they asked, quite heatedly; and they were unanimous that nobody would ever get *them* into uniform. Consequently, I was much amused to see that when they left at the end of the morning, something like two-thirds of this particular class donned bright yellow anoraks of something like p.v.c. That, of course, wasn't uniform . . . it was fashion, which is quite different!

And . . . hair? I have to report that this obsessive topic – as far as English schools are concerned – does not seem to be a great problem in most of my chosen countries. Certainly, I saw a fair number of lads whose hair would possibly not pass muster with a Guards' RSM, but they generally looked clean, tidy and quite acceptable by anyone else's standards. Of those extremes which we have recently learned, if not to love, at least perhaps to live with – pupils with very small heads and spotty faces who make the very worst of their unfortunate situation by growing vast golliwog mops, or demented children who dye their hair scarlet or bright green, I am glad to say that I saw none. Indeed, it was rather a chastening experience to return home and see how much grubbier and scruffier some of our own adolescent children look than do their contemporaries on the Continent. Still, anyone venturing to lay down a standard length or style for what is, after all, the personal possession of another individual human being, had better be warned by the difficulty in which the poet Milton found himself when describing the handsome Adam, in 'Paradise Lost':

> His fair large front and eye sublime declared
> Absolute rule; and hyacinthine locks
> Round from his parted forelock manly hung
> Clust'ring . . .

and then Milton hastily remembers that he is, after all, supposed to be a Puritan, and not very keen on all those Wrong but Romantic Cavalier trends, and he continues the line thus:

> . . . but not beneath his shoulders broad.

Somewhere about the collar was obviously the danger-line, where a 'manly' feature abruptly became abhorrent and subversive of all decency.

So far as I could see, my European colleagues need not yet reach for their shears; though, come to think of it, the Marist College at Jaén did have a completely equipped barber's shop for the boarders: those Spanish schools seem to think of everything!

11
And so...?

As I have admitted already, I knew little about European schools when I began my tour in 1973; now, after a year or more of reflection and digestion, and a large number of further visits, do I know any more? If I do, it is at the price of having discovered how much more there still is to learn; had I the time, money and facilities to undertake several more such tours, I should have just as many questions to ask, though they might be increasingly ones of detail rather than broad principle. Behind the questions I set out in the early pages of this book, to which I perhaps have most of the answers now, loom larger ones: what have we to learn from European schools? Are they doing a better or a worse job than we, and what are the 'hows' and 'whys' behind the answer to that one? If I were a child myself, would I rather go to an English school or to one on the Continent?

I believe that there are indeed some ways in which European schools indeed may be doing a better job than their English counterparts. I do not necessarily mean thereby that they are always, and in all ways, better; as between two cricket teams one could say that this one fields better, or that one runs better between the wickets, without implying that the team praised would inevitably win all its matches. I feel sure, for example, that the average eight- or twelve-year-old child on the Continent will be able to make an altogether better job of writing a page of his own language than will the English child of the same age. It will be better in handwriting, better spelled, better punctuated, better in the grammatical and syntactical formation of its sentences, better in its command of simple stylistic devices. Why and how this is achieved is partly, I think, a matter of professional expertise, and partly a matter of attitude. Many English teachers are far too ready to use the teaching of the native language either as an opportunity to discuss social problems in a vague and unscientific way, or as an activity whose sole end is 'creative expression' such as, say, the art lesson may offer. Consequently, the reading material offered to the pupil is often third-rate or worse, chosen not because it is well-written or capable of enriching the imagination of its readers, but because it deals with some current popular obsession such as the colour-problem, conservation or drugs; and the content of what the child writes (always assuming that it is possible to discover any content) is far more important than the clarity or accuracy with which he says it. But there *is* a difference between an art lesson and an English lesson: the painter need not always have a precise meaning to convey; if his technique is imperfect, the result may be a poor painting, but it is unlikely to be an ambiguous or a confused one; the painter does not have to express complex reasoning or logical processes. Whereas the writer *does*, usually, have a precise meaning to convey; sloppy writing *will* produce confusion and doubt in the reader's mind; the writer must be prepared if need be to convey more than just feeling, excitement or pleasure.

Now, the European teacher realizes these things, and so his approach is different: from the outset he will demand a greater degree of formality and exactness than is generally expected in England today. Accordingly, he disciplines himself and his pupils to use language rather as mathematics may be used – as a set of symbols with definite meanings, requiring to be combined in accordance with precise laws so that they may convey more complex concepts. They do not spend as much of their 'native language' periods as we do on really rather unimportant books, on third-rate poetry, on the acting of dismal little 'One-Act Plays for Junior Forms'. Just recently we read of the great success achieved by some teachers in Bradford who have coached immigrant pupils to a higher standard of English than native-born children, by insisting on such techniques as the use of complete sentences and an embargo on the 'one-word answer'. Of course this produces better results, as any French schoolmistress could have told us – or indeed, as our own grandparents knew. I am less sure that the formal approach to grammar beloved of European teachers would work equally well with our own less highly-structured language, for almost any 'rule' one tries to make in English turns out to have innumerable exceptions, and few of our most characteristic idioms are capable of being satisfactorily classified in orthodox grammatical terms; there may, however, be hope along the new lines suggested by some modern books.*

This high degree of professionalism is, I think, even more clearly revealed in the second lesson I should like English teachers to learn from Europe. This is the great value of a little self-discipline on the teacher's part; for example, in keeping full and formal records of work done, and the results achieved; in studying the individual requirements of his pupils and organizing work suitable to fit them; in discussing their progress and their problems regularly with his colleagues. I feel sure we should be making more use than we do of such tools as the official log-book on the classroom desk, the individual work-sheet for the brilliant or the backward pupil, the class council meeting once or twice in each term. And, as the flesh is sometimes weak, these things should be a statutory obligation upon us English teachers as they are upon our European colleagues, for even the best of us may otherwise neglect these chores.

Ask a layman what he thinks is wrong with English education, and you will find high on his list the charge that many of our pupils leave the schools virtually illiterate, the accusation that many of them also cock a snook at such discipline as their schools may still try to impose, and the charge that teachers are often indifferent to their pupils' difficulties, doing no more than scribble 'Must work harder' on the end-of-term report. I think it highly probable that

*For example, in F. S. Scott *et al.*, *English Grammar: a Linguistic Study of its Classes and Structures* (London, Heinemann, 1970).

some of these grave failings could be largely put right if we moved closer to the European approach.

I should like, too, to see some degree of standardization and co-ordination in our school curricula. I do not want wholesale direction from an official in Whitehall; I cherish as much as the next man my freedom to teach my subject in my own way, to vary my syllabus, to spend the odd period in doing what a very wise old friend of mine once called 'pushing a bit of culture between the cracks of the curriculum'. But that does not mean that I think it sensible, or necessary, to have half-a-dozen quite different systems of secondary education in our one small country; or that a pupil may move fifty miles from a school where he has taken French as his sole foreign language, done biology and chemistry but not physics, studied modern mathematics, and played rugby, and find himself in a school where the first foreign language is German, where he learns physics but not biology, where the mathematics syllabus is strictly 'trad', and everybody plays soccer. This sort of nonsense does not happen in France, or Spain, or Italy.

There are, of course, many lesser details for which one could argue. I should like to see our schools equipped with those plastic-topped desks which I so much liked in Italy and elsewhere; I should far prefer to see our schoolboys attired in Spanish *batas* or French *blouses* rather than the expensive and impractical British blazer; I do not see why we cannot have as good medical facilities in our schools as some European ones have, or why our buildings cannot be designed with the same sense of space as are the best modern German ones. On the other hand, one can point to many things one is glad to be spared: the idiotic Italian school-hours; the cramped and dusty playgrounds of Spain and Portugal; the prison-like interiors of so many French school buildings; the material deprivations endured by so many Portuguese schools; the over-solicitous regulations and rigid 'democracy' of the German school system; the bureaucracy . . .

And one facet of the European school at its best may also reflect its greatest weakness: the very fact that the teachers are so astonishingly good at imparting a controlled amount of formal knowledge and skill to their pupils – the fact that they are so formidably professional, indeed – means that they tend to lack the cheerfully amateur versatility of the English teacher. Few of us in English schools have not turned our hands to producing a play, running a Scout troop, organizing a library, playing in a school orchestra – indeed, many a teacher has in the course of his career done several such things. Our pupils can put on pretty good concerts, stage near-professional productions of *Macbeth* or turn out teams which can give a good game to a strong club side; and we do these things a good deal more frequently than do our European counterparts. There, in general, comes the end of the day, and out troop the pupils; a few minutes later the teachers and the *surveillants* put on their coats and drive off home; the cleaners move in; and soon silence has fallen. The school is a place where one goes to work, and all that happens there is a facet of that work.

This is fair enough, of course; if the extra-curricular activities can be provided elsewhere, there is no absolute need for a school to provide them. But it does make a difference to the atmosphere. If there is more seriousness of purpose and more desire to acquire knowledge, there may perhaps also be more anxiety and more stress.

I should not accept, as some might, that because European teachers are in this respect more aloof from their pupils, they are any less liked or respected by them; indeed, they possibly thereby avoid the pitfall of familiarity breeding a sort of contempt. Anyway, they are very aware of the possible dangers, and many of them are concerned to try to break down the old barriers, to descend from the dais and become more accessible to their pupils. There does, however, remain a gap. And perhaps that is as good a lead-in as any to my question: if I were a child, would I prefer to go to school in England or on the Continent?

Of course, if I really were a child, I might anyway not see the matter as I now do; but if I must try to answer my own curious question, I think the answer must be a doubt. Only one school I visited, a French secondary school, showed me any appreciable number of pupils who were clearly discontented with their lot, and I think I sensed the reasons for that. Elsewhere, I was surrounded by friendly and smiling faces, even at that adolescent stage where a melancholy aspect is almost a fact of life. I have certainly seen many more glum faces coming out of English schools than I did in Europe, for all that the school day here is far more varied and enjoyable than it is there. Perhaps part of the

And so...?

answer to this paradox is that in some of the countries I visited there is still something rather splendid about the whole idea of education: children want it, are serious about it, and will put up with its more austere face because they know it is a Good Thing. So, if I were a Spanish boy, I should be very happy in a Spanish school, and that is generally true of the other countries, though least so in the two most industrially advanced, France and Germany. If I were an English boy suddenly transplanted there, I should also be happy, though I should miss some of the activities of my English school and should probably find the work somewhat more pedestrian. I think the best Spanish schools, and perhaps also some of the best Portuguese, would probably provide the closest approximation in atmosphere to what I had been used to at home: I should probably find the pace of French schools rather too intensive and that of the Italian rather too relaxed. As for Germany, I am less sure; the German schools have many really excellent qualities, but it was there that I felt the greatest difference from the English school. If I had to sum up my doubts about Germany in one short sentence, I might say that I felt there the same uneasy conflict between authoritarianism and freedom in the schools that I also feel in the country as a whole: can the German laugh at himself as the Englishman, the Frenchman and the Spaniard can? For, surely, the capacity not to take oneself too seriously is more necessary for the schoolmaster than for most people?

Perhaps that last reflection brings me nearer to the adult point of view than to that of the pupil, and I must conclude with an attempt to look at matters from the angle of the parent. I think I should be very pleased to see any child of mine entrusted to the schools of Europe. Of course, I might be unlucky: I might find a school which was dull and unimaginative, as I did here and there in France; or materially deprived, as sometimes in Portugal; and as I have said, I have certain reservations about Germany. But the average would, I think, give me little to worry about, and the best would be very good indeed. As to discipline, I should be fairly happy: there are no harsh punishments, and such rules as there are seem to be mostly sensible and acceptable ones; standards of manners, courtesy and behaviour are generally high; I saw no evidence of bullying, and less of that form of cruelty which involves jeering at a classmate who makes a mistake, or teasing one who is somehow different, than in our own schools.

I have heard the phrase 'ordered freedom' used to describe the atmosphere in a good English school, and I would willingly borrow it for most of those I saw on the Continent. Some might find it strange that I can include in that tribute many schools from countries whose political systems and laws are more rigid than our own; yet it is true that pupils in their schools often have more freedom in such matters as dress, coming and going, smoking and so on than our own do. Perhaps the schools there know that they can afford to concede these freedoms because there is a framework outside the school that ensures a high standard of personal responsibility and civil obedience. Perhaps we ourselves need to learn that liberty, of all things, demands a society which can substitute its own self-discipline for disciplines imposed from without; if we cannot provide that self-discipline, we may have to lose some of the liberties we have gained. Certainly, in education as well as in other aspects of our society, we have to work very hard to understand the nature of freedom; and, if we cannot achieve that understanding, I shall have more fears about what may happen to children in some of our own schools than I would have about any of those I visited in Europe.

POSTSCRIPT

I was sorry to learn from a German teacher whom I recently met in Frankfurt that the problem of poor reading and writing is on the increase in Germany. These things are, however, relative, and her standard of comparison is probably a very exacting one.

Appendix I
Curriculum in France

The following details are based on official documents; the data given may be taken as generally representative, but variations do exist.

Primary

There are 27 hours in the school week, divided as follows:

French 10 hrs – Mathematics 5 hrs – *Éveil* 6 hrs – Physical education and games 6 hrs.

(The term *éveil*, or 'awakening', covers all the 'interest' subjects such as history, geography, science, art, music and handicraft.)

Secondary

The allocation of time in the first two years of CES is about $27\frac{1}{2}$ hrs, divided as follows:

French 6 hrs – Mathematics 4 hrs – Science 2 hrs – First foreign language (usually German or English) 4 hrs – History and civics 2½ hrs – Geography 1 hr – Art 1 hr – Handicraft 1 hr – Music 1 hr – PE and games 5 hrs.

From the third year onwards, there are 26 hours of compulsory subjects, plus a varying amount of optional work. The compulsory subjects are:

French 5 hrs – Mathematics 4 hrs – Science 1 hr – Foreign language 3 hrs – Pre-technology 2 hrs – History, civics and geography 3 hrs – Art 1 hr – Handicraft 1 hr – Music 1 hr – PE and games 5 hrs.

The pupil MUST further choose one, and MAY choose two, options from:

Latin 4 hrs – Greek 3 hrs – second foreign language (English, German, Spanish, Italian or Russian, though probably few schools can offer all these) 3 hrs – Additional work in first foreign language 2 hrs.

This is the programme offered to pupils in streams of Type I and Type II. The less able Type III pupil has a simpler version of this curriculum, without the options. His 30-hour week is made up of:

French 6 hrs – Mathematics 5 hrs – Science 1 hr – Foreign language 5 hrs – Pre-technology 2 hrs – History, civics and geography 3 hrs – Art 1 hr – Music 1 hr – Handicraft 1 hr – PE and games 5 hrs.

Lycée

The *lycée* pupil entering the 2e Classe, roughly equivalent to an English fifth form, has four possible routes to his *baccalauréat* (besides certain technical courses, which I am not dealing with here); these are called Courses A, AB, C and T, and the allocation of time to the common-core subjects is as follows:

	Number of hours			
	A	AB	C	T
French	5	5	5	4
Mathematics	3	3	5	5
Physical science	3	3	4	4

Curriculum in France

	Number of hours			
	A	AB	C	T
Foreign language	3	3	3	3
History, civics and geography	4	4	4	2
Physical education and games	5	5	5	5
Total of common-core subjects	23	23	26	23

There is then a choice of further *compulsory* studies:

Course A
1. 3 hrs each of Latin and Greek (beginners in either have 5 hrs).
2. 3 hrs each of Latin OR Greek and a second foreign language (again, beginners have 5 hrs).
3. A second foreign language (beginners only) 5 hrs.
4. 3 hrs of a second foreign language, plus 2 hrs of extra French or extra time on the first foreign language.
5. 3 hrs each of a second and a third foreign language.
6. 3 hrs of music plus 3 of Latin OR Greek OR a second foreign language.
7. 3 hrs of art plus 3 of Latin OR Greek OR a second foreign language.

Course AB
1. 3 hrs of Latin OR Greek plus 4 of economics.
2. 3 hrs of a second foreign language (beginners have 5 hrs) plus 4 of economics.
3. 4 hrs of economics plus 5 of commerce and typewriting.

Course C   No further compulsory studies.

Course T
1. Mechanics and electricity course: technical drawing, technology, and workshop practice.
2. Civil engineering course: technical drawing and geometry, and workshop practice.
3. Laboratory course: technical drawing or biology techniques, and glassblowing, plus extra physics and laboratory practice.
4. Medical/social course: biology plus medical-social sciences, including typewriting.

All the Course T options are of 12 hrs weekly.

Lastly, students may also add the following further *optional* subjects:

Any one of the A and AB courses may add options from: additional mathematics 2 hrs; drawing, music, handicraft 1 hr each.

Courses AB1 and AB2 may also add typewriting (3 hrs).

Course AB3 may add a second foreign language (3 hrs, or 5 hrs for beginners).

The C course may add options from: Latin 3 hrs; Greek 3 hrs; second foreign language 3 hrs (or 5 for beginners); drawing, music, handicraft 1 hr each. Courses T1, T2 and T3 may add as an option 1 hr of drawing; and Course T4 may add an option from the following: drawing 1 hr, music 1 hr, initiation into social and family life 1 hr or second foreign language 2 hrs.

Under the proposals for reform, already mentioned, this specialization would be postponed for one year, and all pupils would continue with the general curriculum, to which would be added economics and technology for all. The final years of the course would offer three *baccalauréat* sections; letters and philosophy; humanistic, economic and social sciences; mathematics and sciences; there would be two sections in the organization of technological education, one for industrial technology, and the other for economic technology. As now, there would be common-core subjects in all these courses, and a range of options within the basic programmes.

Appendix II
Curriculum in Italy

Information about the primary schools is based on personal observation; that for the secondary schools on official publications, though the latter do not always agree either with each other or with what actually appears to happen.

Primary

The week contains about 24 hours. Pupils normally study Italian, mathematics, and some elementary history, geography, science and religious knowledge. Sometimes other subjects like art, music and handicraft may be available, but this is exceptional, though a few schools have begun providing these in additional afternoon sessions.

Secondary

In the first year of the *scuola media*, the pupils work a total of about 25 hours, studying Italian (6 hrs), history, civics and geography

(4 hrs), a foreign language – English or German (2 hrs), mathematics (3 hrs), science (2 hrs), art (2 hrs), handicraft (2 hrs), music (1 hr), religion (1 hr) and physical education (2 hrs).

At the time of my visit the allocations were:

Italian, including some elementary Latin (9 hrs), history, civics and geography (4 hrs), a foreign language (3 hrs), mathematics (3 hrs), science (2 hrs), art (2 hrs), religion (1 hr), physical education (2 hrs).

This gave a basic weekly total of 26 hours, to which pupils could voluntarily add one hour of music and/or two of handicraft, so extending their weekly stint to 27, 28 or 29 hours.

Now, however, I understand that Latin is completely out, which has been called 'a victory for those who regard Latin as useless, divisive, anti-democratic, racist and reactionary'! Music has been added to the compulsory subjects, and technical studies to the voluntary ones.

In the third year, the time for Italian is reduced and that for science increased.

Liceo

Ignoring the specialist schools such as the *liceo artistico* or *liceo linguistico*, there are two main types, the *scientifico* and the *classico*; in these, the allocation of hours in each year of the course is as follows:

	LICEO SCIENTIFICO					LICEO CLASSICO				
Year	1	2	3	4	5	1	2	3	4	5
Italian lang. and lit.	4	4	4	3	4	5	5	4	4	4
Latin lang. and lit	4	5	4	4	3	5	5	4	4	4
Foreign lang. and lit.	3	4	3	3	4	4	4	–	–	–
Greek lang. and lit.	–	–	–	–	–	4	4	3	3	3
History	3	2	2	2	3	2	2	3	3	3
Geography	2	–	–	–	–	2	2	–	–	–
Philosophy	–	–	2	3	3	–	–	3	3	3
Natural science, chemistry and geography	–	2	3	3	2	–	–	4	3	2
Physics	–	–	2	3	3	–	–	–	2	3
Mathematics	5	4	3	3	3	2	2	3	2	2
Art	1	3	2	2	2	–	–	1	1	2
Religious education	1	1	1	1	1	1	1	1	1	1
Physical education	2	2	2	2	2	2	2	2	2	2
Total	25	27	28	29	30	27	27	28	28	29

Appendix III
Curriculum in Portugal

Having been unable to obtain very much in the way of official information about Portugal, I have based the following brief summary upon my own observation in the schools:

Primary

There are 28 hours in the working week. An actual school which I visited had allocated this time in the following way:
Portuguese 5 hrs – Mathematics 5 hrs – Science with geography 4 hrs – History 3 hrs – Religion 2 hrs – Handicraft 2 hrs – Art 2 hrs – Physical education 2 hrs – Music 1 hr – Visits, etc., 2 hrs.

Secondary

At the time of writing there is no basic secondary education in Portugal. The *ciclo preparatorio* continues with a curriculum much like that of the primary school, but introduces a foreign language also.

Liceu

The timetable of a first-year class at the Evora *liceu* was based on the following allocation:

Portuguese 4 hrs – Mathematics 4 hrs – First foreign language (French, begun in *ciclo preparatorio*) 2 hrs – Second foreign language (English, started at *liceu*) 4 hrs – Physics 3 hrs – Biology 2 hrs – History 2 hrs – Geography 2 hrs – Art 2 hrs – Handicraft 1 hr – Music 1 hr – Religion 1 hr – Physical education and games 3 hrs.

Total for the week, 31 hours.

Appendix IV
Curriculum in Spain

The information is taken from official publications.

EGB first stage

The programme is based on the concept of 'areas' as already explained. The periodical *Vida Escolar* (Dec 1970) suggested that about 40–50 per cent of the time at this stage should be spent in a general treatment of the 'areas of expression', through topics taken from the 'areas of experience'; about the same time in specific treatment of the separate areas; and the remaining time on 'complementary activities'. It may however be more enlightening to report that the printed timetable of one class of 10–11-year-old boys provided for about 27½ hours per week, divided as follows:

7 hrs for 'individual work' based on the *ficha* system described in this book, which would normally include some practice in every 'area'.

$20\frac{1}{2}$ hrs allotted to the various disciplines, with the largest allocations ($2\frac{1}{2}$–3 hrs each) going to French, physical education and religious knowledge, and the smallest (1 hr each) to music, art and civic education. The other subjects received about $1\frac{1}{2}$ hrs a week each.

This allocation may seem to give very little space to Spanish and mathematics, but it must be remembered that the 7 hours of work on *fichas* would in practice involve a lot of writing and calculation: the $1\frac{1}{2}$ hours would simply be time spent in giving and receiving instruction.

Other schools might well interpret the syllabus quite differently; both the flexibility and the uncertainty of the new order in Spanish education are revealed.

EGB second stage

The *Vida Escolar* article suggests the following division of time:

		%
Areas of expression 46%	Spanish	20
	mathematics	13
	foreign language	13
Areas of experience 20%	science	10
	socio-cultural subj.	10
The arts 12%	music	6
	plastic arts	6
Physical education and sport		10
Technical subjects		6
Religion		6

It is not easy, however, to translate these curious percentages into terms of a 28-hour working week.

There is little change in this programme during the three years of EGB second stage.

Institutos de bachillerato

The *bachillerato* programme is to be revised by 1977–8; the following information is based on the existing system:

In the first two years, there is a broad general course comprising:

Spanish 3 hrs – Mathematics 3 hrs – Latin 3 hrs – History 3 hrs – Foreign language 3 hrs – Physics and chemistry 3 hrs – Religion 2 hrs – Handicraft (boys) or domestic science (girls) 2 hrs – Civics 1 hr – Physical education 3 hrs.

This adds up to 26 hours, but the pupil must attend for 30 hours a week, the balance being made up with various complementary or voluntary subjects (or, for some, with the 'recuperation' of weak subjects).

After two years of this, the pupil specializes on either an arts or a science course. During the third year, there is a 16-hour common core comprising 5 hours science, 3 each of a foreign language and physical education, 2 each of religion and art, and 1 of civics; to this the arts student adds 5 hours of Latin and 4 of Greek, the scientist 5 of mathematics and 4 of chemistry. In the fourth year, the common core is 18 hours, including 5 each of literature and philosophy; 3 of history of culture; and 5 devoted to religion, civics and physical education. Arts students add 3 hours of Latin and 4 of Greek; science students take 3 of mathematics and 4 of physics.

Finally comes the *curso de orientación universitaria*, involving 4 hours weekly of Spanish; 3 of a foreign language; 2 of mathematics; 3 of each of three chosen subjects; 1 each of religion and civics. Four hours weekly are devoted to 'Orientation Seminars'; and 6 further hours must be spent in individual work, initiation into research, etc.

Appendix V
Curriculum in West Germany

There is, properly speaking, no single system for the whole Bundesrepublik; it is hoped that the information given below will be found reasonably typical, however.

Primary

A specimen school timetable shown to me indicated that the youngest children, aged 6–7, spent about 18 hours a week in school. 14 hours were labelled *Anfangsunterricht* (basic knowledge) and the rest went on physical and aesthetic education. Second-year children followed a similar programme, though rather longer and with the addition (for girls) of some needlework. For the remainder of the primary school course, pupils worked about 22–3 hours a week, spending roughly half their time on the mother tongue, 5–6 hours on mathematics, 2 hours on religious knowledge (it was a Catholic school) and the rest on physical and aesthetic education. Some schools' timetables also include provision for an hour or two of additional work (*Förderunterricht*) in

German and mathematics where this is required. Many schools now begin the study of a foreign language in the last two years of primary education; these years are nowadays regarded as a diagnostic period preparatory to deciding on the best form of secondary education.

Secondary

I give below specimen allocations of time for the first two years of secondary education (classes 7 and 8, for pupils aged 12–14; but if, as is proposed, the age of starting school is lowered to 5, these classes will be aged 11–13).

	HAUPTSCHULE		REALSCHULE		GYMNASIUM	
	Class 7	*Class 8*	*Class 7*	*Class 8*	*Class 7*	*Class 8*
German	5	5	4	5	4	4
Mathematics	4*	4*	4	4	4	4
English	4*	4*	4	4	–	–
1st foreign lang.	–	–	–	–	4	3
2nd foreign lang.	–	–	–	–	5	5
History	2	2	2	2	2	2
Geography	2	2	2	2	2	2
Biology	1	1	2	1	2	2
Physics	2	2	2	2	–	2
Chemistry	1	1	–	1	–	–
Music	1½	1½	2	1	2	4§
Art	1½	1½	1	1	3§	4§
Handicraft	4†	4†	1	1	3§	4§
Physical Education	3	3	3	3	3	3
'Options'	–	–	4‡	4‡	–	–
Total	31	31	31	31	31	31

*Mathematics and English are taught in streamed groups; other subjects in mixed-ability classes.

†This subject is called *Arbeitslehre* and may cover economics, domestic science, various types of craft, simple technology etc. The idea, I think, is to familiarize the pupil with the world of industry and labour.

‡These options include a second language, domestic science, additional periods of mathematics and science, or economics.

§Pupils take one only of these optional subjects.

I

From the third year of secondary education, the picture becomes more complicated.

A typical *Hauptschule* timetable showed that certain optional subjects began, at first with two, later with four, periods weekly. The first group comprised physics, chemistry and biology; the second art, music and handicraft. Pupils chose one subject from each group and studied it for the whole year. At the same time, there appeared what were known as *Arbeitsgemeinschaften*, or 'study groups'. Each pupil could choose one or two subjects from a wide range including typewriting, shorthand, photography, handicraft, swimming, physical education, English literature, domestic science for boys, etc. Subjects could be changed halfway through the year if the pupil so wished.

Basic subjects continued as in the first two years, though PE ceased to be compulsory, and certain subjects were reduced slightly to allow time for the options.

Changes in the curriculum for the third and fourth years of the *Realschule* are only of a minor nature, involving slight adjustments of the time for certain subjects and the introduction of an option system for art, music and handicraft similar to that used in the *Gymnasium*.

In the later years of the *Gymnasium*, a wide range of subjects continues to be studied, as in the *lycées* and similar schools in other countries. Additional languages, such as Greek, may be introduced by pupils wishing to do so; several periods a week are devoted by older pupils to political philosophy; and a certain number of periods in Classes 11, 12 and 13 are set aside for opional studies to meet the students' own interests. The number of tours worked during the week rises from 31 in Classes 7 and 8 to 33 in Classes 9 and 10, and 36 in the three highest classes.

Appendix VI
Numbering of classes

France

The five years of primary school are known respectively as *cours préparatoire*, *cours élémentaire* I and II, and *cours moyen* I and II. Having thus reached the top class of the lowest level of school and called it the 'middle course', there seems to be a good case for a fresh start, and in the CES the first class is called the *sixième* (6th), and subsequent classes number backwards; that is, the second year is called the 5th, the third year the 4th, the 4th year the 3rd, and the 5th year (by which time we are in the *lycée* or other upper school) the 2nd. The 6th year is called the 1st, and as many pupils in fact do a seven-year course, the final year is called, with about the one bit of logic in the whole system, the *terminale*.

Italy

The *scuola elementare* classes are numbered from I to V, and those of the *scuola media* from I to III.

Spain

The lowest class of the EGB is called the 1st, and the numbering is continuous until the highest class of stage 2 is reached, which is known as the 8th.

Portugal

Primary schools run from 1st class upwards, and secondary classes start again at 1st.

West Germany

German classes begin with the 1st in the lowest year of the primary school (*Grundschule*) and nowadays usually number continuously through primary and secondary stages to the 9th, 10th or 13th as the case may be. Classes 1–4 will be in the *Grundschule*; 5 and 6 will form the *Orientierung* stage; 7, 8 and 9 may be in a *Hauptschule*, a *Realschule* or a *Gymnasium*; anything above 9 is found only in the *Realschule* or *Gymnasium*. But sometimes in the *Gymnasium* one finds a determined clinging to an older tradition of giving classes Latin, or hybrid German-Latin, names; the first year pupils are called the *Sexta*, and one then works upwards through *Quinta* and *Quarta*, *Unter-* and *Ober-tertia*, *Unter-* and *Ober-secunda*, to end with *Unter-* and *Ober-prima*. It is all rather like those baffling Shells and Removes beloved of the late Mr Frank Richards.

Appendix VII
Working hours

Many local variations are found, of course, and the timings given below may vary by, say, half an hour at almost any point. The object of the table is simply to give a reasonably accurate picture of typical practice in the five countries.

	Start of school day	Morning session	Midday break	Afternoon session	End of school day
France (primary)	8.30	3	2	3	16.30
(secondary)	8.30	4	1½	3½	17.30
Italy	8.30	4	—	—	12.30
Spain (EGB)	9.00	3½	2½–3	2½	17.30
(instituto)	9.00	4½	2½–3	2½	18.30
Portugal	9.00	3	1½	2½	16.00
West Germany	8.00	5	—	—	13.00

In Germany often, and elsewhere occasionally, the actual hours worked by the pupil may vary from day to day: for example, if the school is open for six teaching periods daily on six days a week, but the pupils' timetable only includes a weekly total of thirty periods, one class may leave on some days after doing only, say, four periods, or arrive on other days only in time for the start of lesson two. Thus, there is a lot more coming-and-going during the day than we should expect in our own schools.

Saturdays are sometimes normal working days; sometimes they are shortened working days; sometimes they are used only for out-of-class activities; sometimes they are not used for school purposes at all. It is impossible to generalize.

French schools have one free day in the middle of each week, either Wednesday or Thursday; this is almost invariably found, even though some heretics have questioned the practice in recent years.

In the hotter regions of Spain, pupils attend school in the mornings only during the last three weeks of the summer term and the first week or so of the autumn term, when the afternoon heat would make work impossible.

Appendix VIII

Some notes on teachers' salaries

Italy

New salary scales come into force in 1976 (with a further increase authorised for 1977). By these scales, a teacher commencing his career in a *scuola elementare* will earn a gross monthly salary of 180,575 lire (about £120); regular increments can bring him to a maximum of 400,620 lire per month after forty years. If he teaches in a *scuola media*, he will commence at 213,037 lire per month (about £141) and can rise to 474,639 lire monthly in his fortieth year of teaching (about £314). Teachers of technical and practical subjects receive slightly higher pay than the elementary school teachers and there are, of course, extra payments (though by our reckoning very modest ones) for *Direttori Didattici* and for *Presidi* (heads of secondary schools). In a working year, a primary school teacher faces a class for some 738 hours, and has no free periods; in the *scuola media*, hours ranged from 468 per year (foreign languages and mathematics) to 540 hours, but are now, I believe, being increased.

Spain

The Embassy in London kindly informs me that in 1974 teachers' salaries were:

Basic salary: 151,632 pesetas (about £1,150) per annum at the minimum and 273,472 pesetas (about £2,070) at the maximum.

Supplements: A married teacher with two children who was required to live away from home might add about £400 to his pay through marriage allowance, children's allowances, and lodging allowance. There are also payments for some special responsibilities.

The teacher at an *instituto de bachillerato* would earn from 324,000 to 720,000 pesetas, according to the number of hours he chose to teach (i.e. about £2,460 to £5,460). Special allowances are also available to him.

EGB teachers at present teach for 29 hours a week. In the *instituto*, a teacher may work either ordinary, full or exclusive hours (the last implies that he renounces any other paid work such as private coaching): thus he may work from 25 to 40 hours, of which about two-thirds is actual teaching, the rest being devoted to administration, evaluation, preparation of lessons, etc.

A 'Teachers' Charter' is on the way, which will officially establish extra compulsory paid duties such as evaluation, staff meetings, training courses, preparation of lessons, etc.

Teachers in non-state schools often earn a good deal less.

Portugal

The Embassy in London quotes (1974) the following rates:

Primary schools: 3,400 to 4,700 escudos (about £60–£82) a month, for about 28 hours' teaching per week.

Liceus: 6,670 to 10,810 escudos (about £116–£188) a month, for about 22 hours a week.

France (1974)

Primary schools: 16,800 to 32,000 francs a year (£1,530 to £2,910).

CES: 20,000 to 44,350 francs a year (£1,830 to £4,030).

Lycées: 25,500 to 61,750 francs a year (£2,320 to £5,610).

Teachers' salaries

Number of hours taught in the week:

Primary schools: about 27; CES: about 21; *lycées*: 15–18.

Germany (1974)

A German friend informs me that a schoolmaster aged thirty, married with two children, would earn 2,100 DM per month in the *Grundschule* (about £350), 2,300 in the *Realschule* (about £380) and 2,550 in the *Gymnasium* (about £425). These are gross salaries before the deduction of taxes, superannuation payments, etc. The weekly hours of teaching are, respectively, 28, 25 and 23 periods each of 45 minutes.

Appendix IX

Blueprint for a Spanish school

The Ministry publication *La Reforma Educativa en Marcha* of 1973, proposes the following provision for a school of 640 pupils (EGB):

	Area in square metres	Total area in square metres
Years 1–3		
Six spaces for class activities, each	50	300
One area for individual work	188	188
Two tutorial rooms, each	13	26
Infants' toilets	22	22
		536
Years 4–5		
Two class-activity spaces, each	50	100
One area for individual work	230	230
Two tutorial rooms, each	13	26
		356

	Area in square metres	Total area in square metres
Years 6–8		
Science laboratory area	180	180
Resources area	50	50
Audio-visual room	94	94
Five class-activity spaces, each	50	250
Two tutorial rooms, each	13	26
		600
Common use		
Library, resources-centre, store	95	95
Multiple activities area (art, music, etc.)	300	300
Interview room (parents)	22	22
		417
Miscellaneous		
Administration (office, headmaster, director of studies, visitors and staff common room)	148	148
Caretaker's room	80	80
Other general services	281	281
Circulation space	322	322
		831
Total area		2,740

Average area per pupil 4·3 square metres

In addition, there is proposed a space of 330 sq. m. for a gymnasium with its necessary changing-rooms, stores, etc.; and 300 sq. m. of covered playing accommodation.

The same booklet also gives figures for a mixed *instituto de bachillerato* of 810 pupils. Here the suggested division is by areas of study, some of which divide further into separate areas for the boys and girls. Dimensions of principal rooms are:

	square metres
Classrooms	50 each
Seminar rooms, for small groups	22 each
Laboratories (three in all)	94 each
Library, with offices and store	155 each
Art and craft area	144 each
'Dynamic expression' area (music)	94 each

Again, there is liberal provision of small spaces for tutorial interviews, preparation of teaching material, offices for departmental heads, etc.

Glossary

Obviously not in any sense a comprehensive dictionary of educational terms, this list is provided to give the reader a rough definition of terms used in this book without the need to turn back to the actual references.

Abitur (Ger.) is the common abbreviation for the school-leaving examination corresponding roughly to *baccalauréat*, etc. The term *Reifezeugnis* is also used, and means exactly the same as the Italian term (*certificato de*) *maturita*.

Additivgesamtschule (Ger.) is a comprehensive school, formed by combining three types of secondary school on one site.

Arbeitsgemeinschaften (Ger.) are the study-groups from which pupils in the upper forms of the secondary school may supplement the more academic part of their curriculum.

Aula (It., Sp. and Port.) is a generic word for a classroom.

Baccalauréat (Fr.) and *Bachillerato* (Sp.), though obviously connected etymologically with 'bachelor', approximate nearly to our GCE A level. But they normally exact a much greater number of subjects than our examination does.

Bata (Sp., Port.) is the name given to the overall or smock which forms the usual school dress for boys up to the age of about fourteen and for girls throughout their school life. In Spain the term *delantal* is also sometimes used.

Bedel (Port.) and *Bidello* (It.): the officials employed in many schools as janitor, caretaker or messenger. The French would call this a *concierge*, the Germans a *Hausmeister*.

Blouse (Fr.): an overall-like garment, usually nowadays of nylon or the like, often worn in French schools by pupils of either sex. Those worn by younger pupils are also called *tabliers*, and an older term is *sarrau*.

Cahier (Fr.) is the word the French dictionary gives for 'exercise-book' but it can also mean a record of marks, or an album such as would be produced in project work. The basic idea is presumably 'a little book'.

Carnet de correspondance (Fr.) is a report-book.

Centro cultural (Sp.): a centre where educational materials and facilities are available, such as film-projectors, slides and records; there will be lecture-rooms, studios and perhaps a library; courses of many kinds will be held there, and also a certain amount of social life. In other words, it combines some of the functions of a library, a teachers' centre and an adult education centre. In France, called a *centre de documentation pédagogique*.

Certificado de escolaridad (Sp.) could literally be translated 'School certificate', but this would be misleading; it is merely a document certifying that the course has been completed, and implies that the holder has *not* gained the title of *graduado escolar* (q.v.). If not very valuable in itself, one probably can't get a job without it.

Ciclo preparatorio (Port.) has nothing to do with the English 'prep school' or the French *cours préparatoire*: it is the stage of education following the end of the primary school at twelve and continuing until the new official leaving-age of fourteen: it is presumably preparatory to entry into a *liceu* or the like.

Circolo didattico (It.) slightly resembles the French concept of a *groupe scolaire* (q.v.); it comprises a number of schools in the same general area of the town, which share their director or headmaster, in common.

Colegio nacional (Sp.) is the common-core school combining our own primary and junior secondary stages, for pupils between six and fourteen.

Collège d'enseignement sécondaire (Fr.) is very much the same kind of thing as the upper part of the *colegio nacional*, or as the high schools in some English reorganized systems: a comprehensive school taking pupils from about eleven to fourteen.

Colonies de vacances (Fr.) are holiday camps for young people, providing a variety of interesting activities; they are not organized by the schools as such, though schools often collaborate with those running them.

Conseil de classe (Fr.): this is a committee of teachers concerned with the work of the class, which meets from time to time to discuss the work and progress of the pupils. It may also have disciplinary functions; other *conseils* found in French schools are the *conseil d'urgence* which deals with more serious cases, and may include representatives of the pupils; and the *conseil de discipline* which is the Ultimate Deterrent and only deals with the very gravest matters.

Cours moyen, *Cours élémentaire* and *Cours préparatoire* are the names of the three stages in French primary education. The child enters in the *cours préparatoire* (CP), then does two years of *cours élémentaire* (CE I and CE II), and finally he moves into the *cours moyen* (CM I and CM II).

Curso de orientacion universitaria (Sp.) is the final stage of education at the *instituto* (q.v.); as the name suggests, it prepares for university entrance. Usually referred to as COU.

Documentation pédagogique (Fr.) is the resonant term given to an extremely valuable service, namely, the provision of teachers' aids, recording facilities, libraries, etc. There may be a *centre régional*, based on the *académie*, or university responsible for the whole region; or a *centre départemental*, roughly corresponding to an English county in its scope.

Doposcuola (It.) – literally 'after-school' – is the name given to extra sessions of school, usually held in the afternoon, to enable pupils to do recuperative work. Introduced some years ago, the system seems to have fallen into disuse in most places, but some schools are now reviving it to cater for subsidiary studies such as music, crafts and sport.

École de neige (Fr.) is a school set up in a winter-sports area, to which whole classes go with their teachers to carry out a programme partly of ordinary work, partly of activities suitable to the locality. There are other similar schools in the mountains

Glossary

(*écoles de montagne*), by the sea (*écoles de mer*) or in the countryside (*écoles de campagne*).

École normale (Fr.) is the training college for primary school teachers. Students formerly joined the *école normale* at a quite early age, thus committing themselves willy-nilly to a teaching career before they were really mature enough to know what they were doing; nowadays, entry is at about sixteen. Students must undertake to serve at least ten years in teaching. In Spain, the term is *escuela normal*, in Portugal *escola do magisterio*, and in Italy *magistrale*.

ERPA (Sp.) is the acronym for *Extracto del Registro Personal del Alumno* (Extract from Pupil's Personal Record). Details are found in chapter 9. The completion of the ERPA, though a very necessary chore, causes many a weary sigh to be heaved at the end of the year.

Etapa (Sp.) means 'stage'. The 1ª *etapa* lasta for five years, corresponding to our primary education, the 2ª *etapa* for the remaining three years of compulsory schooling.

Éveil (Fr.) literally means 'awakening'; it is the term applied to those parts of the French primary curriculum which introduce the pupil to the world around him – science, history, geography, art, music and handicraft. The term is also used in secondary schools.

Fachleistungkurse (Ger.) means roughly 'subjects which are taught in sets', as opposed to the majority of subjects which are taught in mixed-ability classes.

Feuille (Fr.) means 'leaf', but is also a sheet of paper, and hence a test-paper, or an individual task-sheet – the same thing as a Spanish *ficha*.

Ficha (Sp.) is the term usually applied to the testing and practice sheets on which so much of the 'continuously assessed' work of Spanish schools is now based; it can also be an official form of some kind.

Fiocco (It.): this, or *nastro*, is the name of the flowing bows of coloured ribbon worn by Italian schoolchildren on the front of the *grembiule* (q.v.). In a sense, the *fiocco* symbolizes childhood to the Italians.

Förderstufe (Ger.) literally means 'further stage'; this term used to be applied to the transitional period between primary and secondary stages of the *Volksschule*. See *Orientierungstufe* for the current version.

Foyer socio-culturel (Fr.) sounds impressive, but is in fact a fairly simple idea: the assembly of all the school's extra-curricular activities, both social and cultural. It is a concept not unlike that of the 'Amalgamated Clubs' which in my day were a major feature of Cambridge college life.

Graduado escolar (Sp.) is something like our idea of a school certificate. To gain it you must reach a satisfactory standard in all your courses, and if you wish you can then automatically proceed to a *bachillerato* course (q.v.).

Gran grupo (Sp.) in the Spanish EGB course is one of the four suggested teaching-units: it implies a group of anything up to 100 or even 150 pupils taught together – for example, by showing them slides or a film, or by demonstrating a technique which they will later practise in smaller groups. The other three possibilities are the *grupo coloquial*, of about thirty pupils, for discussion or the more detailed explanation of material outlined in the *gran grupo*; the *pequeño grupo*, a small group of perhaps six pupils working together on a project or the like; and finally, of course, the single pupil working at his own individual task.

Grembiule (It.), sometimes in the diminutive form *grembiulino*, is the Italian equivalent of the *bata* or *blouse*, worn by both boys and girls, mainly at the primary stage. Usually it is a loose-fitting overall, black or blue, fastening behind and often enlivened with a broad white collar, sometimes stiff, and a coloured *fiocco* (q.v.); there also exist, mainly for the boys, more modern variants of the outfit.

Groupe scolaire (Fr.) is the term applied to a group of two or three schools sharing the same site. Generally they are primary schools; sometimes one finds a *maternelle* (q.v.) and separate boys' or girls' primary schools, but more often today it will be a *maternelle* and two identical co-educational primary schools differentiated by the suffixes -A and -B. Eminently rational, of course, but perhaps a little unimaginative! In Spain the corresponding term *grupo escolar* is sometimes found.

Grundschule and *Hauptschule* (literally 'ground school' and 'head school') are the two sections of what used to be called a *Volksschule*: the basic, non-selective type of German school for pupils aged six to fifteen.

Gymnasium (Ger.) is precisely what we should call a grammar school, and the name is just about as misleading to the foreigner!

Glossary

Should you want to refer to what *we* mean by 'gymnasium', you must say *Turnhalle*.

Institution (Fr.) has for us overtones of the workhouse or the place where you dispose of the Family Curse, but in France it is a common name for a rather superior sort of private school; the name has the same overtones, perhaps, that 'College' or 'Academy' once had here. Of course, any ordinary primary school teacher may be an *instituteur* (masc.) or *institutrice* (fem.); it is nice to know that the logical French have these little quirks, even if they have never gone so far as to call their most exclusive schools 'public'.

Instituto (Sp.) is not quite the same thing: the *instituto de bachillerato* is the exact equivalent of a state *lycée* in France. But *instituto* can also, of course, be used like our 'institute' in, say, the 'Imperial Institute' or the 'Mechanics' Institute'.

Kernunterricht (Ger.) means, literally, 'kernel-instruction'; the term is applied to those basic subjects that can be taught to the class as a whole without recourse to setting.

Klassenbuch (Ger.) is not a 'class-book' in our sense, but the official log-book of the class, often with registers, records of work etc. also incorporated.

Liceo (It.), *Liceu* (Port.), *Lycée* (Fr.) are all forms of the same word, and of the same thing, namely an upper secondary school attended by pupils hoping to proceed to the *baccalauréat* or its equivalent, and perhaps then to further education. Where there are classical *lycées*, technical *lycées*, etc., they have parity of status but have the bias appropriate to their names.

Maternelle (more properly, *école maternelle*) (Fr.) is a nursery school. In Spain this would be a *jardín de infancia* (a literal translation of the German *Kindergarten*) if the pupils were aged two or three; or an *escuela de párvulos* if they were aged four or five.

Monodocencia (Sp.) is the practice, normal in most countries, of having only one teacher for all subjects for the younger pupils.

ONISEP (Fr.) is the acronym for *Office Nationale d'Information sur les Enseignements et les Professions*, an organization which puts out some excellent information about courses and careers. Connoisseurs of the Numerate Society may care to know that 'the catalogue of publications will be sent on a simple request to O.N.I.S.E.P. B.P.102.05 – 75225 PARIS CEDEX 05'. The word to savour is 'simple' . . .

Organigrama (Sp.) is the name given to those 'family-tree' diagrams which businessmen and with-it people generally like to concoct to show just who is responsible to whom, and for what. The visitor to a Spanish school will inevitably be shown one or more, and should express polite admiration even if he secretly tempers it with a little gentle scepticism.

Orientierungstufe (Ger.) is a new development by which pupils, before passing from the *Grundschule* to a secondary school, will spend two years in an 'assessment stage', to help in coming to the right decision about the type of course they should follow.

Patronato (It., Sp.) may be translated 'sponsorship' or 'foundation'. In Spain, a non-state school is an *escuela de patronato*, the patron being anything from the Catholic Church to the local savings bank. In Italy, a *patronato scolastico* produces funds for such things as school meals, minibuses and other things not quite in the normal educational pipeline.

Polidocencia (Sp.) is the opposite of *monodocencia*: that is, it means being taught by specialist subject-teachers.

Programación (Sp.) means 'planning': an up-to-date word, for it is not in my 1959 edition of the Spanish dictionary. *Dias de programación* come at the start of the school year, before work begins in earnest, and are presumably devoted to finding out exactly what class everybody is going to be in, what options they will take, what special remedial work they will need, and so on.

Prova (Port.) and *Prueba* (Sp.) are forms of the same word, meaning 'test'. The *prova de passagem* in Portugal is the 'going-up test' which every child does at the end of the year to decide if he is fit to move to the next class or stage.

Realschule (Ger.) is another rather untranslatable term; but the status of the school is rather like that of the old 'intermediate' or 'central' schools which we used to have in England long ago: not quite a grammar school, but decidedly more academic than the ordinary secondary school, which is a *Hauptschule*.

Recuperación (Sp.) means those activities which a backward pupil undertakes in order to assimilate him more nearly to his group. Nowadays *recuperación continua* is the watchword: not so much extra penal work, or keeping the pupil down for a year, as giving him carefully graded work to help him catch up at his own pace and in his own time. Somewhat related ideas are:

Glossary

Redoublement (Fr.) which means 'repeating', i.e. putting the pupil back into the same class and making him go over the year's work again; or

Riparazione (It.) which is the second session of examinations, held in September, for those who made a mess of things in June and have (in theory) spent their summer holidays sweating over their textbooks.

Sachunterricht (Ger.) is about what we should call 'general knowledge', if we had such a thing nowadays.

Salón de actos (Sp.) is the name given to the hall where plays, concerts, meetings and other such fiestas take place. I think the term *acto publico* implies 'an occasion' or 'a bit of a do'.

Schülervertretung (Ger.) means 'pupil-representation' and is a pillar of the educational temple these days.

Scuola a tempo pieno (It.) means 'full-time school' – a rather rare thing in Italy.

Scuola media (It.) means 'middle school', i.e. much the same as a *collège d'enseignement secondaire* in France.

Sitzen Bleiben (Ger.): in the absence of a real noun to apply to the idea of repeating a year's work (French *redoublement*) the Germans make do with this compound verb.

Stützkurse and *Liftkurse* (Ger.) are two terms applied to supplementary courses arranged to assist pupils who need extra work to bring them up to standard.

Surveillant (Fr.) is a young supervisory official in a French secondary school, possibly himself intending eventually to teach; he exercises a disciplinary function something between that of a teacher and that of a school prefect. His existence frees the French teacher from some of the more tedious duties such as policing the playgrounds or standing watchdog over the dinner queue.

Surveillant-général (Fr.): a much more important official. You report to him if you arrive late, for example, or wish permission to do something normally forbidden by the rules.

Verbindungslehrer (Ger.) is the teacher appointed to represent the interests of the pupils in staff discussions: a sort of shop steward for the pupils' union, one might say.

Versetzung (Ger.) means promotion to the next class as a result of the annual assessment procedure.

Volksschule (Ger.) is the term applied to the old-style all-age elementary school, now replaced largely by the *Grundschule* and *Hauptschule*.

Wahlpflichtkurse (Ger.) are optional courses from which older secondary school pupils may choose.

Zensurenkonferenz (Ger.), about the same thing as the French *Conseils de classe*: meetings to discuss assessments of pupils, attended by all the staff who teach the class.

List of schools

As previously explained, this book does not mention by name every school which I visited. Those mainly referred to are listed below, with references to the page on which appears a brief description of the school; other references in the text are listed in full in the Index.

Abbreviations
B: boys' school   M: mixed school
S: secondary school   P: primary school
T: technical school   G: school of grammar type (*lycée* etc.)
AA: all-age school   I: non-State school (Church, etc.)

Country	*Town or Village*	*Name of School*	*Type*	*Page*
France	Avignon	La Barbière-B	P M	43
France	Avignon	J. H. Fabre—A	P M	41
France	Avignon	Frédéric Mistral	G M	47
France	Beauvais	CET (Bâtiment)	T B	131

Country	Town or Village	Name of School	Type	Page
France	Beauvais	J. B. Pellerin	S M	47
France	Beauvais	Saint-Esprit	AA B I	63
Italy	Cremona	Leonida Bissolati	P M	52
Italy	Cremona	Virgilio	S M	73
Italy	Perugia	A. Fabretti	P M	26
Italy	Perugia	Pestalozzi	P M	89
Italy	Porcellasco	Pietro Pasquali	P M	28
Italy	Soresina	Scuola Media	S M	59
Portugal	Braga	São Vitor	P B	44
Portugal	Evora	Liceu Nacional	G M	64
Portugal	São Gregorio	(Village School)	P M	91
Spain	Gerona	Juan Bruguera	AA B	53
Spain	Gerona	La Inmaculada	AA B I	53
Spain	Gerona	La Salle	AA B I	97
Spain	Gerona	J. Vicens Vives	G M	58
Spain	Jaén	Ramón Calatayud	AA M	120
Spain	Jaén	Marist College	AA B I	19
Spain	Jaén	Martin Noguera	AA M	72
Spain	Jaén	Santo Tomàs	AA M	94
Spain	Jaén	Virgen del Carmen	G B	39
Spain	Salt	Menendez Pidal	AA M	71
W. Germany	Emden	Früchteburg	P M	49
W. Germany	Emden	Realschule	S M	46
W. Germany	Emden	Treckfahrtstief	G M	46
W. Germany	Emden	Wallschule	S M	56
W. Germany	Trier	Hindenburg	G B	118
W. Germany	Trier	Zewen	AA M	41

As well as the above schools, the following also receive occasional mention; it appeared simpler to provide brief notes on these here, rather than to attempt to work them into the text:

École Normale d'Institutrices, Beauvais: a primary school and *maternelle* attached to the women's training college. About 130 pupils and six teachers in the primary school.

Lycée Technique, Beauvais: a big modern school on the outskirts of the city, with 850 pupils in the *lycée* and 250 more in the attached CET; staff of ninety-six. Some pupils come from outside the Beauvais area.

École Maternelle Jean-Moulin, Beauvais: nursery-type school serving the ZUP Argentine, a large housing estate. There are 225 pupils and six teachers.

List of schools

Scuola Media San Paolo, Perugia: mixed secondary school of about 700 pupils aged ten to fourteen in an ancient building adjacent to Perugia Cathedral.

Technical School, Evora: a fine modern school, opened in 1970; there are about 1,400 boys and girls, with a staff of nearly 100.

Colegio La Salle, Palma de Mallorca: a school very similar in every way to the La Salle College at Gerona (q.v.).

Colegio Nacional Miguel de Cervantes, Ecija: a well-built modern school in a small Andalusian town; about 850 pupils, with twenty-three classes; the staff comprises a headmaster and twenty-three other teachers.

Escuelas Profesionales Sagrada Familia, Ecija: another quite recent school, built 1970. There are about 950 pupils, whose ages range from six to seventeen; pupils in the fourteen to seventeen age-range do a technical course with an emphasis on motor-mechanics.

Index

absence inquiries, 172
absences, 96, 190, 193, 197
Acebrón, Jaime, 116
Additivgesamtschule, 23
address, forms of, 206
admission form, 172
age of compulsory schooling, 8, 9
age-range of class, 104
alcoholic beverages, 136
ancillary helpers, 100, 101
animateur technique, 152
Arbeitsgemeinschaft, 151, 158
architecture of schools, 113–24, 217
archives, 100, 135, 163, 164
areas (Spanish system), 29
arithmetic, 48–54
art, 131, 132, 153, 158
art gallery, school, 132
assembly, 133
assembly halls, 114, 133

assessment, 102–8, 165–7, 171, 174, 175, 178, 193
athletics, 140, 150
attendance certificate, 172
attendance register, 169, 191
attitudes of pupils, 25, 70, 71, 74, 204, 205, 218
audiovisual methods, 64, 94, 144
aula, 115

baccalauréat, 30
bachillerato, 10, 30
badges, 209
barber's shop, 213
Barbiana, Italy, 8, 76, 78, 103, 203, 211
BARBIÈRE, LA (AVIGNON), 43, 52, 70, 84, 94, 120, 132, 138, 187
Bari, Italy, 111, 152
bars, 136
basketball, 149, 155

Index

Bassano del Grappa, Italy, 146
Bassi, Signor (teacher), 52, 76
behaviour of pupils, 204–7
bells, 22
Bernardini, Aldo, 76, 203, 204
bicycles, 20, 191
biology, 56–60, 128
BISSOLATI, LEONIDA (CREMONA), 52, 76, 171
blackboard, 143, 144
blackboard, use of, 54, 59, 90
Blanco Rodriguez, A., 178
board cleaning, 144
boarding education, 19
Böhme, Herr (teacher), 56
Bonvilliers, France, 156
books, provision of, 145–7
brackets, for satchels etc., 141, 142
break, midday, 138, 141, 237
break, recreational, 21, 22, 155, 237
Breteuil, France, 156
BRUGUERA, JUAN (GERONA), 53, 139, 140, 147, 165, 166, 176, 196, 197
building, college of, 133
buildings, layout of, 115–18, 217, 242, 243
buildings, school, 113–24, 217
bureaucracy, 163, 171, 217
bursaries, 173

cafés, 136
cahiers, 41
CALATAYUD, RAMÓN (JAÉN), 28, 111, 120, 210
calendar, school, 20
Camino, El (novel), 197
carnet de correspondance, 174
Catalan language, 153, 156
Cecarini, Signor V. (teacher), 194
Centenary Plan Schools, 91
Centre Départemental de Documentation Pédagogique, 93, 135
Centro Cultural, 93
certificado de escolaridad, 10
CERVANTES, MIGUEL DE (ECIJA), 95, 139, 145, 150, 255
chalk, 144

chalkboard, 54, 59, 90, 143, 144
chapel, school, 134
chemistry, 55
chewing-gum, 198
Chirignago, Italy, 183
choirs, school, 151, 152
Cicchi, Signor (teacher), 26, 27, 76
ciclo preparatorio, 10, 11
cinema, use of, 92, 94
circolo didattico, 84
civics, teaching of, 36, 46
class council, 162, 169, 192, 200, 216
class-lists, 169
class numbering, 235, 236
class prefect, 95, 190, 191
class secretary, 27, 95
class teacher, 85, 86
classes, size of, 16, 17, 87
classrooms, dimensions of, 242, 243
classrooms, layout of, 72, 124, 125
cloakrooms, 136
clocks, 144
club rooms, 155
clubs, 151, 152
co-education, 15
coffee machines, 137
Colaço, Maria Rosa, 79, 80, 157, 178
colegio nacional, 10
collective salute, 193, 194, 206
collège d'enseignement secondaire, 11
COLLÈGE D'ENSEIGNEMENT TECHNIQUE, BEAUVAIS, 15, 127, 131, 133
colonies de vacances, 154
commercial subjects, 133
committees, 95, 96
common rooms, staff, 81, 200
compositions, 46, 47
comprehension lessons, 44–6
compulsory schooling, 8
concerts, school, 151–3
concierges, 101
conduct marks, 171
conseil d'éducation, 163
conseil d'études, 105
conseil d'urgence, 195
continuous assessment, 102–8
cookery, 133

Index

cooks, school, 100
'cornets', 23
corporal punishment, 197
Corriere della Sera, 78
Costa Ribas, José, 86
courtesies, 193, 194, 206
craftwork, 29, 94, 95, 132, 158
Criança e a Vida, A, 79, 80, 157, 178
crossing patrols, 173
crucifix in classroom, 143
curriculum, 26–33, 217, 221–36
curso de orientación universitaria (COU), 10, 108, 231
cycles (Spanish system) 87, 116, 117

day, school, 21, 22
decoration of schools, 118–20, 132
délégué de classe, 96
Delibes, Miguel, 197
democracy in schools, 95, 96, 199–201, 217
departure from school, 173
desks, 141–3, 193, 217
desks, arrangement of, 72, 124, 125
dialogue method, 26, 88
diary, educational, 147
dimensions of classroom, 242, 243
dining halls, 81, 134, 138
direct method language teaching, 65
disciplinary code, 201–4
disciplinary council, 192
discipline, 27, 53, 66, 71, 185–213
discussion lessons, 46, 89
doctor, school, 181
domestic science, 133
doposcuola, 78
dossier, personal, 165–9
drama, 48, 151–3
drawing, 132, 153, 158
dress, pupils', 180, 190, 193, 194, 196, 198, 205, 207–12, 217
dress, teachers', 82, 208
duties of teachers, 97–9

ÉCOLE NORMALE, BEAUVAIS 70, 254
écoles de campagne (... *de mer, de montagne, de neige*), 154

écoles maternelles, 40, 41, 126
Elche, Spain, 128
Elternbeirat, 183
emergency council, 195
end-of-term activities, 155, 158, 159
English, teaching of, 62–6
enrolment, 23
Enseñanza General Básica (EGB), 9, 10, 87
enveloppe-navette, 191
ERPA, 165, 176
essay writing, 46–7
evaluations, 165–7, 171, 174, 175, 178, 193
examinations, 102, 108–11
excursions, 153–6
exercise-books, 148
exercise-paper, 148
experiments, science, 60, 61, 128
Extracto del Registro Personal del Alumno, 165, 176

FABRE, J. H. (A) (AVIGNON), 41, 43, 132
FABRETTI, A. (PERUGIA), 7, 26, 76, 161, 205
Farga, La (school magazine), 149
FAURE, FÉLIX (BEAUVAIS), 195, 196
Feder (school magazine), 149, 150, 158
fees, 10, 11, 179, 180
fichas, 105–8, 171, 216
Figuière, Mme Simone (teacher), 84
films, use of, 92, 94, 134, 152
fiocco, 208, 209
Floral Games, 153
football, 150
form teacher, 161
Formicaio, Il (School magazine), 73–5, 149, 154, 155, 173, 184
Forni, Scuola Media, 122
foyer socio-culturel, 151
Fracassi, Signor Rino (teacher), 76, 205
free activity, 88
Freinet, Célestin, 89, 156
French numerals, teaching of, 51

260 Index

French, teaching of (in Italy and Spain), 66, 67
FRÜCHTEBURG (EMDEN), 45, 49, 70, 84, 85, 100, 118, 125, 165, 198, 207
furniture, 134, 141–4

games, 141, 149–50
games clothing, 130, 196
gardening, 152
Gazzettino, Il, 122, 183
general knowledge, 39
geography, 36
Gesamtschule, 23
graduado escolar, 10
graffiti, 207
grammar, 43–6, 216
grants, 179, 180
grass, 140
grounds, school, 140
Grundschule, 13
Günther, Herr (teacher), 130
Gymnasium (German grammar school), 14
Gymnasium (sports hall), 129, 130

hair, 213
half-class groups, 17
handicraft, 29, 94, 95, 132, 133, 158
handwriting, 34
Hauptschule, 14
Hausmeister, 101
head teachers, 83–5
Henkelmann, Herr (teacher), 46
HINDENBURG-GYMNASIUM (TRIER), 118, 157
history, teaching of, 41
holiday-tasks, 186
holidays, 20, 21
homework, 22, 23
hour (lesson), 22
hours, school, 21, 22, 217, 237, 238
Huck, Frau (teacher), 45

individual assignments, 105–8, 216
indoor games, 150, 152
Información, 123

INMACULADA, LA (GERONA), 34, 53, 81, 106, 120, 123, 124, 129, 141, 142, 144, 145, 150, 172, 179, 186, 197, 209
inspectorate, 83, 84
instituto de bachillerato, 10
insurance, 179, 181
interest groups, 124, 125, 178
interviewing of parents, 99, 135, 161
interviews by pupils, 89
intonation, English, 62

jargon, educational, 168
João Paulo (pupil), 44
Jordana, Ricardo, 72, 73

Kakaotrunk, 137
Klassenbuch, 165, 201
Klassensprecher, 96, 200
Kremer, Frau (teacher), 41

laboratories, 55–9, 127, 128
Lamoretti, Signorina (teacher), 26, 27
language laboratories, 135
languages, modern, teaching of, 62–67, 73
languages, native, teaching of, 33–5, 40–8, 215, 216
Lanternino, Il (school magazine), 155
late arrival, 190, 197
Latin, teaching of, 68, 226
Lattanzi, Massimo (pupil), 75
layout of building, 115–18, 217, 242, 243
layout of classroom, 72, 124, 125
leaving age, 8, 9
leaving card, 190
length of lesson, 22
length of term, 20, 21
Letter to a Teacher (book), 8, 76, 78, 103, 203, 211
librarians, 100, 134
library, pupils', 134, 135
library, staff, 81, 134
liceo, liceu, lycée, 11, 12
LICEU NACIONAL (EVORA), 64, 70, 96, 113, 136, 139, 152, 164, 169, 171, 180, 205

Index

locked doors and gates, 119, 136, 140
logbook, classroom, 165, 169, 170, 191, 201, 216
Lörscher, Frau (teacher), 42
lunch break, 138, 141, 237
LYCÉE TECHNIQUE DE BEAUVAIS, 131, 138

magazines, school, 28, 29, 89, 154–8, 199
Mainardi, Signor (teacher), 48
Mallorca, 48, 123
marbles (game), 141
Marchi, Cesare, 202
MARIST COLLEGE (GERONA), see INMACULADA
MARIST COLLEGE (JAÉN), 3, 19, 132, 152, 213
marking, 97
marks, 166, 170–2, 174–6, 193
materials, shortage of, 45, 61
maternelles, 40, 41, 87, 126
mathematics, teaching of, 35, 36, 48–54
Mazzolari, Maurizio (pupil), 74
meals, school, 137–40, 180
media, scuola, 11
Mediavilla, Alberto, 72
medical facilities, 180, 181, 217
Medina (pupil), 54
MENENDEZ PIDAL (SALT, GERONA), 15, 71, 106, 123, 128, 139, 149, 153, 156, 162
menus, 137, 138
Méru, France, 156
methods, teaching, 65, 73
midday break, 138, 141, 237
Miguel, Señor (teacher), 63
Milani, Father, 76
MISTRAL, FRÉDÉRIC (AVIGNON), 47, 127, 194
Mittlere Reife, 14
mixed-ability classes, 17, 171
modern languages, teaching of, 62–7, 73
modern mathematics, 35, 36, 53
monitors, 95
monodocencia, 85

monotony of buildings, 118, 119, 121
Moreira, Victor Barroca (pupil), 157
motor engineering, 133
MOULIN, JEAN (BEAUVAIS), 40, 41, 126
murals, 120
museum, school, 132
music, 129, 130, 133, 151–3
music, background, 145

nastro, 208, 209
native languages, teaching of, 33–5, 40–48, 215, 216
Navarro Higuera, Juan, 86
needy pupils, 179
newspapers, 78, 79, 109–11
NOGUERA, MARTIN (JAÉN), 22, 72, 123, 140, 155
noise of traffic, 120
non-specialist teachers, 85
note-taking, 95
numbering of classes, 235, 236
numbering of pupils, 96, 171, 209
nursery education, 7, 8, 16, 40, 41, 87, 132

Oggi, 79, 181, 202
Oise (French *département*), 156
Oliveira, Senhor Carlos (teacher), 91, 92
Oliveira de Aziméis, Portugal, 159
open-plan buildings, 71, 128
organigrama, 163
organization of school, 87
Orientierungstüfe, 13
outings, 153, 154, 156
out-of-school activities, 25, 156, 218
outside organizations, links with, 128
overall, as school dress, 82, 180, 190, 193, 194, 196, 207–12, 217
overhead projectors, 143

paper, squared, 148
parents' associations, 183, 184
parents' days, 183
parents, contact with, 162, 176, 181, 182
pastoral care, 160, 161

pay, teachers', 78, 79, 81, 239–41
pegs, 136, 143, 155
PELLERIN, J. B. (BEAUVAIS), 47, 64, 68, 120, 133, 134, 138, 151, 158, 168, 189–92, 208
Peñamefecit, Jaén, Spain, 120, 123
PESTALOZZI, (PERUGIA), 89
pets in classroom, 126
philosophy, teaching of, 39
photography, teaching of, 129, 152
physical education, 107, 129, 130
physics, teaching of, 56, 57, 128
Pietralata, Italy, 76, 203, 204
pinafore as school dress, 180, 190, 193, 194, 196, 207–12, 217
plants in school buildings, 120
plastics, use of in equipment, 128, 142
playground games, 150, 188
playgrounds, 140, 141, 217
play park, 152
plays, school, 151, 152
poetry, children's, 81, 155–7
police, 173
polidocencia, 86
Pons (school magazine), 157
PORCELLASCO (CREMONA), 18, 28, 76, 121, 132, 137, 144, 155, 162, 189, 205
Potier, Mme (teacher), 47
Pozzéra, Mme (teacher), 52
précis-writing, 47
precision, insistence on, 43, 48, 69, 215
prefects, class, 95, 190, 191
printing, as school activity, 28, 29, 155, 158
private study, 134, 196
prizes, 173
professionalism of teachers, 69, 84
project work, 27, 71, 89
promotion of pupils, 102, 103, 105, 108, 112
promotion of teachers, 82, 83
prova, 108, 109
punishments, 191, 192, 194–7, 201–204
pupil-representation, 95, 96

pupils' views on school, 24, 73, 74, 155, 156
puppetry, 94

qualifications of teachers, 75, 82
questionnaire to parents, 168

reading, teaching of, 34, 40–44
reading-matter, 43–4
REALSCHULE (EMDEN), 46, 56, 65, 66, 104, 114, 121, 125, 150, 172
record cards, 165–8
records, 161, 164
recreational breaks, 21, 22, 155
recuperative work, 12, 104–6, 176–8
registers, 165
relations, pupil–teacher, 70, 99, 218
religion in schools, 134
reports, 172–6
responsibilities of teachers, 97, 98
retirement of teachers, 83
Ringewaldt, Frau (teacher), 56
roll of honour, 155, 172
rules, school, 174, 185–213

Sachunterricht, 39, 198
SAGRADA FAMILIA (ECIJA), 10, 71, 133, 184, 210, 255
SAINT-ESPRIT, INSTITUTION DU (BEAUVAIS), 15, 63, 131, 134, 135, 162, 208
salaries, teachers', 78, 79, 81, 239–41
SALLE, LA (GERONA), 97, 105, 106, 127, 128, 134, 140, 145, 164, 171, 184, 209
SALLE, LA (PALMA DE MALLORCA), 48
salón de actos, 134
salute, collective, 193, 194, 206
SAN PAOLO (PERUGIA), 15, 140
sanctions, 191, 192, 194–7, 201–4
SANTO TOMÁS (JAÉN), 94, 116, 120, 123, 140, 152
SÃO GREGORIO (near EVORA), 91–3, 115
SÃO VITOR (BRAGA), 44, 45, 60, 61, 115, 136, 140, 145, 154, 208, 210

Index

satchels, 142
Saturday morning activities, 153
Schultze, Frau (teacher), 133
science, teaching of, 30, 55–61, 128
scuola media, 11
seating arrangements, 72
secretary, class, 27, 95
secretary, school, 100
sexes, separation of, 15, 16
shift-system, 122
shortages, 45, 60, 61, 85, 121, 122, 145, 147
singing, 129
size of classes, 16, 17, 87
size of school, 18, 19
sketching, 153
slates, 96
smock, as school dress, 82, 180, 190, 193, 194, 196, 207–12, 217
smoking, 98, 191, 195
social activities, 158
social studies, 107
sociograms, 162
Soms (pupil), 54
SORESINA, SCUOLA MEDIA DI, 59, 60, 66, 127, 135
Spanish, teaching of (France), 63
specialist teachers, 86, 127
spectacles, provision of, 181
spectator galleries, 130
sponge for cleaning chalkboard, 144
sport, 149, 150
sports grounds, 140
squared paper, 148
staff, shortage of, 85
staff meetings, 99
staff rooms, 81, 200
staffing ratios, 17, 18
stationery, 145, 147, 148
Stefano (pupil), 27
streaming of classes, 17
structure of education, 9–13
Strybny, Frau (teacher), 66
Strybny, Herr (teacher), 46
Sürm, Frau (teacher), 49
surveillants, 101
swimming pools, 130, 131

syllabuses, 33–8, 58
symbols on doors, 120

teachers' centres, 93, 94
teachers, deployment of, 86, 87
teachers, professionalism of, 69, 84
teachers, qualifications of, 75, 82
teachers, work conditions of, 76–9, 81, 97, 98
teaching groups, 87
team-teaching, 71, 87
technical education, 133
TECHNICAL SCHOOL, EVORA, 70, 124, 127, 132–6, 152
technicians, 101
television, 144, 145
terms, dates of, 21
testing, use of slates for, 96
tests and test papers, 111, 112, 148, 170
textbooks, 49, 53, 60, 61, 63, 145–7
theatre, 48, 151–3
Thiemann, Frau (teacher), 84
tiles, use of, 128
timetables, 28, 148
toilets, 136, 188, 193
Tortosa, Spain, 114
traffic noises, 120
transfer documents, 167
transport of pupils, 19, 20
travelling teachers, 91–3
TRECKFAHRTSTIEF (EMDEN), 46, 56, 85, 118, 125, 129, 133, 140, 141, 151, 165
truancy, 109, 110
tuckshops, 136

uniform, school, 180, 190, 193, 194, 196, 198, 207–12, 217

vandalism, 204
Vatio (pupil), 29
Verbindungslehrer, 163, 200
Vergoni, Gianfranco (pupil), 27, 35
Vida Escolar, 33, 72–3, 86, 116, 128, 178, 184
VIRGEN DEL CARMEN (JAÉN), 39, 67, 70, 81, 127, 134, 138, 195

VIRGILIO (CREMONA), 48, 73–6, 94, 120, 132, 145, 149, 153–5, 161, 162, 164, 170, 173, 184, 192–4
visits, educational, 153–6
visual aids, 91–4
VIVES, J. VICENS (GERONA), 58, 67, 70, 91, 127, 129, 134, 136, 138, 152, 170
vocabulary of primary school pupils, 70
volleyball, 150

walls, use of, 91, 120, 126, 127
WALLSCHULE (EMDEN), 95, 114, 129, 141, 143–5, 179, 183
warning systems, 22
washbasins, 144

week, school, 237, 238
welfare, 179–81
Wittneben, Herr (teacher), 151
work-groups, 28
work rooms, for staff, 81
writing, children's, 27–9, 35, 47, 75, 81, 154–8
written observation, 194, 195

year, school, 21

Zelarino, Italy, 122
Zensurenkonferenz, 172
ZEWEN SCHOOL (TRIER), 14, 41, 48, 66, 70, 128–30, 149, 151, 158, 183, 207
Zimmer, Herr Reinhold (teacher), 66